FINDING OURSELVES AT THE MOVIES

Finding Ourselves at the Movies

PHILOSOPHY FOR A NEW GENERATION

Paul W. Kahn

Columbia University Press
New York

Columbia University Press
Publishers Since 1893
New York   Chichester, West Sussex
cup.columbia.edu
Copyright © 2013 Columbia University Press
All rights reserved

Library of Congress Cataloging-in-Publication Data
Kahn, Paul W., 1952–
Finding ourselves at the movies : philosophy for a new generation /
Paul W. Kahn.
pages cm
Includes bibliographical references and index.
ISBN 978-0-231-16438-2 (cloth : alk. paper) —
ISBN 978-0-231-53602-8 (ebook)
1. Motion pictures—Philosophy.   I. Title.

PN1995.K255   2013
791.43'684—dc23   2013016275

Columbia University Press books are printed on permanent
and durable acid-free paper.

This book is printed on paper with recycled content.
Printed in the United States of America

c 10 9 8 7 6 5 4 3 2 1

Jacket design: Catherine Casalino
Jacket photograph: Nejron Photo-Fotolia.com

References to websites (URLs) were accurate at the time
of writing. Neither the author nor Columbia University Press
is responsible for URLs that may have expired or changed since
the manuscript was prepared.

CONTENTS

PREFACE

Two men encounter each other near the law courts. One is there to defend against a charge of impiety; the other is there to accuse his own father of manslaughter. The former asks the latter to help him to understand the nature of piety. A conversation on family, justice, and law begins. The conversation does not resolve any of this, but it moves through a variety of possibilities, creating a kind of space, or pause, in the daily routine. In that space the speakers examine what they believe and how they should act. On another occasion the same questioner has gone to the suburbs to watch a festival. The son of an old acquaintance invites him home to see his father. After greeting the father, the younger guest asks his host to tell him what it is like to be old. The conversation quickly leads to questions of justice, which involve both young and old. Again, there is a pause in the daily routine, while the participants take a hard look at their own beliefs and practices. They exercise their imaginations, as well as their critical faculties, for they try to imagine an ideal political arrangement—a project in which they are only partially successful. At the end of the conversation they return to the business of their daily lives.

These are the framing scenes of two of Plato's dialogues, as familiar to many as the scene of Abraham taking Isaac up the mountain. Philosophy's origins are no more esoteric than the biblical stories. Just as religion begins with narrative, not theology, so philosophy begins with narrative, not abstraction. Plato may have done philosophy, but he wrote dramas. In his dialogues we are offered an imaginative construction that has a narrative line, as well as philosophical arguments. The narrative is not just something that gets in the way of the arguments. Because narrative and argument are always intertwined, these texts require interpretation, not reduction to abstract propositions. We are asked, just like the characters in the dramas are asked, to pause, to try to answer questions, to reflect on what is said, and to respond.

One of the messages of these dramas is that philosophy is a conversation that can happen anywhere. It is an engagement that can take place on the street or over dinner. Philosophy is not extraordinary, but a continuation of reflective practices that are, or can be, a part of our lives. I want to recover something of this tradition for philosophy. Today, we no longer have the time or the knowledge of each other that would make possible a pause for argument on our way to court or anywhere else. We live in different communities spread out across the nation and, increasingly, across the globe. The people we deal with are more than likely strangers. We husband our time and cannot simply take a break for reflective inquiry in our busy work schedules. Yet we are not so far from the world of Plato that we no longer recognize the point of the dialogues. We still have an interest in serious reflection and self-examination. We do want to examine our beliefs; we do want to understand ourselves better. We want to ask each other why we think and act as we do. Our curiosity about ourselves remains as strong as ever.

To engage in this conversation today, we need common objects to talk about. We are not all going to read Plato's dialogues. Nor do we have the easy familiarity with each other that comes from living in a relatively small city with little contact with the larger world. Increasingly, what we have in common is the movies. Here we can find a point from which to begin a conversation about our shared beliefs and practices. Philosophy can begin as we leave the theater and talk to each other about what we just experienced. Today, we often do not even share the space of the theater, yet still we have the movies as common texts. The movies connect us across generations—here I find a common ground with my students, as well as with my parents. Movies give us a ground on which to strike up a conversation with a stranger. We ask each other, "Have you seen any good movies lately?" and find we have something in common to talk about.

A philosophical work that discusses popular culture is not itself a work of popular culture. I am not taking up the role of movie critic. I have little to say on whether any of the movies I discuss are worth seeing. Neither is this a work in film theory, although I hope that those interested in that discipline will find something of value here. I spend no time on the history of film or even with the recognized film classics. I emphasize narrative over the other aspects of creativity and production that go into a film. This is not because narrative is more important but because my questions go to what a film means and what that meaning tells us about ourselves. The film theorists rightly point out that narrative does not stand alone, that a film's meaning relies on its many other elements: for example, music, lighting, cinematography, editing, composition. I don't disagree. My ambition, however, is not to study film or the experience of film but to explore the accounts we give of ourselves and our communities.

This book will strike some readers as fitting neither the genre of philosophy nor that of film studies. I avoid the scholarly apparatus of both disciplines because my intended audience is not the professionals. It is my hope to do serious philosophy while speaking of one of the most ordinary elements of our common life—what is playing at the local cinema. For that reason I avoid the form and style of conventional scholarly texts. I keep notes to a minimum, crediting sources of specific ideas and providing basic information on the films I discuss. For those readers interested in the broader literature on which I draw, I provide some orientation in the bibliographic essays that follow the notes.

Socrates reminds us that the stakes are always high when we try to understand even our daily routines. I don't expect anyone to suggest that I drink hemlock, but I do expect a lot of professionals to tell me that this is just not the way it is done. That, however, is just the point: we need a new beginning to get back to what has been most important in the Western practice of philosophy. One place to begin is at the movies.

ACKNOWLEDGMENTS

Over the past few years I have talked about the themes of this book in many places, both in the United States and abroad. I discovered a level of enthusiasm that surprised and delighted me. Listeners everywhere wanted to talk about the movies. They quickly understood what I was doing and responded by suggesting other movies to consider and new interpretations of those films I discussed. I greatly appreciated their suggestions. Many of the films that I discuss in this work were brought to my attention by people whose names I never learned. These conversations also confirmed my belief that in the movies we find a common ground for the critical, self-reflective discourse that is philosophy.

Alongside these helpful, brief encounters I also received sustained criticism and advice from many people, to whom I want to express my appreciation. An early draft of the manuscript was the subject of an ad hoc gathering of fellows at the Yale Law School, which included Amnon Lev, Jonathan Schell, Steven Jensen, Daniel Bonilla, and Robert Diab. I owe a special thanks to Kiel Brennan-Marquez, who was a member of this group but also provided valuable research assistance and advice throughout the project. My colleagues Owen Fiss and Bruce Ackerman labored through the manuscript and helped me to shape the project. Benjamin Berger carefully reviewed the whole manuscript and offered detailed advice on every chapter. Early conversations with my friends Tony Kronman and Ulrich Haltern helped a good deal more than they could have realized. On many occasions I discussed the project with Tico Taussig, who helped me to broaden my view. The manuscript was the subject of discussion among an extraordinary group of graduate students at Yale, including Itamar Mann, Or Bassok, Han Liu, and Lucas McClure. Helpful reviewers included Samuel Moyn, Stanley Hauerwas, and Alan Stone. I also received helpful advice on which movies to consider from both of my children, Hannah and Suzanne—as well as from Noah Kazis. Blair Greenwald and Talia Kramer helped to bring the manuscript into final form. Catherine Iino delivered useful doses of skepticism, as well as needed support. Finally, I thank Barbara Mianzo for managing the production of this manuscript through countless drafts.

FINDING OURSELVES AT THE MOVIES

Part I

FROM PHILOSOPHY
TO FILM

Philosophy, broadly conceived, is a practice of critical reflection on our beliefs and practices. In this sense we all philosophize at some points in our lives. We may think that little will come of it, but we are all concerned with understanding ourselves and with finding meaning in our own lives and in the lives of those about whom we care. Everyone confronts death and wonders how to make sense of this ending to the enterprise that is his or her own life. Similarly, we all confront issues of justice: we wonder what we should do for others or how much we can demand that others do for us. These are issues in the home, the community, the church, and the workplace; they are subjects of deliberation and decision in politics and law.

Philosophy begins with these common experiences. It takes these moments of inquiry further and adds to them an element of critical self-reflection. Socrates wants to know the nature of justice, courage, and piety, but he wants also to understand what it is to know and why it matters. Philosophy situates itself. Classically, it did so by detaching itself from the particularity of the philosopher's actual circumstances in order to explore the universal. When we ask, "what is justice?" we are asking more than what do I happen to think it is. Lately, some philosophers have questioned this effort to achieve a universal perspective, moving instead in the opposite direction: they have embraced the particularity of a contingent position.

Both classical and contemporary inquiries begin by thinking about the nature of inquiry itself and the conditions that make it possible. So do I. Accordingly, I don't begin by asking directly what we can learn about ourselves from film. Instead, I begin by asking what the background conditions of such an inquiry are. What is it to learn about oneself, and how, if at all, might we expect such knowledge to be useful? These are the subjects of part 1, in which my primary effort is to turn philosophical inquiry toward an examination of the imagination as the common source of action and understanding.

In chapter 1, I assess the need for a new direction in philosophical inquiry. For those who believe that something serious is at stake, the need will be clear. I explain the stakes of the inquiry and the reasons why I approach it as I do. Philosophy has become an academic discipline, addressing a professional readership. Philosophy should be exciting. It should be, at least in substantial part, an accessible form of self-discovery. After all, everyone has a deep interest in the traditional subjects of philosophy: the nature of the self, the meaning of life, the possibility of free action, the character of justice, and the nature of truth. We are born with a great capacity for wonder, and philosophy should engage that wonder.

Chapters 2 and 3 situate my inquiry with respect to the traditional philosophical problems of action and knowledge. In both cases I shift the point of inquiry, looking at the way in which we occupy a meaningful world, a world created by the imagination and maintained by narrative. We can think of narrative as the account I give when explaining who I am or what I am doing. We cannot really answer the question of whether the imagination is a faculty of action or of knowledge, for narrative always links the two. Explaining who I am sets forth a range of possible actions that express my identity; conversely, explaining what I am doing will lead me to offer an account of myself.

Chapter 2 argues that we misunderstand the nature of freedom if we think that the role of philosophy is to discover principles or values that are to be applied at moments of decision. Freedom is indeed a matter of taking responsibility, but this is misunderstood if seen as a sort of practical syllogism in which an abstract, normative proposition is applied to a discrete set of facts. Rather, we decide when we see our way forward, and we see our way forward when we have been persuaded. Focusing on the imagination, the problem of action becomes that of understanding what it is to persuade and to be persuaded. This is no less a problem of freedom, for only a free subject can enter into this exchange of reasons that is the process of persuasion. Philosophy, I argue, won't tell us what to do, but it can illuminate how our practices are situated in a complex world of norms, values, and meanings within which we find our way.

Chapter 3 extends the inquiry into the imagination from action to interpretation by looking directly at the nature of narrative. We have a meaningful world by virtue of our capacity to offer narratives to ourselves and others. Meeting someone, I get to know that person, and she or he gets to know me, as we reciprocally construct accounts of each other. The same process is at work when we locate ourselves in a community. We know the various communities of which we are members when we can give an account of them. Those communities extend from family to town to nation to world; they include religious and ethnic groups, as well as unions, corporations, and churches. Each is sustained by an imaginative project of narrative construction: each has a history that leads us to see distinct, possible futures. These narratives are not descriptions of causal chains, as if we were describing a natural process. Rather, narratives describe free subjects who have created their communities by choosing some possibilities over others. Thus, narrative invokes the possible to explain the actual.

My objective is not to resolve the traditional, philosophical problems of action and knowledge. I don't try to explain how free will is possible in a causal universe; I don't try to explain the nature of scientific truth. These, after all, are subjects that have generated argument and controversy for thousands of years. Nevertheless, part 1 orients the inquiry into specific films(part 2) by breaking with certain assumptions about the nature of decision and knowledge. I reject the idea that abstractions exist as principles to be applied either in the act of deciding or in the moment of comprehension. Thinking and acting are ways of occupying an entire world of meaning, which is always a product of the imagination.

We act freely when we can give an account of ourselves. To give that account is to construct a narrative.

The first three chapters, part 1, might be of particular interest to philosophers. These chapters can stand on their own as philosophical reflections on the problem of meaning as it shows itself in action and knowledge. Nevertheless, the chapters are intended to interest the nonphilosopher in the possibilities of this project. My intention in part 2 is to put my conclusions to work by turning directly to popular films. I hope to demonstrate what philosophy can be by actually doing it. Thus, I take up a practice of critical self-reflection by looking at the work of the social imaginary as I find it in contemporary popular films.

Films offer a common resource throughout this study. Nevertheless, because the questions I ask in the two parts are different, the way in which I make use of films differs as well. In part 1, I use films to illustrate my arguments about the nature of practice and interpretation. I choose examples that offer access to these issues. The arguments and analyses that I offer in each chapter must stand independently of the films I use to illustrate my points. In part 2, however, I interrogate films not to understand the way in which the social imagination works but to understand its products. These products include not just films but the meaningful world within which we find ourselves. Part 1 focuses on the way in which the social imagination works, while part 2 examines those historically contingent products of the imagination that constitute our own lives.

Just as part 1 can stand on its own, so can part 2. There, however, the question is not whether I have properly analyzed the nature of action and knowledge but whether I have convinced you of the meaning of the popular films that have captured your attention lately. Just as those interested in philosophy might stop after reading part 1, those interested in film might skip directly to part 2. My hope is to find a common ground in a democratic enterprise of philosophy that will convince both kinds of readers to attend to the whole.

CHAPTER 1

Philosophy, Democracy, and the Turn to Film

In a democracy we are entitled to ask of any organized pursuit whether it contributes to our collective activity of governing ourselves under the rule of law. This is not the only question we want to ask; nevertheless, it is an important question because a democratic polity's first obligation is to preserve the conditions of its own operation. Politics is, in this sense, the condition of all other activities, public and private. We know this not just from Hobbes's theorizing of the state of nature but from the history of great wars of the twentieth century. Total war really does mean total. When politics turns deadly, it can destroy everything and everyone.

This political demand made on philosophy is no different from that made on the financial system. We want to know not whether bank practices make individuals a lot of money but whether they contribute to the well-being of the entire community. We ask the same question of other cultural and social pursuits: do their contributions serve a public purpose, or do they undermine public purposes? Philosophy, particularly political and moral theory, has not convinced many people of its public purpose. Some suspect that philosophy breeds a kind of ideological conceit that tends to polarize the community; others suspect that it is likely to lead people astray, forsaking common sense for ideology.[1]

The democratic challenge to philosophy is both ancient and familiar, beginning with the trial of Socrates. He was charged with and convicted of corrupting the young with false beliefs relating to those entities—the gods—that were thought necessary for the political cohesion and effectiveness of the city. His defense failed, but it showed us something important about the nature of philosophy's defense. He offered no list of Socratic doctrines, the political impact of which could then have been evaluated. Rather, his defense was an effort to engage his accusers—and judges—in the activity of philosophy. The defense of philosophy, in other words, is the practice of philosophy. This is exactly the task I plan to take up in this work: to defend philosophy by engaging the reader in philosophy.[2] Philosophy is a practice of discourse, not a set of doctrines. We don't learn philosophy by learning what philosophers have believed. We learn philosophy by engaging with each other in a critical examination of our own beliefs and practices.

Philosophical engagement needs a common object of discourse. I propose that we turn to popular films for two reasons: first, because they are popular, they are widely known and easily accessible; second, because they are popular, the imaginative resources they deploy are responsive to the audience's expectations. We are that audience. Talking about popular film is, therefore, a way of talking about ourselves.

What does such a philosophical inquiry look like? We could begin with literally any film playing at the local cinema. I will begin with a recent winner of the Academy Award for Best Motion Picture of the Year (along with four other Oscars): The Artist.[3] I choose it not for its content but only because its success suggests familiarity.

The plot of The Artist frames a particular moment in the history of film: the transition from silent films to talking movies. The narrative traces the fall of a silent-film star, George Valentin, and the rise of a talking starlet, Peppy Miller. It forces us to think about the transition from silence to sound by taking us back across the divide, for the film is itself (mostly) silent.[4] The film takes the point of view of silent film, reflecting on its own demise. We experience a kind of guilty pleasure, for we know that such films are "primitive" and that we are no longer supposed to like them. They are artifacts for historical study, not contemporary forms of entertainment. Enjoying the film, we indulge in a double break: the break that every film offers from the ordinary demands of our lives, but also the break with an expected form of contemporary entertainment. We appreciate the aesthetic quality of the film, and we are proud of ourselves for achieving that appreciation. It is as if we decided to read Latin for a few hours instead of turning on the television—except that it turns out that it is the television that is presenting the Latin, and it now fits our contemporary expectations.

The Artist is nostalgic in form, but the entire deployment of the techniques of silent film is done with a certain irony. There is no sense, for example, that the film is meant to inaugurate a wider return to silent films. This is not traditionalism or romanticism. The experience aimed for is not the lost aesthetic virtues of the silent actor, as if they were something to be recovered. We are never unaware of the artificiality of the film's denial of voice. Neither does the film examine the diverse technical, economic, and social factors that figured in the moment of transition. The transition is really just the background against which a very familiar story is played out. That story would be the same on either side of the transition; thus, it can easily span the transition itself.

The film's return to silence is not exactly a gimmick, but neither is it serious. It is a form of play. As such it startles us. It gives us access to a certain joy in the visual representation of narrative, where the sound of dialogue gives way to the sound of music. From the very first scene of an audience watching a silent film accompanied by a live orchestra, we are aware that music is going to carry us along the plotline. Music signals emotional investment, as well as continuity and disruption. There is no doubt a pleasure in coupling the visual to the musical, without the disruption of speech. But there is also a point: we don't really need speech to understand the narrative of the film and to experience the impact of plot and characters. We know exactly what is going on and who these characters are, but not by virtue of anything they say—or, at least, hardly by virtue of language, since there is an occasional intertitle offered.

The film juxtaposes the technical change of the medium—from silence to talkies—with the personal drama of actors whose successes and failures are products of these changes. Valentin, the Artist, begins as a wildly successful silent-screen actor. Because he refuses to speak, he is left behind by a changing Hollywood. His personal life disinte-grates—divorce, poverty, alcohol, loneliness—as his professional career collapses. At the same time, Miller succeeds. The two meet in a chance encounter that ends with a kiss, when he is still a star and she has yet to begin her career. He helps her with her initial steps into the business of silent film. We already expect that by the end, she will return the favor. Soon, she displaces him as the face—and voice—of the new cinema. Of course, she is silently in love with him and continues to do her best to protect him during his self-imposed, destructive exile. In the end she saves him by finding a new medium of sound that is neither voice nor silence, in which the two can perform together on a common ground: tap dancing.

The audience can make sense of this film-without-voice because we know the plot so well. We recognize a world filled with egotistical men who must learn of their dependence on women; corporate agents who make decisions based on money, not friendship; and servants who act out of care rather than for money. Most of all, we know the story of the triumph of love. Valentin would be self-directed as an artist in control of his creations. He fails because no one is in such control. Looking at his own shadow projected on a screen—the null point of his "screen image"—he reaches his moment of self-awareness, describing himself as "stupid" and "proud." His sin has been pride. He has confused the adulation of his fans with genuine love.

He thinks people love him because of his artistry, but what they love is the movies. They love his screen self, of which the real artist has been just the momentary and accidental beneficiary. Thus, when he realizes his sin is one of pride, his film image literally walks off the screen, leav-ing him alone, which is just what he is outside of the studio's production capacities. Change the production output, and the people move on. That the audiences move on to Peppy Miller is just an accident. She is no more in control than he is.

What is not an accident is that he cannot regain control and find meaning in that life until he opens himself to the love of another. To be alone is to be nothing at all.[5] For the Artist, to be alone is not to be seen; it is to have no projected image of himself. In this state he acts to complete his own negation by violently destroying himself. To become someone again, he must admit his vulnerability; he must give up his pride. Only then can he love. Thus, the end of the film—a raucously joyous production of a tap-dancing number by Valentin and Miller—contrasts vividly with the opening of the film, in which he comes onstage to the enthusiastic reception by an audience and then deliberately slights his costar, who is also his wife. Valentin's redemption occurs through the process of his first being humbled and then his recognizing that only love can make us whole. To get to this position, he must choose to trust Peppy Miller. "Trust me" is just what she says to him, as she brings him out of the depths of suicidal despair.

Shortly before the end of the film, there is a suicide scene in which Valentin puts a gun to his head, while Peppy races to reach him. Here, the film deploys the oldest Christian theme: through death is life. She is the agent of his rebirth. Romantic love has taken over the imaginary space of Christian faith. This, of course, is the theme of countless films: we must give up an image of the self alone in order to find the true self through love. Trust establishes the genuine bond to another, which is completely different from the solipsistic relationship between the artist and his screen image. Thus, the name of the new movie in which Valentin and Miller star as a tap-dancing team is *The Sparkle of Love*. That sparkle is both internal and external: in love, the two of them can now recreate the world.

This is a very old story. We can cast it against political change, economic change, technological change, or even the change that is personal aging. Change, which we cannot prevent or avoid, defeats any claim that we are masters of ourselves. The film brings the point home by linking the cinematic change to the collapse of the stock market. The movie star and the Wall Street mogul both learn that they are decidedly not "masters of the universe"—to use a contemporary expression. The film tells us that we must accept our vulnerability and meet it through our reliance on love. We learn this lesson from the least among us: servants and women. Against change and the threat of change we have only the steadfastness of love.

The Artist succeeds because we are so familiar with this story of the sin of pride, the experience of fall, and the recovery brought about by love. This story has as good a claim as any other to be the founding narrative of the West. It is still preached in our churches; it fills the airwaves; it is there at the movies. Do we not want our children to take it to heart? It was no accident that *The Artist* was produced while the entire West was reeling from the economic collapse of 2008. Behind its play of nostalgia we see the imaginary resources that we bring to bear in our own reflections on the meaning of economic collapse today. *The Artist* tells us that we must learn anew to dance together. The Oscar goes to the film that shows us yet again who we are or, at least, who we should be.

The film is, of course, entirely implausible. It offers melodramatic exaggeration, as well as anachronism. We don't care, though, for the film is not trying to describe the world but to tell again the myth of the redemptive power of love. If we press the film for its political vision, however, it yields a somewhat darker result. For there is one group, of which we catch a glimpse, whose silence is not merely a matter of technology. These are the nondescript, shadowy figures of the corporate board, who decide without bothering to speak—at least to us. They control the studio, and against them Valentin has nothing to plead. We know, even if we are not quite aware, that they control Valentin's fate, just as they control Peppy's. Interestingly, the film cannot help but let in this glimpse of power, even as it indulges the myth of love and redemption.

Power penetrates the fantasy but only for a moment. The visible narrative of the film adheres to the myth or what I will call an "archetype." Thus, when Valentin tries to produce a silent film that can hold off the new world of talkies, he utterly fails. Our glimpse of that film-within-a-film, however, produces the one moment of genuine surprise in *The Artist*. As Valentin is sinking to his death in quicksand, he says (in a dialogue box) to the presumed heroine, "I never loved you." We are shocked, for we expect the last words always to be of love. With such a final line, how could his film not fail? That unsuccessful ending is contrasted with a number of endings we see of the new, talking films of Peppy Miller, which offer just what we expect: the success of love. She always gets her man. To this story even the men of power must pay their respects. Power is always complicated; it is rarely unidirectional.

Valentin fails as an artist because he has failed at love. His wife has left him; he has no children. He has only a dog, whom he obviously does love and who requites that love. Most of all, however, he loves himself. He is doomed to fail until he learns to love another. We do not need words to understand this plot. It is a part of who we are. It was there, we might say, at the beginning. If we ask why we imagine the world in this way, the answer is not simply because this is the way the world is. That would be the answer of religion. Neither, however, is the answer that our imaginations are stuck in a prerational world framed in childhood. That would be the answer of psychoanalysis. Philosophy's role is to help us grasp the archetype and to understand how it works as we navigate our common world of meaning. Philosophy's role is not to judge this as good or bad. That determination depends on whom we love and how we love.

What would we say if asked to explain our lives? Many of us would begin to offer a narrative not unlike what we find in *The Artist*. We, too, struggle for the redemptive promise of love; we, too, fear the emptiness of a self alone and powerless before a changing world. Even as we offer this narrative of fall and redemption, however, we are suspicious of the play of power that we cannot quite grasp. Philosophy follows these narrative paths and brings them to our attention. It does not tell us how to respond: we might choose to abandon or reform some of these beliefs and practices; we might affirm them. It is enough for philosophy that we come to know ourselves.

The Artist is structured around a powerful imaginative configuration that is widely shared. We appeal to it in explaining not just our own lives but those of others. The narrative often grounds a feeling of trust: we can trust those who have learned this lesson of love. Often, the narrative is configured as one of a dissolute youth who almost succumbs but is rescued by love. George W. Bush offered this story, but so did Edward Kennedy. Change the context and we have Saint Augustine. The narrative can be used to describe entire societies.[6] They, too, are tested when individuals pursue only their private interests. When the crisis—change—occurs, they are not prepared. They succeed only as they learn again the lesson that we must love one another. How often was this imaginative construction used to give sense and direction to the national project that began on 9/11? In *The Artist* we see the story as comedy, but it is also powerfully present in tragedy. Listen to the narratives offered in the wake of the killings in Aurora, Colorado, in July of 2012. There the deaths were real, but the lesson we are to draw is the need for love. Philosophy's object of inquiry is the meaning created and maintained by the narrative. It is distinct from the efforts of "experts" to explain the causes of the shooting, whether in individual personality disorder or in social factors such as an absence of gun control. Philosophers are distinct, as well, from those who use the event as an occasion to express an opinion—for example, we have become too irreligious or too permissive. Philosophy lies between science and opinion.

BETWEEN SCIENCE AND OPINION

Promising more than it could deliver, traditional philosophy has lost its audience. Most people believe it has also lost its point. Who thinks that metaphysics has more to teach us than physics about the nature of the real? If space is curved and time slows down at the speed of light, what are we going to learn from the metaphysicians? Physics is stranger and more puzzling than anything metaphysics has to offer. Does philosophy do any better with morality? Moral theory seems to have been stuck on the same debate for more than two hundred years: should we follow the utilitarians or the deontologists, Bentham or Kant? Too much Bentham, on the one hand, and we may start cutting up individuals to use their body parts to save others. Why not trade the one for the many, if we are strict utilitarians? Too much Kant, on the other hand, and we start speaking the truth to the Nazi at the door asking about the Jews hiding in the attic. Which of us would ask a philosopher for advice in a tough case?

What about political theory? Surely here philosophy can help us to get our principles right. There has been no lack of philosophical work on the basic principles that must inform a liberal polity. Those principles, however, have been deeply challenged by the communitarians and are now questioned by the multiculturalists. Arguing against both are the postmodernists, who tell us that there is no distinction to be made between philosophy and ideology or ideology and power. Can philosophy do more than provide arguments in support of the political positions we already hold?

The actual political injustices of our day—and every other—are so evident that philosophy seems beside the point. The most pressing problems of politics today are less of the sort "What should we do?"

than of the sort "What can we do?" We don't know how to make our actual political arrangements function effectively, even with respect to the goals that we agree on. We don't need to theorize about health care to know that we need to reduce its price and increase its coverage. The same is true of the dislocations threatened by global climate change. We don't need complex inquiries into the demands of equality to know that the distribution of wealth in this country is deeply problematic. We don't need to inquire into the nature of justice to know that there is something wrong in a society that imprisons so many of its young minority men. We don't need theory to condemn genocide, torture, and corruption.

Political paralysis and moral uncertainty cannot be cured by philosophy. Even when philosophy has interesting and important things to say about the nature of our political problems, it does not have any particular insight into how to make ideas effective as political practice. Today, however, we have a great need for people who can practice a political art, whether or not they are well grounded in theory. That art requires situated judgment, for the scope of possible action is a matter of context and history. Theory will not tell us how to move people to act; rather, it is a call for them to stop acting while they take the time to reflect. It will not tell us how to mobilize to create a movement or to seize an opportunity.

When we turn from the United States to Europe, there is a stronger argument to be made that theory has mattered to politics. The last century was the great age of political theory. Who would care to repeat it? If Kant led to Hegel, Hegel to Marx, and Marx to Lenin, who can trust theory? The problem is not just on the left. Whatever else we might say about Carl Schmitt and Martin Heidegger—two of Weimar's greatest philosophers—they did support Hitler. Our own philosophers were slow to identify the problems of racism and quick to protect property. The judgment of our age seems to be that when it comes to politics, philosophy is either worthless or dangerous.[7]

There is very little evidence to suggest that we should trust philosophers with power, but of course power is not on offer. If not power, what about advice? Hasn't the role of philosophy been to "speak truth to power"? Philosophy, however, is not going to settle our arguments over the requirements of justice or the procedural arrangements that adequately meet the multiple demands of fairness, recognition, and efficiency. It has had thousands of years to resolve such issues. Still today, we can do no better than to read Plato and Aristotle, if we want to think philosophically about these problems.

Even if we thought that our politics would be aided by clarifying the basic norms of political life, few would think that philosophers could help us. Most people probably think that philosophy would just make the problem of disagreement even worse. Philosophy, they think, is just another forum for the expression of opinion, and opinion is relatively impervious to argument.

Philosophers inadvertently support this common view, because they do not reach a consensus. Philosophy is not like science, in which experts converge on common answers. Scientists converge because they share an immense body of knowledge, as well as common disciplinary rules for what counts as a contribution. Philosophers share neither. If the philosophers do not agree, does that suggest that there is no knowledge to be had here? If there is no knowledge, must it all be opinion?

The political reception of philosophy today is actually burdened by the fact that its practice is a form of speech. Philosophers produce nothing but talk. In America, where speech has such a privileged political position, there tends to be a flattening of all forms of discourse. In terms of legal regulation, this may be a good thing. Its effect is to extend the protections of the First Amendment well beyond the parameters of formal, political debate.[8] Nevertheless, one consequence of this broad protection is a failure to draw distinctions. Every argument becomes an expression of opinion, a point of view.[9] We find ourselves puzzling over the speech rights of creationists. Are they not entitled to express their opinion just as much as the supporters of evolution?

If speech is speech, then everyone has a philosophy in the same way that everyone has a religion: "a philosophy of life."[10] The very meaning of philosophy has been inverted: instead of a practice of critical inquiry, philosophy now delineates a set of privileged beliefs that need not be defended. To suggest otherwise seems an expression of undemocratic elitism. Why should it matter how one reached one's opinions? What matters is the expression of them. With the recent extension of free speech rights to corporations, even a corporation can have a philosophy.

It is just more speech, and are we not all better off when we have more speech competing for our attention?[11]

These views about freedom of speech—more speech is better—are increasingly difficult to explain. In classic First Amendment jurisprudence an unrestricted domain of free expression was thought to lead, in the long run, to truth.[12] The competition among ideas—not the regulation of expression—would be the most effective way of moving from falsehood to insight. But this mode of thinking presumes that people are listening to each other with a certain openness. Ironically, the Internet may have dealt the deathblow to the marketplace of ideas as the justification for free speech. The Internet invites a turning to the like-minded in the reception of opinion, not an engagement with others.[13] This is a market without exchange. The very idea of critical exchange can get no foothold when every instance of public speech becomes simply a way of reaffirming an opinion.

Reflecting these changes in the economy of speech, more recent justifications of free speech tend to rely on values of autonomous self-expression.[14] It's not about persuasion, and not about truth, but about authenticity. I should not have to keep from public display any aspect of myself. That would render me effectively "in the closet." The public sphere becomes a place for recognition rather than deliberation. Under the norm of recognition difference is no longer measured on a scale of truth because there is no truth to be had apart from the difference itself. The result is a kind of aestheticization of speech, which finds its political expression in our contemporary practice of identity politics.

When philosophers come to the public sphere pedaling the products of their own inquiries, they will be treated just like any other merchants of opinion. If they are "lucky," they will be invited onto the talk shows alongside the religious claimants and the political ideologues. Each has an opinion. No matter how successful they are personally, this will be the end of philosophy. Philosophy's claim is that it is not simply another moment for the expression of opinion but rather a form of inquiry into what opinion is worth having. Its role is critical, not expressive. Philosophers should have no settled opinions, because they cannot know in advance where that practice of critical deliberation will lead. Whatever respect the philosopher is due attaches to his or her pursuit of discourse as a practice of freedom—not freedom in the sense of a lack of external constraint but freedom as a quality to be earned by an openness to engage, reconsider, and experiment.[15]

Philosophy is neither science nor opinion. If these are our only alternatives, then philosophy has simply disappeared. The first problem for philosophy today, then, is to defend the possibility of a free practice of critical self-reflection that disavows the universal claims of science but insists that it is more than a personal opinion.[16] What philosophy has always promised is an "examined life." What this might be I have begun to illustrate in my discussion of *The Artist*.

One comes out of the theater with an opinion: the movie struck you as good or bad. It left you feeling good about Valentin's success or bad because you know that tap dancing has no more of a future in the movies than silent films did. Or perhaps you thought the movie boring because in some sense nothing happened; there were no surprises. Philosophy won't tell you whether your opinion of the film was right or wrong, but it will lead you to see that your opinion relies on an entire world of meanings without which not just the movie, but everything in your life, can make no sense. To come to understand the nature of this world is the task of philosophy.

PHILOSOPHY AND POLITICAL LEGITIMACY

Philosophy, I am arguing, should return to its Socratic roots. At stake is "an examined life," not some grander scheme of truth, whether at the foundation of knowledge or of political and moral practices. Recent political philosophy, however, has offered a very different democratic defense of itself—one grounded in the discovery of the first principles of a legitimate political order. We need to consider the strength of that claim before we head to the movies.

Here is the most compelling argument I can imagine linking philosophy to political legitimacy. It is important in a democratic political order that somewhere in the society there be an ongoing conversation about the grounds of political authority. The importance of that conversation does not arise from its direct impact on particular policies. We are not waiting for the outcome of that conversation in order to know what to do. Rather, the argument for the political importance of this conversation is that politics is the sort of activity that gains legitimacy by inviting an open and transparent examination of its first principles. Habit and tradition alone are not enough. While those qualities are important for long-term stability, with stability comes the threat of perpetuating the unjust and the inefficient. A modern, democratic practice of governance rests on a faith in its own legitimacy, but that faith will fail without the belief that the question of legitimacy is not just potentially open but actually engaged. In short, the modern political order requires an acknowledgment that fundamental issues are being addressed by someone, even if not by everyone.

There is, no doubt, an aura of legitimacy that comes from the knowledge that someone is subjecting our political practices to examination. The Supreme Court is arguably the institutionalized presence of this role in the United States.[17] But the Court is part of the political order. There are, therefore, limits on its critical capacities. In particular, it addresses discrete problems and only as they come to it in the form of justiciable controversies. It asks whether laws and practices are constitutional; it does not ask whether the constitution is itself just or whether the government it creates is legitimate. A broader critique serves the broader purpose of sustaining our political faith in the basic forms of our political life.

How this air of legitimacy actually arises is less than clear. Perhaps it arises from the conviction that this conversation must continue in the background so that it remains available at moments of crisis. Or perhaps political legitimacy arises in exactly the opposite way: the continuation of such a background conversation prevents the emergence of a crisis of political legitimacy. Our faith in scientific inquiry would fail if we thought the first principles of a field could not bear reexamination when new problems arise. Political legitimacy may be like scientific inquiry in this respect. These two possibilities loosely correspond to Thomas Kuhn's view of scientific investigation, moving between episodes of revolutionary paradigm shift and ordinary science.[18] A similar parallel might be drawn to religious practice. The ordinary church member may not see the direct relevance of theological speculation to the claims of faith. But the idea that faith can support a deep theological inquiry may lend some sort of legitimacy to ordinary practices. Just imagine the opposite: a religious practice that could not bear such an examination.

Contemporary political philosophy lays claim to just this sort of foundational role, identifying and defending the first principles of a democratic polity. The dominant works of political theory over the last generation, those of John Rawls and Jürgen Habermas, arguably fit here. Rawls saw that there is nothing about the political order that cannot be questioned from the perspective of justice. For him this meant that we had to develop a theory of justice that went all the way down. Most dramatically, one is not necessarily entitled to the benefits of one's personal endowments. Those productive capacities may be in part natural, but the distribution of the benefits must be measured by a norm of justice.[19] We need, then, to agree on a theory of justice to move from production to distribution. Agreement, he thought, could be reached if we all imagined ourselves behind a veil of ignorance. At that point we could rely only on the voice of reason, which will speak in the same manner through each of us. In that original position, to which we return in philosophical argument, we will consent to basic norms of governance that are themselves the product of pure, practical reason—pure because nothing apart from reason can penetrate the veil.

Habermas's work is similar to that of Rawls in substance and form. Instead of distributive justice, Habermas focused on the legitimacy of political outcomes: what are the conditions under which we are legitimately bound by a political decision?[20] Just as Rawls saw that there is nothing natural about distributions, Habermas saw that there is no self-evident, Archimedean point from which we can construct a political order. Once we realize that everything about the polity is entirely artificial—that is, man-made—there is no premise that cannot be questioned. Instead of understanding legitimacy as a foundational point from which all political order derives, he located legitimacy in an open process of discourse in which we seek to justify to each other our political arrangements. The first task of philosophy is not to specify a substantive norm of justice but to articulate the norms of discursive justification. Those norms offer a discourse ethics that must then be used to create— or evaluate—a viable institutional structure. We need not imagine a veil of ignorance; rather, we need to create institutions in which citizens can exchange arguments in an effort to persuade each other by speech alone.

Both Rawls and Habermas operate at the foundations of political order. Both are committed to individual rights of equality and recognition. Both ask under what conditions a political order can legitimately exercise coercion over an individual. Both are doing fundamental philosophy at a point close enough to our actual institutions that their work speaks critically to our practices. Both present their work in massive tomes that are inaccessible to all but professional philosophers. The substance of their theories is democratic, but this is hardly philosophy for a democratic audience. Indeed, one has to go to graduate school just to have the time to read the books. Nevertheless, each has had an enormous impact on the practice of political philosophy. Political theory became largely commentary on their work.

The question remains whether the political philosophy spawned by Rawls and Habermas has served the democratic purpose of grounding belief in the legitimacy of our practices and institutions or of encouraging reform of these practices in the direction of legitimacy. In the end this argument seems weak and close to apologetics. Can we really claim that the philosophy department is the center of critique upon which the legitimacy of the political order depends? Writing commentary on John Rawls is hardly the same as writing commentary on the Bible—after all, the Bible has been in popular circulation for millennia, while nonprofessionals will never read Rawls.

My argument for the legitimizing role of philosophy may have let the philosophers off too easily. Unable to show how philosophy is relevant, I have argued that philosophy is a condition of any sort of legitimate politics. The argument defends philosophy in the abstract, without offering any way to know whether the professional discourse of philosophy that we have today actually serves this purpose. How could I even begin to give a demonstration of this point? We do know that, despite the work of Rawls and Habermas, our actual political practices have deteriorated in both of the dimensions on which they focused. The distribution of wealth has moved dramatically in the direction of inequality; our political discourse is driven, if not controlled, by vested interests.[21] Philosophers are not at fault. But of what use is philosophy when it is cast as the construction of ideal norms, whether of justice or process?

The problem for engaged citizens, including holders of public office, is not that they have no interest in fundamental norms. Rather, they don't know what to make of the ideal types that are generated by contemporary theorists, and they have no interest at all in the professional discourse that has developed around those ideal types. Our political practices have become far too complicated and interrelated for us to believe that such first principles can help us going forward. After all, the dominant political development of the age may be the embrace of capitalism by a communist country, China. In the confrontation between theory and practice, theory has turned out to be a weak force both here and abroad. A philosophy of first principles is neither capable of, nor suitable for, doing actual political work.

Contrary to Rawls and Habermas, fundamental theory has no special place in determining the shape of a political practice.[22] There are also values of commitment, care, faith, and love, which are no less at issue in our political communities but may be incommensurable with the claims of justice. These norms do not appear as abstract propositions. We don't come to a conclusion about the nature of love behind a veil of ignorance; we don't find our commitments through discourse ethics. Political theorists tend to believe that the abstract determines the possible, but this is exactly backwards. In politics the actual produces the possible. Finding myself committed to the nation, my possible world is shaped by the actual. Commitment cannot compete with justice if theory sets the terms of the debate. But why should it? It was love that moved Adam in the Garden and faith that moved Abraham as he went to sacrifice Isaac. We are not so different in the range of our beliefs and commitments. Was this not the message of *The Artist:* to insist on principle looks like pride, and there is no reasoning with love.

If we claim that with respect to political acts and institutions all of these values should be subordinated to justice, and that justice is a matter of reason, we still need to persuade others to that position. Reason's superior role is not a self-evident first principle with which all must agree. That claim will always be contested by those who worship other gods, literally or metaphorically. To observe the plurality of values at work in the community is not an argument against justice or a claim that justice is irrelevant. Rather, the point is that justice is one value among others. A political practice surely should take account of justice, but it is not the case that it must seek to realize a theory of justice. *The Artist* ends with trust, not justice.

Politics arises out of the diverse practices and beliefs of the members of the community. If we argue that these should all be subjected to the ordering of an abstract norm of justice, then we are announcing that we are people who maintain certain beliefs about the good and about ourselves.[23] We may be such a people, or some of us may believe this about ourselves some of the time. Surely, philosophy has a role in elaborating what those beliefs are, but it is beyond its mandate to say that people who do not share those beliefs should. Would they become better if they did so? How would we answer that question when the issue is what constitutes the basic norms by which to evaluate the quality of a life?

It is hard, of course, to speak of justice without implicitly assuming that it is *the* norm that is to govern our relationships with others. But as soon as we make that assumption, we have to bring theory into contact with the actual community. Philosophers often imagine this as a contrast between religious particularity and the universality of reason. They think that all of modernity—history itself—is on their side. They believe that what is self-evident to them will be self-evident to others, as soon as the blindfolds of particular cultures are removed—thus the veil-of-ignorance metaphor. Reason, they argue, is universal exactly because it requires no prior commitments of faith, only an openness to arguments that meet standards to which all can, and therefore should, agree. But religion is not the only source of particular values that stand up against reason. As we saw in *The Artist*, we are more likely to speak of love than faith, but the conflict between the universal and the particular is the same.[24]

I am not going to be moved by an argument for justice when it stands against the love I feel for particular individuals. I literally do not care if the acts I take out of love are in conflict with justice. For those whom we love, we will sacrifice our all, even if that means injustice to others. What parent would abandon a child for the sake of justice? Of course, we hope that the choice will not have to be made, but in small ways it is made all the time. Each time I choose to favor my own family over the claims of equality for others, I am choosing love over justice. Most of us would not have it any other way. But this tells us a great deal about the way in which meanings actually create and sustain our world.

There is no natural hierarchy of norms that puts justice first. We don't assess the relative merits of different nations on a scale of justice when we identify ourselves politically. We know who we are quite independently of the justice of our nation's policies. We find ourselves already committed because we literally find ourselves in a world. That world is not a product of reason, as if we built it from behind a veil of ignorance. Peppy Miller simply shows up for no reason at all. We are not behind the veil but in front of the screen. None of this means that we are indifferent to injustice or to issues of reform—only that the place of justice in our normative universe is not self-evident. Its place is not fixed by abstract argument.

As a democratic, political community we don't need a theory of justice. Rather, we need something far more modest: a critical capacity to orient ourselves toward our own beliefs and practices. Philosophy's role, if it is to have one outside of the university, is not to ground but to disrupt. It does so not by turning to first principles, as if its grand topics can be settled once and for all; rather, it disrupts by asking each of us to take up the task of examining who we are, what we believe, and to what we are committed.

PHILOSOPHY AND THE SOCIAL IMAGINARY

Philosophers cannot make people other than they are, but philosophers can help them to understand better who they are. The promise cannot be that critical self-understanding will make people more politically effective or morally virtuous, for we have no idea of the nature of the connection between self-awareness and action. Thinking too much is a familiar source of inaction. Virtuous action may arise from character and impulse as much as from reflection.[25] Nevertheless, the pursuit of self-knowledge remains a deeply attractive course to many people. Self-understanding remains a form of wisdom, and this is the only knowledge that philosophy can promise. Like Socrates, we must act with faith that, introduced to the possibility of an examined life, individuals will take up the invitation. The disruptive discipline of philosophy can promise no more than to make us individually and collectively a problem to ourselves.

Is there, then, any public role for philosophy? Not if we mean by this some form of application of theory to practice. But this is to measure philosophy by a particular understanding of what constitutes a public role. In this view there is no public role for art or even for liberal education. Yet we believe that art and education are critical for the character of our political life—not because they are a means to some other end but because they constitute a part of that life. Art and education are activities we perform together, and doing so, we constitute a public domain of meaning. The same can be true of philosophy.

Politics, narrowly, is the work of the institutions of governance. But democratic politics, broadly seen, is our living together in a common domain of meaning—a culture. Our political institutions reflect and contribute to our identity, but that identity is first of all a matter of finding ourselves with a shared social imaginary.[26] Together we imagine a common world that binds us to each other through shared values, practices, and meanings. The social imaginary sustains our history, as well as our sense of the future; it establishes the boundaries of home and homeland; it tells us what is the nature of the family and the community; it offers the variety of forms in which we each think it possible to realize a meaningful life. Many of these points are already evident in a film as narratively simple as *The Artist*, the interpretation of which requires inquiry into love and death, pride and loneliness, change and commitment, as well as myth and power.

The social imaginary is that which sustains what Clifford Geertz referred to as "webs of significance."[27] Referring to the social imaginary, rather than simply speaking of culture, is a way of emphasizing that the human world of meaning is a product of the imagination and that imagining the world is a collective project. The world within which we live has no existence apart from our imagining it together. A film is just such a common imagining, and philosophy's role can be to bring to light the web of significance that the film simultaneously creates and maintains.

People do not occupy the world as if they were dropped into an environment upon which they now do experiments to determine its nature and limits. We can study the world in that way, but this is not the way we occupy the world first of all and most of the time. The world in which I imagine myself is one in which I am bound by a geography of emotional space. Space has a meaning to me that is established by the multiple narratives that make sense of my place in the world. I think of my country not as a geographical formation but as the site and consequence of a history. I think of my more immediate home as the site of my family history. The same is true in every dimension of our experience. Lived time is not that of the chronographer. Rather, it is history and hope, duration and completion. We remember and we plan. We mourn for loss and hope for redemption. Of course, I can make a time line from the beginning of the universe to the end. I can take up the attitude of the scientist toward time, just as I can take the geographer's attitude toward space, but the lived significance of that time line begins when I place myself on it. My time becomes the reference point from which I imagine all other time.

Modern science had to work very hard to free itself of the idea that human beings and the earth are at the center of the universe. The modern era arguably began with the realization that humanity's perspective on the world was not a privileged point from which to determine truth. Indeed, absent the capacity to transcend that perspective, to take the view from nowhere, science is not likely to find any truth at all. But the discovery of the necessities of science is misunderstood if taken as a statement about the way in which the subject lives in the world or about the shape of the world as a matter of lived experience.[28] The sun may not go around the earth, but surely we live as if it rises and sets each day. Science did not change that; it did not put the poets out of business, and it did not render the imagination merely a source of falsehood.

A useful analogy to other organisms can be made. When we ask how the bird finds its way south or how ants know how to build a nest, we are imagining them as subjects acting on an external world. How, we ask, do they know how to do this? But we don't ask how a liver knows how to produce bile or lungs know how to breathe. We don't say that the liver works by "instinct." But what does *instinct* mean beyond our observation that the organism pursues certain functions? The boundary between inside and outside is something that we bring to our perception of the organism.[29] It is not simply there. The organism is in the world not as a ball is in a box but rather as an organization of functions. It does not see a world and decide how to act. Rather, it is always being-in-the-world. There are, we might say, as many worlds as there are organized ways of being. Biologists speak of an ecological "niche," but it is wrong to think of this as some place that precedes the organism, which then adapts itself to it. The niche is only a niche to an organism, and the organism is only such to the niche. Neither exists without the other, not because they are well matched but because each only makes sense with respect to the other.

People are not so different from other organisms in their relationship to their world. That world does not precede us as a niche into which we enter. It comes into being only with us, and it lasts only as long as we last. We are not separate from it nor it from us. It is easiest to see this with respect to language. Language is simultaneously an objective feature of our world and something that only exists for and through us. We cannot conceive of ourselves apart from language, yet it is not in us. It is an aspect of our way of being-in-the-world. We can say the same thing of history and other aspects of our culture that together constitute our world. The important difference between us and other organisms is not culture versus nature but rather our capacity to take our world as an object of thought. It hardly follows, however, that our world is entirely plastic, as if a world that relies on symbols is one that can be reformulated at will. Many of our ways of being in the world are more durable than any possible project of reconstruction: for example, language and family.[30]

The work of the social imaginary in creating and sustaining a world is not different in kind from the work of the artistic imagination. Entire worlds are at stake in the imaginative work of artistic creation. A novel or a film does not just present us an issue to think about. When we are watching a film or reading a novel, we often stop thinking of ourselves as observers on the outside. Rather, we have a sense of the whole from the inside. A film is not a commentary, and it is not theory. It is rather a showing forth of a world that is its own construction. Of course, that world does not come from nowhere. It is no less dependent on the social imaginary. For that reason a film can be used as an initial point from which to engage in critical self-reflection on our common beliefs and practices.

Philosophy must find its place as a critical form of the same imagination that creates the work of art, the historical narration, or the discourse among family or friends. Its function is critical not in the sense of offering a practical critique but in the sense of exposing to view that which we take for granted. Philosophy can aim to show us how the imagination constructs the world that we find ourselves within and that we share with others. It can do so only by offering an interpretation in the same way that one speaks intelligibly of a work of art only by offering an interpretation.[31] Philosophy's role is to interpret in a way that brings to deliberate awareness how the social imaginary creates and sustains meaning.

We inherit the world as a form of social capital; we join in the project of the social imaginary. We come to ourselves and others with commitments to language, families, religions, politics, arts, and forms of knowledge. We come with friends and enemies, with lovers and teachers, with parents and children. We come understanding roles and responsibilities. At no moment are we simply a self alone in a natural world. We come already so deeply attached to this imagined world that we can only say that it is us and we are it.

We want to know how these different imaginative structures intersect and interact with each other, for our lives are complex and rich because of the multiple strands of meaning in our world. Traditional philosophy assumed that politics and morality could be well ordered, but in fact, the world that we occupy does not even follow the principle of noncontradiction. We maintain and pursue multiple values, some in contradiction, some in tension with each other. Rarely do we have to choose between them. When we must, we may face tragedy.

We know all of this intuitively. We operate in the world through a kind of innate sensitivity. The artist creating his work does not first analyze the elements of a world that he or she wants to create. Abstract principle will not produce any particular work. Creating the work is the creation of a world. Each of us takes up the role of artist of our own lives. We do so in the multiple small choices we make each day but also in those moments when we know something important is at stake. We don't apply a rule. We create meaning.

Just as the meaning of my life is not something different from my life, the meaning of our common life is not something different from that life. The community is a means to our individual ends, but it is at the same time a common practice of meaning. In our political life, meaning does not precede the act. We learn who we are by being it. This is true of all products of the imagination. For this reason a theory of art won't produce good art, and a theory of politics won't produce a good polity.

Interpretation begins from the particular—the actual products of the imagination—and explores from there the shape of the possible. When we interpret a work of fiction, we explore the possible world that is brought about by the work. We have no access to that world other than through the work itself. That world sustains the text, but it does not exist apart from the text. In this way the meaning of the work exceeds the boundaries of work. We can, for example, ask of the characters in the story why they acted as they did or what might have happened had they acted otherwise. We see the possible through the actual whenever we deal with the work of the imagination. The same is true of each of us: our possibilities do not precede us but are the consequence of our actual lives.[32]

This structure is at stake when we write history as narrative. History is not the realization of abstract possibilities that somehow exist alongside the facts. An account that is a mere chronicle of facts sees no possibilities at all. What might have been emerges only as we interpret what actually happened. The narrative imagines a meaningful world, one in which the account of what happened gains its sense against what might have happened. Historians cannot locate their narratives at too abstract a level. If they do so, they risk becoming theologians, explicating the unfolding of a divine plan. The idea of unrealized possibilities is always difficult to assign to a perfect God. Neither, however, can the narrative simply stick to the facts as if they were individual events causally related to each other. Human events are not the subject of actual causal demonstration: there are no experiments to be run, no repeat of conditions, no testing.

Of course, one can study large-scale change over time; one can study the human as an aspect of a world determined by causes. Human events have underlying conditions, for example in geography, technology, and economy.[33] The possibilities created in narrative, however, refer not to these structural conditions but to possible decisions or courses of action. A historical narrative holds forth these possibilities, which may not even have been present to mind for the actual actor. The narrative offered by a historian shows us the meaning of events by reading them as the consequences of individuals or groups acting for reasons. The only measure of the historian's success is whether he or she convinces us to see ourselves—or others—in this way. We move from the actual to the possible through an interpretation. History has reasons, not causes, and reasons only are such to a free agent.[34]

Philosophy can no longer hope to convince by drawing on reason alone, as if there were an abstract, normative science to be applied to our community and individual lives. Political theory goes astray as soon as it assumes that the internal aspiration of a community is to realize the ideal of reason, wherever that might lead. If anything, this is a theological construct asserting itself as a secular truth. The normative claim of reason was once grounded in the idea that here we approximate the mind of God. Without that the claim is simply ungrounded. Our life—communal or private—is not a science experiment. It is not fact at all but a grand work of fiction.[35]

Philosophy can take as its task the critical work of the social imagination turned in on itself. A philosophical interpretation differs from other forms of critique in its disregard of disciplinary lines and conventional boundaries. The art critic's role, for example, is to locate a work in its genre and assess whether it is a good or bad performance within that genre. The critic asks whether it is a well executed example of its kind. The philosopher wants to know about the "elementary forms" of the imagination—to understand how they evolved, where they are challenged, and how they fit together. He wants, in other words, to reveal the imaginative world within which the particular both has a meaning and creates possible meanings. His end is to bring some critical awareness to this world. What happens after that is no more up to him than it is to the rest of us. Stopping here, before the project of reform begins, the philosopher shows himself to be a true democrat.[36]

In taking up popular film as the object of a philosophical study, I am translating into contemporary form one of the earliest moments of philosophy. In the *Republic* Socrates asks what justice is. He decides that the direct pursuit of the nature of justice in the soul of man is too difficult a task. He needs, at least at first, an object in which the features of justice will be cast larger and therefore be more evident. He looks, therefore, to justice in the city, as an enlarged image of justice in the soul. He hopes to be able to work the argument back down from the macro to the micro, from the constitution of the city to the constitution of the human being. We face the same problem in asking how it is that the social imaginary constructs and maintains our common world. Rather than pursue the issue directly, we can take up an enlarged image of that world—popular films. The self-contained world of the film will place some boundaries on our inquiry and provide a concrete object with which to explore the patterns and forms of meaning within which we pursue our ordinary lives together.[37] Until and unless philosophy gets out of the ivory towers and back into the streets, it will continue its slow death from lack of care and, even worse, lack of respect.[38]

CHAPTER 2

Freedom and Persuasion

Philosophy, I have argued, must defend itself in a democratic society. If it cannot do so, it risks being dismissed as antiquarian, elitist, or both. Dismissal is hardly the same as prohibition, but those who believe that there is something important at stake in philosophy must make the case. That case has to convince without appealing to claims of some sort of special knowledge that is to be applied in and through our political practices. A political practice is not an effort to implement a theory, and philosophy is not a study of the possibility of political reform. Theories of justice are not irrelevant to politics any more than they are irrelevant in our personal lives. But in both cases justice is one among many values—some of which are incommensurable—that constitute a way of living.

Philosophy does not offer a program of political reform: it cannot promise to make people, collectively or individually, better. It is not like going to a physical trainer or a physician. If successful, the trainer or physician helps the individual in ways that are visible to friends and relatives. Socrates, apparently, had just the opposite effect on his young followers: their friends and parents thought they had taken a turn for the worse. Heidegger was an enthusiastic supporter of National Socialism and tried to convey his enthusiasm to his students. This should not make us reject his philosophical work. Rather, we should condemn his political judgment. The point is that theory and judgment are not the same, and in our collective, political life the latter is far more important than the former.

Philosophy is a form of critical reflection. As such, it is the site of a characteristically human freedom—free thought. We can ask what this exercise of freedom tells us about the exercise of a different sort of freedom: political freedom.[1] But we should not think that free thought and free practice are the same or that the latter is an application of the former. In the end philosophy stands to political life as it stands to every other aspect of life. We seek to understand ourselves because we can. Exercising this capability, we know ourselves as free because we literally claim our beliefs and practices as our own. Without understanding this relationship of critique to freedom, we will always tend to ask too much (or too little) of philosophy. The demand for action will overwhelm the activity of thinking, which is simultaneously the most fragile and enduring of human activities.

PHILOSOPHY AND THE PROBLEM OF FREEDOM: CAUSES AND REASONS

Philosophers often take up the issue of freedom by seeking to understand how free action is possible in a causally determined world. This is indeed an important and difficult issue. It may be even more pressing today as the scientific attitude penetrates ever more deeply into our ordinary experience. Scientific inquiry proceeds under the belief that every event has a cause; an event is explained scientifically when we have identified its cause.[2] Social scientists, too, work under a version of this belief when they search for testable hypotheses regarding the empirical causes of political, economic, or social phenomena. Implicit in the scientific framework is the assumption that if we knew everything about the world right now, then we could predict exactly what will happen next. Scientists realize, of course, that it is not possible to know everything, but this idea of a comprehensively knowable world operates as a kind of regulative ideal in their work. Thus the puzzle: if everything that happens is caused by that which preceded it, how is freedom possible? Does our sense of freedom only reflect the limits of our knowledge of causes?[3]

To hold persons morally accountable for their actions, we have to believe that they had a choice—a free choice—whether to act. Absent an appeal to some idea of divine creation or dispensation, by which human actions are different from all other events, how can we explain the possibility of that free act in a causally determined world? If everything that has happened since the big bang of cosmic origin has had a cause, how can human agency form an exception? Yet the moral demand on human action—a demand we experience as just as compelling as the demand for truth in our knowledge of the world—makes freedom a necessary condition of our own self-understanding. Practically, we cannot lead our lives under the regulative ideal of causality.

We cannot help but act with the belief that we face choices to be made under the guidance of principles and values. When we explain our actions, we speak of reasons, not causes.[4] If we turn to causes, we imply a failure to take responsibility for the self—for example, I was drugged or I was ill. When we try to persuade others, we offer them reasons for deciding one way rather than another. We judge others, legally and morally, under the assumption that they, too, acted for reasons. Thus, the experience of acting for a reason quickly leads the philosopher to the metaphysical problem of determinism: do we live in a causally determined world in which our sense of freely deciding on the basis of reasons is an illusion?

Posing the question in this way is bound to leave us feeling dissatisfied, for we already know that we are equally committed to both answers—freedom and causality. This was Kant's insight: a knowable universe must be one in which causality holds universally, but a person must be capable of acting for a reason. Kant tried to show how both of these answers could be true. His double answer gave a sophisticated new form to the classic distinction of body and soul. The body exists in the world of causes, the soul in that of reasons. Because Kant thought he had to keep these radically separate, he offered a very formalistic account of what it is to act morally. Acting for a reason must come as if from nowhere because the world of objects and interests is determined by causes.

For Kant and most of his followers, morally appropriate reasons for action are those that apply equally to everyone. When we act morally, we do not favor ourselves. Rather, we take up an "objective" or "neutral" position, asking what any rational agent should do under the circumstances. A moral principle, for Kant, has the same compelling quality as a logical proposition. Both present themselves to us as necessarily true; both are quite independent of causes in space and time. Indeed, each carries the indicia of its truth in its formal structure of universality. Thus, his famous categorical imperative: "Act only according to that maxim whereby you can at the same time will that it should become a universal law."[5] For a finite subject, on the one hand, it is a burden to act as reason demands. For a fully rational being, on the other hand, the moral act would be the only possible act. We must will—decide for—the moral act, but a fully rational agent would not be tempted by the alternatives.

It may seem odd today that Kant's answer to the problem of causal determinism was to appeal to the compelling character of reason itself. He stands here in a long philosophical tradition that thinks freedom is realized in the power of reason to compel assent—whether in thought or practice. This suggests the lingering presence of a theological ideal: we realize the truth of ourselves only when we transcend the finite character of the body. Ideas of the body as a "prison," of the senses as offering a merely "perspectival" view of the real, of the material world as one of illusion are all quite familiar.[6] They illustrate that the idea of freedom brings with it a special kind of fear—the fear of an irresponsible use of that freedom. Freedom can look like arbitrariness. The response is to identify freedom with truth, and truth with reason. The cost of freedom, in this view, is literally the abandonment of the particularity of the individual. We are promised immortality, only to learn that it is not personal. When we fall into error, we also fall into sin. At least the sin is our own.

God is the anchor of this entire idea, for God is perfectly free and perfectly ordered.[7] There is a complete overlap of His will and His reason: "In the beginning was the word." We are an "image of God" and must, therefore, strive for a similar overlap of reason and will. He wills the regularity of nature into existence; we must will the regularity of the moral order into existence. This theological background continues not just in moral theory but also in contemporary political theory. When John Rawls argues that the basic order of a political community must be founded on an imagined contract formed behind a veil of ignorance, he is imagining the overlap of reason and will.[8] The point of the veil is to prevent all persons from knowing anything about their particular circumstances, including their character and beliefs. Behind the veil we can rely only on reason, which is the same for everyone. Behind the veil we are before the Fall. Speaking to each other, it is as if we can hear only the voice of God, for we are not yet there. The particularity of the subject has nothing to contribute, apart from error.

Understanding freedom as the product of reason, we miss entirely the experience of free choice as an expression of personal identity. Following a proof, I don't make a decision whether or not to believe its outcome. There is not some further step at the end of a mathematical demonstration in which I decide whether to accept its conclusion. If I don't accept the conclusion, it is because I have doubts about the proof. If I have doubts about proofs in general, then I don't understand what a proof is. The proof is the same for all; there is no place in the construction of a proof at which the identity of the subject enters.[9] The same is true of an analysis of causes. The personhood of the scientist does not enter into the explanation of causes. For this reason an experiment is a demonstration that is repeatable by anyone. Neither logical form nor scientific explanation offers a space for that ordinary experience of freedom as self-realization.

Missing from this account of freedom is the experience of decision. The only moment of decision seems to be the turn to reason itself. That, however, looks more like an act of submission than a decision, for there is only the singular truth of reason to which we must conform our will. That freedom is linked to submission is, of course, an idea with a long history in both Judaism and Christianity.[10] The former links law to freedom; the latter links sacrifice to freedom. Western philosophy continued in this tradition when it saw freedom as a struggle to free the soul of context, beginning with the body itself and then extending to every source of particularity. Stripped of everything, we are to find in ourselves the image of God: a subject of whom we can say nothing apart from the universal truth of reason.[11]

Freedom cannot be distinguished from submission once God and reason coincide. We begin to escape the pull of this image only when we look at how we actually exercise judgment. We find that the decision is a function of neither mind nor body—neither proof nor cause—but of an engaged imagination. We decide when we see the world one way rather than another. This way forward, we are persuaded, makes sense. Principle alone cannot do the work of persuasion, because I can have any number of attitudes toward a principle.

Acknowledging a moral or legal principle is hardly the same as accepting the premises of a deductive proof. Little follows from an argument deploying such a principle, because it is not self-contained in the same way as a proof. First, a moral principle is only one norm among many that I might maintain simultaneously, any two of which might resolve a situation differently. Indeed, I may harbor an aspiration for evil. Second, just as there is disagreement among norms, there is disagreement on how an abstract norm applies to any set of facts. Third, even if we could agree on starting points and on application, there is still no reason to believe that we will reach agreement on what to do.[12] That reason alone should be the source of action is not a self-evident truth of human nature. Instead, it is a proposition that we either do or do not find persuasive given everything else we believe about ourselves and our relationships to others under particular circumstances.

We may have no answer to a moral argument, but still we may be convinced that the right way to act lies in another direction. We may, for example, decide that, under the circumstances, the particularity of love is more important than the universality of a moral rule. We may even acknowledge that what we are doing is morally wrong but still believe that it is what we should do—for example, an act of revenge or of mercy. Moral reasons are not the only reasons; particular relationships may be more important than universal norms. I may have no proof to offer, but proof is not the only sort of reason to which we respond. If to act for a reason is to be persuaded, we must keep in mind the whole range of arguments, examples, intuitions, beliefs, and relationships that can be deployed in order to persuade someone. My reasons for acting refer to more than reason alone.[13]

No principle will tell me whether I should act on care or justice when they point in different directions. That hardly makes me a passive observer of the diverse causes of my own behavior. Out of this contestation of reasons I must decide what to do. The metaphysical possibility of decision itself may be mysterious, but that does not mean that the experience of decision is mysterious. Just the opposite: we are entirely familiar with our own freedom. When asked to explain a decision, I will speak of what I found persuasive and what I did not. Principles will be mixed with analogies, examples with proofs, personal relationships with universal norms. The more dense the reasons, the more I feel that a whole world is at stake in the decision. It always is, even if we are using shorthand expressions, heuristics, and rules of thumb. We decide when we have been persuaded. We are persuaded when we have considered arguments for and against a decision and come to see the world a certain way. Judgment is intertwined with character. What we see is a function of what we believe, and the range of beliefs is without limit. This does not mean that we cannot be surprised or change our minds. Indeed, precisely because the possibilities are open, we can be surprised at where we come out.

Persuasion is at the center of *The Sweet Hereafter*, a film about a lawyer.[14] Lawyers operate at the intersection of causes and reasons. Their task is to bring us to see the world a particular way. They must persuade a decision maker to see the facts as the expression of a norm or as the violation of a norm. Seeing it that way, the decision maker knows what to do. *The Sweet Hereafter* offers a kind of modern theodicy, investigating the worst kind of loss—the death of children. Do we offer reasons or causes to explain such events?

A small town suffers a terrible accident when a school bus bursts through a guard rail onto a frozen river, where it quickly sinks. Many children die. A lawyer from the city shows up. He is there to convince the bereaved parents to join in a lawsuit. The parents had not been thinking of legal action. Their reaction had been that the tragedy was simply an accident. They are not inclined to hold anyone responsible, for they know and trust the bus driver, as well as the mechanic responsible for the bus. The mechanic lost two children; the bus driver survived with injuries. There was, on this initial view, no reason, only a cause, for the accident—a patch of ice. The parents' response is grief, not anger.

The lawyer must persuade the parents to see the event differently. He tells them that there is no such thing as an accident. Somewhere, someone acted for a reason for which he or she should be held accountable: there must have been negligence, deliberate indifference, or a decision to save money instead of considering safety. Tragedy like this does not simply happen as if it were a natural event in the world. The accident is put in a moral framework in which the appropriate response is anger, not grief. We grieve over a death caused by illness; we are angry over an immoral or illegal act. The lawyer's job is to shift the frame of perception. He must persuade them to see an injustice. Wrongdoers must be held accountable. Entering the lawsuit, the parents become agents, not merely passive victims.

The lawyer's commitment to reasons—there are "no accidents"—is juxtaposed to the tragedy of his own life. A second narrative runs through the film, one that involves his relationship to his own adult daughter. She is a drug addict, with all the pathologies that implies. She lies to him; she is involved in crime; she sells herself; and, in the end, she has AIDS. She constantly interrupts his life with phone calls that always become shouting matches as she asks for money. This familial relationship stands as a counterpoint to his legal practice. It shows us that terrible things happen for no reason at all. They happen despite our best efforts.

The lawyer loved his daughter; he was willing to do anything for her. As a child she filled his life with limitless meaning. He remembers in particular an event when she was a toddler. She had been bitten by spiders and had an allergic reaction that threatened to close her windpipe. He and his wife had to drive her forty miles to a hospital. During that entire journey he held a knife ready to cut open her throat in an emergency tracheotomy. He is remembering an Abraham-like moment: Abraham, too, was willing to use the knife on his own child in a mysterious working out of God's command. For love, each would do this.

Outside of the Abrahamic myth things don't always work out. In the lawyer's personal story there is no God whose reasons are real even if inscrutable. Instead, there is only loss for no reason. He has tried every response to his daughter's addiction, every therapeutic intervention. Nothing helps. He, too, is grieving over the loss of a child. This binds him to the parents. But whom is he to hold accountable? There is no one to sue, no one to persuade. Grief is as much a part of our world as anger. We frame different possibilities of response as we register causes or reasons.

He recounts some of his tale of familial loss to a young woman he happens to be seated next to on a plane. She had been a childhood friend of his daughter's and is now working in her father's law firm—she, too, is the daughter of a lawyer. We wonder why she succeeds in life while his daughter fails. There are no reasons. The loss of a child for no reason can throw us into an awful loneliness. We learn that the lawyer and his wife have divorced. In the town of the school-bus tragedy we see that the one father who resists the lawsuit ends up alone. But in a world of loss there is a certain integrity in loneliness. That father takes responsibility for his grief, without displacing it on to anger. The lawyer, too, must find integrity in accepting his loss without blame.

The film offers another parallel in the character of an adolescent girl who survives the crash but ends up in a wheelchair. She had been a wonderful child, portrayed as the much-loved babysitter to two children lost in the accident, as an aspiring singer, and as someone sympathetic to all. She is also seen, however, in a scene of sexual abuse by her father. How can he have such a wonderful daughter, while the lawyer's love for his child is met only by failure and loss? This adolescent is also the key to the entire lawsuit, for she is the most important witness. At the critical moment, when she is giving a deposition describing the accident, she lies in order to subvert the lawsuit. Lying, she chooses the grieving father who refused to join the suit over her own father.

We were not exactly prepared for the lie, but we do have a sense that she took responsibility at this moment. She did not apply a norm. Rather, she saw the way forward, returning the town to a world of silent, lonely grief. She was not persuaded by the lawyer. She was not persuaded because she knows what we suspect. The motivation for the lawsuit is less justice than opportunism; it is about cashing in on the opportunity for gain created by the accident. She knows her father, and she sees through him. She judges him, and judges harshly. The audience is persuaded by her, not by the lawyer. We see the world as she sees it, for despite their loss, these people, including her abusive father, are not entitled to make claims of compensatory justice. They should be grieving, not plotting.

Our view is supported by the reaction of the lawyer, who tells her father that he has more important issues than the lawsuit if his daughter is willing to lie in this situation. Indeed, he does. We think at this point that the lawyer realizes what we already know: that his professional role is a displacement of his parental role. Unable to find a reason for the tragedy of his own life, he looks for reasons in the tragedies of others. In the end he, too, must take responsibility for a loss without reason.[15]

PERSUASION AND ANALOGY

There is in *The Sweet Hereafter* a critical moment when the lawyer confronts the father who lost two children. The father is the bus mechanic and the most sympathetic adult that we see. He will have nothing to do with the lawsuit. This may be because he had already lost his wife to illness. He is an expert on loss. He knows that family tragedy has nothing to do with justice, and he knows that the other parents are not moved by justice. The lawyer, nevertheless, tries to persuade him. He does so by appealing to his own life as an analogy. He, too, he says, has lost a daughter. He can be trusted because they are similarly situated.

He fails to persuade, but we do see more clearly the nature of persuasion. Analogy, not deduction, models the decision of a free subject. Analogy precisely lacks the force of deductive proof. About any situation there are endless analogies that could be drawn. Some I reject as unconvincing; others I pursue. I inquire further, developing yet more analogies, deploying yet more distinctions. Doing so, I construct a web of meanings. At some point the way forward seems clear enough to me. I see things one way rather than another. Because the construction of this web is a matter of analogy and distinction, people always exist in a state of pluralism. Furthermore, because we don't see the world the same way, we don't agree about what we should do. We don't come to the same conclusions, even when we have each fully considered the other's arguments. For example, perhaps the lawyer should draw the analogy the other way, learning how to respond to grief from the mechanic.

Analogy is also at work when the teenage daughter chooses to misrepresent the facts in order to end the lawsuit. She has seen that the lawsuit is itself the creation of a huge fiction. It is a reconstruction of the event that makes it look as if there were a reason for what she believes was only caused. However, the only reason she sees is in the construction of the suit itself: the pursuit of gain. If the lawsuit is a fiction, why not create a counterfiction? Is her lie different in kind from what the lawyer is doing? She, more than the actual clients, has been persuaded by the lawyer's behavior, even if her conclusion is not what he intended. Freedom, personhood, and decision are all at issue. We cannot know what she will decide to do until she does it. At her deposition we learn who she is, just as she does.

We would like to interrogate her to see how she explains herself. We would like to take yet another deposition beginning where the last one ends. This endless questioning is a necessary aspect of our experience of freedom. Offering an explanation of a decision, I implicitly open myself up to a reconsideration of those reasons. I may find that I no longer agree with the reasons I had, or I may find that those reasons are even better than I had imagined. Explaining myself, I acknowledge that the decision is not founded on proof but on persuasion. There is never "nothing more that can be said." My interlocutor may challenge my reasons; he or she may ask for further support or explanation. The lawyer is tireless in his talk.

I cannot explain myself without entering into a free space of discourse. Explaining, I recognize that the decision is neither caused nor determined. I believe I could have decided otherwise. This is the essential quality of freedom: it rests on persuasion. Finding myself open to persuasion—having to make up my mind—I know myself as free. The elementary site of persuasion, and thus the site of freedom, is the conversation. Ordinarily, the conversation is with others. But, of course, each of us becomes capable of holding a kind of internal dialogue with the self. I can "debate" my own reasons; I can criticize my own decisions.

Just as I know myself as free when I open myself to persuasion, I understand others to be free when I seek to persuade them. Absent freedom, persuasion makes no sense. We don't persuade slaves; we coerce them. As soon as we try to persuade them, we know that they are free agents just like ourselves. In this way the entire drama that the lawyer initiates, even though he fails to persuade, is a kind of recovery of freedom for the grieving parents.

Sometimes persuasion can look like deductive proof. As a general matter, however, we have no reason to model persuasion on deduction in place of narrative or to prefer the reasoning of the engineer to that of the politician. I may be convinced by an example, or I may be convinced by an appeal to a norm. I may simply trust a close friend or someone I think deserves my trust. Does the lawyer deserve our trust? Asking that question leads us to a more fundamental question: has the film persuaded us to see the world one way rather than another?

When we reject a moral rule, we have not abandoned our freedom or fallen into sin. There is no simple hierarchy among reasons by which we can judge the decision to be right or wrong. Our reasons—good and bad—depend on what we are doing and why we are doing it. Thus, when the teenage witness lies in her deposition, we judge her to be doing the right thing. We may worry that in such situations we have acted for the wrong reasons, but we answer that worry by examining our reasons: we either affirm them or change our minds. In either case we take responsibility for the reasons that persuade us; they are our reasons. A responsible individual is one who is willing to give an account of why she decided as she did. She becomes more responsible as her account becomes richer. We can, for this reason, respect individuals for their character even as we disagree with their decisions.

Freedom first appears to us as a political idea because we discover it not in an inward turning from body to soul but in the discursive engagement with others. It is something that we do with others, not something we find in ourselves. We ask a question or respond to another person's proposition. We try to find out what it is that we should think about a problem by actually thinking it. The paradigmatic free space was the Athenian agora, because there citizens engaged each other through reciprocal acts of persuasion.

The agora was not coincidentally the original space of both democratic politics and philosophy—free action and free thought. They differ from each other not so much in the role of persuasion and critique but in the circumstances of decision. A political decision, including a legal decision, may be required before the conversation is over. We must decide now, even under conditions of uncertainty. We call the vote; we poll the jury. Philosophy is without such external constraints. There is no vote to be called, only an openness to renew the debate.

Precisely because persuasion is not logic, it is difficult to persuade and to be persuaded. We talk until we are persuaded or until we have persuaded our interlocutor. At that point I know what to do. I might still fail to act, but that does not create a new kind of problem. All I can do is take up again the question of what I am doing by examining my reasons, that is, by opening myself up to persuasion. If my beliefs are really not capable of determining my action, then I am not free. It may well be that we all lack freedom in some respects: no matter what we say to ourselves, we cannot change certain patterns of behavior. The lawyer's daughter, who is an addict, is not free. The father bound to his lost daughter by love is not free in that relationship. No matter how determined he is not to give in to her demands for money to feed her addiction, he always does. Love can shape a world just as much as addiction. We draw this analogy all the time.

FREEDOM AND IDENTITY

Often I find myself acting without knowing what I think. I may respond to a situation as a matter of habit—for good or bad. I may be influenced by unconscious factors, or I may be carried along by "false consciousness." I might find myself challenged, or I might ask myself why I am acting as I am. I examine my reasons; I talk to others, and I debate with myself. I may find that I am not persuaded that what I was doing was right: I have no good reasons. I change my mind, or perhaps more accurately, I come to know my mind. These are the capacities of a free subject.

When we carry on a conversation, we listen and we respond. The conversation shapes a world in which we are both participants and observers. My next sentence is not something I plan in advance. It is not the realization of an abstract possibility. Before I got to this point, I could not predict what I would say because it is the actual conversation that creates the possibility. When we critically examine our reasons for speaking as we do, we bring into deliberate awareness this world of meaning. We do so by offering a narrative. The free act always appears in a narrative of possibilities—a point well illustrated by *The Sweet Hereafter*. The predicate of the lawyer's narrative of the accident is that the persons responsible could have acted differently; they failed to do what they should have done.

In the natural world there is no category of "what might have been." A natural history is actually not a history at all: it is a description of causes and effects. We cannot look back to the time before human beings and speak intelligibly of the possible: there is only what happened. When we ask, "what if the meteorite had not hit the earth and the dinosaurs had continued?" we are placing a human perspective inside a natural history. We are close to science fiction. In contrast, in a person's life— as in a political community—the most important tense is that of what might have been. We cannot write a human history without invoking the possible, because that history is an account of decisions. Decisions rest on reasons, and reasons imagine the world one way rather than another. We cannot understand history without imagining what might have been. About this we speak with each other; without this we would have nothing to say. We construct the possible, in other words, when we describe the actual.

In a causal world whatever will be is already determined by what is. A world of reason alone similarly has no dimension of possibility. A mathematical proposition is true or false; it is not one possibility among others. Because we know ourselves as free, however, we never appear to ourselves without possibilities. I understand my present situation by placing it in relation to what might have been. Only so can I understand my present as the product of my own decisions. Without this thought I could not believe myself free. A condition in which we cannot give such an account is one that we characterize as "slavery"—whether real or metaphorical.[16] Slavery is the null point of the human condition, and for that reason it is never an absolute condition. Even the slave engages in conversation, explains himself to others, imagines the possible, and makes choices—across some range.

To say that our world always exists in relationship to the possible is to recognize the deep relationship between the human world and the imagination. What might have been and what might be exist only for the imagination. Plato's account of Socrates's trial, for example, portrays Socrates saying that the outcome might have been different had he been a bit more persuasive. The point is no different in our practice of recording judicial dissents. The dissent represents what might have been. It tells us that law is not a matter of proof but of reasons. It might have been different had others been persuaded.[17] Indeed, it might still become different. To understand the decision as a decision, we must imagine the possible. To imagine the possible is to construct a narrative.

When we produce a narrative of our reasons, we understand our world as the product of our own freedom. Those reasons are the beliefs and practices of which we have been persuaded. I hold to this account, not some other possible account. Asked to explain myself, this is what I say, and this is what I will defend—forcefully if necessary. When we can no longer identify our world with our freedom, we suffer from anomie, depression, and ultimately a sense of meaninglessness. We seem to have no possibilities apart from what is; we are subject to causes. The loss of freedom that comes from penal incarceration is less about a bounded space—the jail cell—than about the failure of the world any longer to be the product of our freedom.[18] Without possibilities I am no longer an agent.[19] The free subject, however, is always writing and rewriting the narrative of his own life.[20] Doing so, he is creating his own possibilities retrospectively and prospectively.

The forms of persuasion change across fields and across time.[21] Once, it was enough to say that one had been persuaded by the presence of Christ; more recently, one might say that one was persuaded by a course of psychoanalytic therapy. The character of a persuasive argument is not the same in politics as in the family. A political truth is not a scientific truth, and neither is a religious truth. When one applies the same standard of truth to different kinds of questions, one ends up with the creationist in place of the scientist or the ideologue in place of the democrat. We are wrong to require more proof than a field can offer. We are equally wrong if we think that all knowledge claims must meet the same standard. I might be persuaded by an analogy in making a political judgment, while in a scientific investigation I might conclude that analogies are more likely to mislead than to clarify.

In political life the forms of persuasion constitute our public rhetoric. For example, the meaning of the American Constitution is not something apart from the set of arguments that persuade us at any particular moment. It is not something to be discovered; it is not timeless. It is not a matter of political science: it is not a matter of recovering a past intention. It is the set of beliefs in circulation and to which we—or, more importantly, the courts—appeal in explaining what the law is. Arguments about the Constitution are right when they persuade. We know that they have persuaded when individual citizens and government institutions organize their activities to align with these representations of the Constitution's meaning. At that point we see the Constitution as the product of our freedom. Of course, any particular individual may not be persuaded. He or she may, however, still be persuaded to comply for other reasons.

There is no escaping this. If I ask what the Constitution means, I cannot simply assert that we are bound to the plain meaning of the text, or to the intent of the framers, or to the latest precedents of the Court. That is, I cannot say this without offering an argument as to why this is the correct approach. I must persuade my interlocutor that I am correct. If I claim that I have reached my own understanding of the meaning of the Constitution, regardless of what anyone else thinks, that no longer counts as a political argument. No one has any reason to pay attention to my claim of truth, until and unless I try to persuade them. I can only persuade by entering into a dialogue, which means to offer reasons that make sense in light of our common world of beliefs and practices. I cannot short-circuit this conversation by claiming a privileged point of truth, for the truth of the Constitution is exactly what is at issue. A political theory does not carry its own warrant; it must persuade.

We cannot get outside ourselves and start over. We have only the conceptual materials at hand, which means we always find ourselves already in the middle of a conversation—actually multiple conversations. Even John Rawls must persuade us to go behind the veil of ignorance. Of course, I can turn from persuasion to coercion, from argument to force.[22] But when I do so, I no longer treat my interlocutors as free, and they, in turn, will see no relationship between my reasons and their own identity.

Persuasion is contingent, but it is not arbitrary, for it is embedded in an entire world of meaning. To be persuaded is neither an interior nor an exterior experience. Deciding, I bring myself and my world into a sort of alignment. That alignment can be, but is not necessarily, the application of a general rule to the particular. The relationship can just as easily run in the other direction: through the particular I come to understand the general in a new way. We make arguments in both directions all the time. On the one hand, I might decide what is just under particular circumstances by applying a general rule of nondiscrimination. On the other hand, I might learn what nondiscrimination entails by deciding that affirmative action on behalf of a particular claimant is unjust to others. Indeed, we may not know in a particular case which way the argument ran. This is why judges will always accuse each other of "result oriented" jurisprudence.[23]

Persuasion is always bound to context, but that hardly means that we are not capable of taking up a critical attitude toward our beliefs and practices. It does mean that we go wrong if we think that we can subject the whole of our beliefs and practices to a single, simultaneous critique. Then, we are back at the traditional Cartesian project of trying to find an Archimedean point from which we can reason with certainty. There is no such point from which we can build our entire world anew. What we can do, however, is pause with respect to any particular belief or practice and ask whether it survives a critical examination. We ask ourselves whether we remain persuaded. Pursuit of that question is the task of philosophy. We must answer the question honestly. If we fail to say what we actually think, then we will not see ourselves in the discourse. We will not be persuaded, because we are not there.

PHILOSOPHY TODAY: FROM AGORA TO CINEMA

Today we no longer find persuasive a claim that freedom and truth coincide in the ideal of a universal subject. We know that we are bound to history and that history is as much the product of our own thoughts and actions as their cause. Ours is an age in which claims to an authentic particularity compete with those to universality. We don't privilege the logician over the artist, the scientist over the poet. Who and what we privilege is a function of context, of what we are seeking to do and whom we are trying to persuade. The claim that I am free when I act as if I were an expression of universal reason appears now as a contingent belief, to be explained by its place within the social imaginary of Enlightenment intellectuals, which itself reflects a long history of theological thought.

The free act can only appear to a consciousness prepared to see reasons, not causes. Reasons only exist in a network of meanings. We inherit this world of meaning, just as we inherit a language. Indeed, the two aspects of this double inheritance are inseparable. I don't learn a language and then apply it. I learn a language in learning my way around a world. That world is an ongoing project of imaginative narration. Representation makes nature possible. It is not the other way around. Nature is a product of science; science does not simply emerge from nature. For that reason we often turn out to be wrong in our representations of the natural world. We are persuaded, but we know that we might change our minds as we learn more. The same is true of our representations of each other, of our political practices, and of other aspects of our lives together. They all make sense to us—they constitute a world—but we know that we might change our minds with respect to any particular belief. Over time, we might change our minds with respect to most of what we believe.

We understand that who we are is inseparable from our use of language. We don't, however, think that the givenness of our language is an unchangeable fact of nature. We could speak a different language, both in theory—"what might have been"—and in practice. It might be difficult to change our primary language, but we don't think it impossible. We don't imagine the possibility as some sort of contradiction of a law of nature. We understand, in this way, that we are free with respect to our language. We inherit it, but when we deploy it in a self-conscious manner, we take possession of it as our own. Indeed, we may come to see the relationship in the opposite way: deciding to speak a language, I keep it in the world. Then, I can no longer say whether I am the product of my language or it is the product of my decision. Something like this happened with modern Hebrew. Poets, we say, make the world, but so do we all.[24]

Every cultural form has this double character of inheritance and free creation. We cannot start over, making a symbolic order as if we were ourselves a creator god—at least, it is rare that we can do this.[25] But we can and do take possession of the world in which we find ourselves. The artist does this no less than the scientist. Every time we enter into a conversation in which we honestly open ourselves to persuasion, we take responsibility for who we are.

Philosophy is one form of freely taking responsibility. It is simply the conversation writ large. It is a speaking further and is, in this sense, the internal possibility of every conversation.[26] I can always take my action and my thought as the objects of further reflection. We ask how belief and action have created a common world—where it comes from, upon what it relies, and how it is structured. We take up an aspect of our common world of meaning; we bracket our commitment to that way of seeing the world long enough to make it the object of our discourse. Speaking about it, we re-present it in ways that clarify its meaning. If we come to think differently, then we have reconstructed our world. There is not some further step in which we apply our thought.

The philosopher asks whether one will take responsibility for one's beliefs. Unlike the lawyer, he does not seek to persuade. He has no particular outcome in view. Rather, he asks what it is that persuades and whether it continues to do so after we have examined it. Socrates approached individuals in the street, asking what it was they were doing and why. He asked them to explain themselves. He responded to what they said. In our age of mass communication we no longer have the easy familiarity with each other necessary for this practice. Nevertheless, the philosopher's role remains that of creating the conditions for a conversation that critically examines forms of practice and belief. The contemporary philosopher needs a subject matter that can draw us into that common conversation. That subject matter must locate us in a normative universe yet also enable us to detach ourselves for the purpose of conversation. Film offers just such a site of simultaneous engagement and distance.

A film offers at least three dimensions of freedom: that of the artists, the characters, and the audience.[27] First, a film is a product of the freedom of the writer, the director, the actors, and everyone else involved in its creation.[28] It is the product of an interaction among a number of free agents who respond to each other as they persuade and are persuaded. Were the film not a free production, the interpretive enterprise could not begin—reasons come into the world only through a free act. Nevertheless, we have no particular reason to privilege the artists' perspective in the interpretation of a film.

Second, a film is a representation of free action. We would have no interest in the film—or not the same sort of interest—if we did not think that the characters could have acted otherwise. Because decisions could be otherwise, we are engaged by the world created in the film in the same way that the characters are engaged. To understand a character, we must apprehend a narrative that creates the possibilities against which his or her behavior makes sense. For this reason a film must be plausible. Its setting need not be realistic, but the decisions made must fit within a normative framework that we recognize.[29] Of course, some films take up the question of the relationship between a narrative of free decision and causal determinism. This plot goes all the way back to Oedipus.[30] We are, however, not uninterested in Oedipus's reasons for action, even as we struggle with the issue of fate. If his reasons simply did not count, then there would be no problem to think about.

Third, we are never so engaged by a film that we cannot bracket our experience, separating ourselves from the narrative as it appears to the characters. That is the Socratic moment of opening to philosophy. We can take the narrative of the film as the object of a new discourse. We are free then to think about the film in a way that the characters are not. We can range widely or narrowly, connecting it to or distinguishing it from other possible worlds.

We can imagine this movement from the second to the third moment of freedom as shifting our interlocutor: before, we imagined ourselves talking to the characters in the film; now, we are talking to others in the audience. We make just the same movement in our own lives: for the most part we are engaged in the ordinary life realm, but on occasion we step back from that engagement and speak to others—whether friends, therapists, or philosophers—about the forms of meaning in that world. A film is successful not when it closes off critical engagement but when it opens it up. We want not only to be drawn in by the film but also to be provoked to think about it.

In its plot and characters the film sets before us a situation of moral complexity. The narrative that sustains our attention is one in which the characters' own freedom is at issue. They must decide. We want to know what they will make of themselves. The successful film creates a moment of moral suspense that holds us in its grasp. Even if we are confident that we know what the choice will be, the film must create a situation of difficulty such that we experience a sense of resistance to this outcome: it requires sacrifice, imposes dangers, or demands the overcoming of temptation. We must have a sense that it could have been otherwise. Because we understand that it could have been otherwise, we come out of the theater arguing about what we have seen.

Consider *The Secret in Their Eyes*, winner of the 2010 Academy Award for Best Foreign Language Film.[31] The action of the film centers on the brutal rape and murder of a beautiful young woman in Buenos Aires. The case is pursued by the prosecutorial arm of a court, as well as by the victim's husband. These events take place in the mid-1970s, in what a powerful judge refers to as "the new Argentina," meaning one in which law has given way to brutality, torture, and corruption. The investigation is continually hampered by this judge, who first tries to frame the innocent and then closes the file. When, despite these subversive efforts, the murderer is caught, he is quickly released from jail and becomes a powerful member of the "security services." At each point in the film the characters must overcome obstacles—sometimes procedural, sometimes threats of violence—to their pursuit of justice. In their public roles they mostly make the right choices but at great cost, including the murder of one and the internal exile of another. In their private lives they lack a similar courage. The two main characters—the lawyer and her lead investigator—cannot quite proclaim their love for each other. Unable to speak, they each enter unhappy marriages, only acting on their love twenty-five years later.

All of the drama of decision, of recognition, and of accountability is occurring at what I described as the second level. The film, however, asks us to take up the third level as well, for the main character, the investigator, is writing a novel about the murder and the events surrounding it. It is twenty-five years later, and he is still trying to write the narrative, although part of what he learns is that the story is hardly over. We, too, must interpret the events.

At this third level I offer an account of the film that sees it as an investigation of the relationship of the private and the public under authoritarian conditions. The movie—and the investigator's novel—begins with the loving, young couple at breakfast on the morning of the murder. That life of domesticity is destroyed by a horrendous act of private violence. The murder can be solved, but under the political conditions justice cannot be done. The failure of justice penetrates all of the characters' lives. It is as if love itself is killed, for all of them fail in their familial lives. Only twenty-five years later, when democracy has returned, is love again possible. We find then, as well, that love—private love—has worked justice, for the husband of the victim has kidnapped and incarcerated the murderer over all of these years. Thus, the murderer has been punished. "It's complicated," the characters say, but love can reground the world.

Of course, we cannot really keep separate the two moments of discursive engagement with the film—what I have called the second and third moments—any more than we keep these moments of action and reflection separate in our lives. The characters have reasons for their actions. Reasons are only accessible through the construction of a narrative. When we argue about the film, we are pressing competing narratives upon each other. We do so in the service of explaining why the characters did what they did. We try to persuade others to see the film as we do. Entering that conversation, we may find that we are the ones persuaded. If we fail to respond when asked, this is simultaneously an act of disrespect of others and a failure to realize our own freedom. We are free not because we have opinions but because we engage each other in reciprocal acts of persuasion and being persuaded. If we had no one to talk to, we could make no sense of the idea of freedom.[32]

Engagement and critique are roles of the arts more generally, but in our democratic age the art form we share most is film. We no longer have a common culture of live theater or of fiction. We can make no assumptions about common points of reference in painting, music, or dance. We often come out of an art exhibit or a concert in silence. We think of a painting as working its meaning in the solitude of the individual gaze. We no longer have a common idiom for discussion of paintings or music. We can and do argue about books, but few books find a substantial audience. This is even more true of the stage. Film has become the singular art form that we share as a community. Watching a film, we enter a common community of viewers. This is what Benedict Anderson calls an "imagined community": we are linked to unknown others through our knowledge that each of us has experienced the same films.[33]

That which is rendered on film becomes accessible and even familiar. Thus, films become reference points by which we organize our experience. We develop common attitudes toward cultural and historical phenomena by framing them in terms of specific representations in films. Think, for example, of the popular memory of World War II. For most people now, this is not a memory at all. It is an imaginative construction that emerges from the countless war films that my generation has watched. It has been shaped more recently by films such as *Saving Private Ryan*, which put that war back into popular awareness.[34] Suddenly, we find ourselves speaking of the "greatest generation," with its implicit comparison to the present generation. Contrast this with the Korean War, which has made virtually no imprint on the popular imagination. That war remains largely outside of the cinematic world.[35]

We need, however, to be clear here. When the Second World War enters the public imagination as the site of the greatest generation proving itself, we are not studying the strategic course of the war or investigating tactical decisions. War films are not writing history; they are not documentaries. *The Secret in Their Eyes* is not an account of legal practice during the dirty war in Argentina; westerns are not historical inquiries into the expansion of bourgeois market-order on the frontier.[36] A film may make us curious to learn more, but its point is not to do the work of the professional historian. *Saving Private Ryan* is not trying to tell us what happened in the Second World War. It offers a narrative of moral choice framed as a historical account. The film provides a context in which we confront again the possibilities of sacrifice, the demands of friendship, the nature of courage, and the success or failure of a life. We sustain the popular memory of a war, a place, or an era as the site at which such meanings become a common possession of the community.

Memory and ignorance go hand in hand in all cultural phenomena. A hundred years ago Ernest Renan wrote, "Forgetting . . . is a crucial factor in the creation of a nation."[37] We commonly find a popular celebration of past events alongside tremendous ignorance of the "facts." Consider the boisterous celebration of July 4 marking the birth of a free nation—a celebration undeterred by ignorance of the actual political difficulties of the Continental army, of the role of the French, of the liberties of the British, or of the importance of southern slave interests.

Whether an event happened—or happened in the way represented in the film—is not particularly important to this process of symbolic creation. The Second World War becomes a resource for considering the way in which political crisis offers the possibility of realizing an ultimate meaning for the individual and of the need for a community to will its own existence. Conversely, Vietnam becomes a resource for thinking of the way in which political crisis can lead to meaningless death for the individual and to division and disorder of the community. Together, they frame a common understanding of success and failure in the use of political violence, of the threat and promise of the state. We can juxtapose *Saving Private Ryan* to *Apocalypse Now* when thinking of our recent intervention in Iraq: to which narrative do we turn in trying to persuade ourselves what to think and what to do?

As I write this, *The Hurt Locker* has just won the 2010 Academy Award for Best Motion Picture of the Year.[38] It is a film about the war in Iraq, which relentlessly denies the possibility of heroism, inverting any easy understanding of the relationship between success at war and the virtues of character. It works through the contrast between the character of the traditional hero and the individual pathologies required for success in a war in which there is always threat but rarely confrontation. Already, we are learning of the meaning of the war in Iraq through film. If World War II was about freedom through sacrifice for nation, and Vietnam was about freedom as a form of countercultural defiance, then Iraq is about freedom as detachment of the individual. Not surprisingly, World War II gave us the image of the GI, Vietnam gave us that of the draft-dodger, and Iraq has given us that of the military contractor. Or so I would argue were I to try to persuade you.

FILM AND MORAL NARRATIVE

The very structure of a film offers an especially accessible point for philosophical interrogation. A film is literally constructed of a series of scenes that we must hold in our imagination.[39] We must link the scenes to each other through the construction of a narrative. We can think of the film's narrative as how we would recount the film to someone who has not seen it. In fact, remarkably little is actually offered in the film itself by which to construct that narrative. The scenes are like the illuminations of a flashlight on a dark night. We see a series of settings; we have to put them together into an entire landscape. We have to fill in the connections, and we must do so quickly while watching the film.[40] If we get stuck, we lose the thread.

We see an opening scene: a man alone on a highway, looking weary and disheveled. We immediately try to place him: is he fleeing from or traveling to somewhere? Where is his family? Is he traveling for business or for crime? Is he poor? In a hurry? The possibilities are not infinite; realistically, there are not many possibilities at all, for we need to get our bearings quickly. We pose a set of questions to the scene, and we start getting our answers immediately in the next scene. We get the setting, the character, and the possible plotlines. We need to pick up quickly the dramatic tension, the problem around which we are going to orient ourselves over the next two hours.[41]

How do we do all of this? We rely heavily on cues of genre and form. We understand that there will be a narrative beginning, middle, and end. We probably know if we are watching comedy or tragedy. We understand that there is a drama to be worked out, so we come in looking for the point of tension that must be resolved. We understand the way character development works, so we are quite willing to allow a compression of years into minutes. We see the same character across different scenes, yet we do not expect to learn all that has happened in between. We know that we cannot ask, "What was he doing in the years when we did not see him?" At least, we cannot ask this with reference to anything outside of the text of the film itself. We are not creating a biography; we are watching character development. There is no research to be done, only a creative product to be interpreted.

In the first place, then, we know what a film is, by which I mean that we share a common cinematic culture. We need, however, to share more than an understanding of how a film works. We need, as well, a common set of archetypes within which to frame the substance of the film.[42] These are ways of organizing experience. Sometimes, we understand them by reference to a paradigm case—Christ is our best example. Sometimes, there is no single paradigm but an endless repetition of instances—for example, family. The archetype sets a general frame within which variation is possible. We know, for example, the general contours of family, friendship, state, love, and crime. We make the film work by juxtaposing the particular scenes with these archetypes. Out of the juxtaposition we develop the narrative.[43]

The narrative is more than the sum of its parts. It is the unity that is revealed through the parts. The scenes remain our point of access to the whole. Indeed, the whole only exists as that which we see through the particular representations. But without narrative unity the scenes fall apart and the film is likely to fail. Each scene is, in this sense, a representation of the whole. Consider how we imagine the arc of our own lives. We remember particular scenes or events; we constantly have the task of seeing through them to the whole that is our identity. We are sure of our own identity—we must be a subject—even though we have no access to that identity except through particular events. I don't remember or imagine such a thing as "my life." Rather, I imagine particular events, acts, moments that represent that life. We write and rewrite our personal narrative by juxtaposing different scenes, emphasizing different elements, telling the story differently. We keep rewriting because we never have hold of that identity that necessarily stands behind, but extends beyond, every representation.

Narrative fills the space between representation and identity. It is the means by which representation reaches toward identity. Even a photograph must be placed within a narrative, if I am to see it as a representation of someone. Narrative, I argued above, is the work of the imagination, and imagination is a faculty that belongs only to a free subject. Discussing the meaning of a film both models and realizes what it is to think freely. We come to the discussion with a set of shared symbolic resources that make it possible for us to understand the work as a unity—even as we disagree about its meaning. Knowing what to expect, we can argue with each other—and, indeed, can be surprised by each other.

Alongside *The Hurt Locker*'s Oscar for best movie, Jeff Bridges won the Oscar for best actor for his performance in *Crazy Heart*.[44] Bridges plays Bad Blake, an aging, alcoholic, country music singer whose life has already fallen apart at the beginning of the film. He is alone in a car, moving between pathetic performances before inattentive audiences in small towns. He has not spoken to his child in decades. He has had four wives but now has nothing and no one. He does not recover any of them: his son will not talk to him even at the end. But he reconstructs his life by finding generationally appropriate substitutes for the family he has lost. His son's role is filled by his musical disciple. He becomes a grandfather figure to the child of the woman with whom he becomes involved. The woman has a transformative effect on him, but their affair cannot last, for she is more appropriately his daughter than his spouse. By the end of the film she has found someone of her own generation, and Blake is content to bless the marriage. The formal family seems not as important as the familial relationships. These establish an order among the generations, an order of love. To violate the order is, in the end, to be doomed to failure and loneliness. Recovery from his broken life is not a matter for the self alone but rather one of reconstructing familial relationships, even if in nontraditional terms.

Contrast *Crazy Heart* with another contemporary film, *Elegy*.[45] This film, too, is about the relationship among generations and the reconstruction of family. A popular professor—a public intellectual—refuses to accept the fact that he is aging. The generational relationships of family, after all, are about the span of life from birth to death. A person who cannot accept the fact that he is approaching death cannot really participate in the life of a family. The professor fled his family long ago. Now his son speaks to him only to shout his disapproval. The professor himself seems to go from one affair with a student to another: perpetual youth. The drama of the movie is that he actually falls in love with one student and she with him. They violate the age norms. He, however, cannot fully enter into the relationship as long as it requires him to see himself as what he is: old. When she wants to introduce him to her family, he fails to appear. He cannot force himself to do it, even if his failure to appear means the end of the relationship. He knows that they will look at him and ask, even if only silently, why their daughter is in a relationship with someone who is old enough to be her father. That is an unbearable thought for him. The surprise of the movie is the trick that mortality—the thing itself, not the endless worry about it—can play on each of us. He may be old—his best friend, a poet, has a heart attack right beside him—but she is diagnosed with cancer. This brings them back together at the end of the film. They now share a proximity to death, which allows a violation of the generational norms. In our relationship to an unpredictable death, we are all equally old.

What we expected was that he would be stricken and she would come back to attend him, affirming a role more like daughter than lover. That would have been the story of *Crazy Heart*. But *Elegy* surprises us by reminding us of the possibility of the exception. *Elegy* only works because we understand the norm. We come to both films with a set of expectations about family—the archetype at work—that makes it possible to draw our attention to the significance of the violation. Each man violates the generational norm of family; each must construct his own identity in light of the violation. Sometimes a violation should be corrected; sometimes it should be embraced. Either way, we do so understanding that through the exception, we are also recognizing the norm.[46] *Elegy* builds in the direct reference to the norm in the friend who suffers the heart attack. He, too, was having affairs with younger women. When he is stricken, however, it is the suffering wife, not any of the young women, who is at his side. The young have no interest in the dying poet.

Both of these films rely on and create a common store of meanings. They deploy the archetype of family but also illustrate how it operates across a range that we recognize as norm and exception. They affirm and they surprise. If we did not come to the films already understanding the archetype, we would not be able to narrate them so easily. The scenes would lack connection. We might miss entirely the drama of age that is played out in each. We might try to read them as commentaries on the music world, in the one case, and the academic life, in the other. Such readings might be possible. We are free to try, but sustaining those readings would take a lot of effort. We might, for example, argue that each of the young women made the wrong choice: the aging musician was worthy of love; the hypocrite professor was not.

As an object of popular culture a film must rely on narrative structures—archetypes—that are in common circulation. Those structures do not constrain the freedom of the project. Rather, they provide the common context that makes variation and interpretation possible.[47] These simple dramas are dealing with some of the most basic structures of our experience: family, love, death. These are subjects for philosophical inquiry, and film is a readily available and shared resource that we possess for such an inquiry.

The store of these archetypes is not very large.[48] We all learn them early in our lives; we learn them by constructing narratives. Young children want to see the same film or hear the same story over and over. Repetition does not bore them; it reassures them. They are not quite convinced that the story will be the same each time through. They are shockingly disappointed if you vary the story. They are learning to stabilize their imaginations by learning to recognize the parts within the whole, which means that they are coming to construct a whole out of the parts. Knowing the whole, they can comfortably forget themselves within the drama. They need not make only a partial commitment, keeping one foot out just in case they have to flee if things start moving in an uncomfortable direction. Unable to pick up the cues for narrative construction from the start, and uncertain about the reliability of the world, children need repetition in order to begin to make sense of their world.

This childhood repetition resembles the practices of an oral tradition. The same stories are repeated until they become a repertoire available to an entire community. We still see this in the repetition of religious stories: the weekly Jewish service reads through the entire Torah during the course of the year. The Passover story is repeated each year. We don't repeat because we have forgotten or because we literally need to be reminded. We repeat in order to focus, as a community, on this particular story. From here we can begin our own interpretive discourses. These repetitions do not constrain freedom; they make it possible.

We might think of literal repetition as the primitive working of unity. In an oral culture the listener recognizes a story as one of a stock of stories. That stock of stories is, in large part, constitutive of a culture. Who were the Jews? Those who told a set of stories about themselves. They were "the people of the book."[49] Repetition in a culture that can memorialize through writing or other forms of representation does not disappear. It becomes, however, more complicated. We are less dependent on specific repetitions and more dependent on the repeated use of archetypes. We know the kind of story, even as we are presented with new characters and new situations. Nothing is actually that new. The narrative unity comes easily. In this dimension, at least, our common life cannot be a struggle.

We see a pictorial representation of this relationship between repetition and freedom when we enter the churches of Europe. We discover, right up to the modern period, endless repetitions of the same scenes of Christ, Mary, and the saints. Why was there not more curiosity about a variety of themes? To ask that question is to miss the point entirely. It was the very familiarity of the stories that made it possible to represent moral complexity. Familiarity made possible interpretation. Only because the viewer understood the norm could he or she see the free act that is the unique painting. We no longer have the same store of archetypical understandings. Therefore, we look at the paintings and ask what they are about. We are told the same thing about painting after painting. We don't see the realization of freedom but narrow repetition.

Just as churchgoers in an earlier era had a stock of stories that they expected to see represented in their art, we have a stock of archetypes that we rely on when we see a popular film. That stock makes it possible for us to understand quickly who is before us and what is being said. Understanding that, we can proceed to appreciate the actual work. We can sight its mastery of the theme, identify the subtle variations, and consider the way in which our expectations were both met and challenged. We could not reinvent the saints every Sunday. We could not do it in paintings, and we cannot do it at the movies.

So I interpret *Crazy Heart* as an inquiry into the way in which the value of familial form—generational relationships—transcends the specific, ordinary practices of a society, while *Elegy* is about the enduring possibility of the exception to generational expectations in the face of our common mortality. I bring the films into contact with each other, and together I use them to think about the nature of family and familial relationships. I am sketching the boundaries of the familial as it structures the social imaginary. Those boundaries are not hard. Rather, they are a set of resources for both the filmmakers and ourselves.[50]

Thinking about the films this way, I connect them to larger, contemporary controversies about the nature of family. How to think about rule and exception in imagining the order of love is deeply at issue in our disputes over the recognition of gay marriage and our concern with single-parent households. What, I may wonder, happens to family as the site of love in a culture that increasingly celebrates youth? More deeply, I may wonder about the possibilities of love in a society in which family can seem so fragile and concerns for individual identity so strong. The films are not commentaries on such problems. Rather, they are sites for a critical, democratic engagement with our own beliefs, practices, and values.

If we did not share a social imaginary, we simply would not know how to make sense of the representations that constitute the films. We would not know what to say. We would be like the man who finds himself in a place in which he does not speak the language or like the Christian in a mosque. He might think it beautiful, but he has no idea what is being said, for what reasons, and in what way. He does not know if he is in a typical scene or at an extraordinary moment. He does not know whether there is argument or agreement around him. He is lost because he lacks a common world. In such a strange world he might recognize only repetition and wonder why the artistic production seems so constrained. But, in fact, it is he who lacks freedom.[51]

CHAPTER 3

On Interpretation

If we imagine a situation in which there is no consciousness—the universe before the emergence of life forms—we cannot make sense of a claim that anything is distinct from anything else. We have problems of scale and problems of boundaries. We know that the elementary forces in the universe bind everything to everything else. What would constitute a unit in and of itself? There is nothing "natural" about where one unit ends and another begins. Time and space are not divided into segments by nature. What makes something the same through time? What are the spatial boundaries of the unit? Can we even speak of change, since there is no baseline against which to measure? We face the metaphysical problem of the ancient atomists: if we keep dividing material, what do we find to be the smallest unit? If we found such a thing, then we could build new unities from that singular, natural unit—rather like Lego blocks. Unlike the ancients, we know that there is no such elementary unit to be found. We find instead interacting forces, uncertainty, and particles that do not behave like stable units at all.

If we shift our imagination to a larger scale, we again have no reason to think that there is an "in itself"—an essence or form—that establishes a natural unity. I look at a plant outside my window. I know it is an azalea. But I know that I am representing as a single thing what only exists in a system of relationships: no earth, no plant; no water, no plant; no carbon dioxide, no plant; no sunlight, no plant. It is not the plant but the system that maintains itself in the world. The system, we might think, then, is the basic unit. The system, however, is linked to other systems, just as the plant is to it. Starting anywhere, we quickly find ourselves everywhere.

Nothing just is something. It is always something to an awareness. The unit, we can say, is what we make of it. Ideas make the world, not because there is nothing out there but because whatever is out there is neither one nor many until it exists for a consciousness.[1] The sociological form of this proposition is easy to grasp: there is no social unit—whether nation, town, union, family—except as an organization of the imagination. There are as many ways of organizing persons into groups as there are ways of representing them. We represent people as citizens, members, neighbors, parishioners, relatives, age-cohorts, or consumers— the list goes on indefinitely.

The simplest function of consciousness is to create one out of many— or, more accurately, to create one out of what is otherwise undifferentiated. The function of consciousness is to cut. Every cut establishes a border, and every border brings into being a relationship between inside and outside. Persons are not unique in this function. They are, however, unique in being able to take as an object of reflection the cuts that they make. They are not just aware of a world; they represent the world to themselves and to others in their use of symbols. They not only cut; they recut as they construct meaning one way or another. Our access to the world is mediated by this symbolic capacity.

We possess an indefinite number of symbolic currencies.[2] I enter a store, and everything is represented by a price. I enter the store for the purpose of writing an essay on modern design, and everything is represented as an aesthetic value. I enter looking for a present for my spouse, and now everything is represented as pleasing or displeasing to her. How we see is a function of what we are prepared to see, and that depends on what we are up to. I might enter the store as a lawyer in a bankruptcy proceeding, as a competitor, as an agent of a possible buyer, as a tourist from abroad, or as a public health officer. Rarely am I doing just one thing when I enter. There is no finite list of possibilities. In each instance I represent objects and actions differently by setting them into different relationships. I can represent along a dimension of price, beauty, function, interest, age, religion, or science—just to name a few. None of these symbolic resources is simply an abstraction. About each I can offer an account of its structure and history. I can explain what I am doing and why. This is what it is to live within what I referred to in chapter 1 as "webs of significance."

We ordinarily live so completely in this symbolic world that we do not think about it. We think that our world of representations simply is the world, and for the most part we are right. The world as it is appears to me is not somehow "in me," any more than language is in me. Socrates was in Athens; Athens was not in him. We really do live in history, but history is not something that exists apart from our individual and collective imaginations. History is in the world in the same way that language is in the world. Both are objective, but that does not mean they exist independently of the human imagination. Each is a world constructed and maintained through our representations.

The forces that knit us together—language, religion, family, morality, politics—are no less strong for the fact that they are symbolic. For the sake of love I will determine the course of my entire life. Indeed, if I want to describe my world, I must start with love, not gravity. We should not mistake the objective for that which exists independently of all of us. Rather, the objective is that which exists independently of my particular claims about it. Objectivity does not refer to a world without us but rather to the world that we collectively find ourselves already within.

DIALOGUE AND THE CONSTRUCTION
OF THE WORLD

I am aware of myself not as an object moving through physical space— intelligently directed as I may be—but rather as a person with a character, a store of knowledge, a way of relating to others, and a way of seeing the world. Most important, we each locate ourselves in an emotional time and a space populated by particular persons, groups, and others of varying degrees of closeness. We each have a past and a future, just as we each have a home, a community, a nation, and a world. All of these are functions of the imagination. About ourselves and everything in our world, we strive to give an account. We want our lives to "add up." We want to be able to see ourselves as whole, as living a certain sort of life that has a beginning, a middle, and a direction, if not an end. This is neither the unity of a logical argument nor the unity of production. It is, rather, the unity of the narrative.

This narrative construction of myself is not something I do alone. Indeed, I take myself as an object of representation, at least in part, because I am constantly engaged with others. They want to know, and I want to tell them, who I am and what I am doing. If we did not make commitments to others, we might not have the same sense of the need for unity of ourselves over time. The question of one self or many is at least as much a question for those with whom we live as it is for ourselves. Arguably, it becomes a question for us because we need to be someone for them.

We can get a sense of how this narrative function works by thinking through a familiar example of its failure. Imagine coming across a strange artifact from a civilization of which we know very little. We don't know if the artifact served as a tool, a decoration, or an instrument of religious ritual. We don't know how it was used or what it was used for. We don't know if it was a part of something else or served a unique function. We can probably say something about how and when it was constructed. We can subject its material elements to tests that may enable us to determine their origins. We can use that information to understand the technical skills and geographical reach of this civilization. With that we can begin to place these people in a narrative that relates them to others. But about the object of our inquiry, we still cannot advance into the world that brought it forth. We imagine a person shaping this object for a reason. But because we don't know what he was up to, we can't imagine how he would answer our questions. We have nothing to say about how he imagined his life or why he made this as opposed to something else. We know that the artifact was the product of a free act, but we cannot move from causal accounts of its production to a narrative of the reasons for its coming to be.[3] Facing the artifact, we are only at the edge of the human.

The experience I am describing is an extreme instance of an entirely common occurrence. I live on an old farm in New England. In the woods I come across the remnants of an old implement. I ask what it is. I answer that question when I understand how it was used or at least the purposes for which it was built to be used. Describing that use will take me into the technical and social economy of farm life in New England one hundred or even two hundred years ago. The farmer had it ready to hand, precisely because it made sense in his world.[4] It was simply a part of how he did things. For me to understand this, I imagine a conversation with him in which he answers my questions about the tool. I imagine him telling me about the free act that brought it about. To account for that act, I must construct a narrative that has both a bounded and an unbounded quality. It is bounded because it is an explanation of this object, of why some particular person decided to make this particular thing. It is unbounded because there really is no end to the depth and complexity of the narrative I might offer. I can say, "It was used in the milking of cows." But I can always go further, locating the raising of cows in a farm economy, in an account of family life, in the history of New England's development, in a story of the relation of humans to animals, or in an indefinite number of other symbolic dimensions.[5]

These everyday puzzles often take dramatic form in mystery or detective films in which the police must determine the meaning of some bit of evidence. They must construct a narrative within which that evidentiary object has some function in relation to the crime.[6] An interesting and sophisticated version of this theme is presented in the French film *Caché* (*Hidden*).[7] A bourgeois Parisian family's ordinary routine is disturbed by the appearance on their doorstep of a series of videocassettes. At first the videos are nothing but surveillance tapes of the entrance to their own home. Someone has been observing them. Later, childlike depictions of violence are added. We, like the family, need to understand why these objects were produced if we are to understand what is going on. George, the father, traces clues found in a later cassette to an apartment in a run-down neighborhood. There he locates Majid, an Algerian man who had lived with his family as a child. George had, at age six, mistreated him by using an act of deception to cause George's parents to send Majid to an orphanage. Eventually, Majid, through his own use of deception, gets George to return to the apartment, where the Algerian slits his own throat in front of George. We never quite know what is going on, but neither does George. We struggle to fit the pieces into a narrative that must span space and time. George falls back on his brief and episodic memories of childhood, which appear to us as flashbacks. Like him, we struggle to place the cassettes and the pictures in a narrative. George attempts to interrogate Majid and his adult son, but both deny knowledge of the cassettes. Can we believe them?

While we never fully penetrate the world of the Algerian—a world of political and personal discrimination—we do better at penetrating George's world. His belief that these events have to do with his childhood poses a disturbing puzzle for his wife, Anne. George and Anne have together constructed a rich and meaningful world. They have a child and close friends. She needs now to understand his strange behavior, which means coming to understand the narrative he is constructing for himself: how does he imagine the relationship of the strange contemporary events to his past? She repeatedly interrogates him, just as I suggested I would interrogate the farmer. Unlike the ordinary detective film, there is no single revelatory moment. There is only the continuing puzzle of bringing to light the hidden world of memory each of us maintains, aptly represented in the surveillance tape.

If human awareness cut the world only one way, there would be no problem of understanding the found artifact; evidence would not be puzzling. To have symbols, and particularly language, is to have an unlimited range of representational possibilities. The unlimited character of possible human worlds is evident in the interrogation, which can go off in an unlimited number of directions. I don't know what my imagined farmer will tell me or how far he might be willing to carry on the conversation with me. Similarly, I don't even know what my spouse will tell me when I ask about her past. We might talk for minutes, hours, days, or a lifetime. The same is true of each of our own self-interrogations.

The unbounded character of the symbolic function arises not just from the multiple dimensions of representation but also from the way in which meaning arises within each dimension. There is no such thing as a singular representation.[8] We cannot have a word without having a language, a historical incident without an entire history, or an implement without an economy of production. Thus, in *Hidden* the Algerian child is living with George's family because his parents were killed in a Parisian demonstration in 1961 over political events in Algeria. Has George become the symbol of French injustice? Is the suicide an act of political resistance? Are the surveillance tapes a form of witnessing? All of these meanings are present because this is the web of associations that begin to appear as we witness the various interrogations. Meaning is like monetary value: it arises from a network of relationships. Like money, as well, the symbolic value (meaning) constantly shifts as the single proposition shifts in relation to other propositions.

Interpretation pursues this process of "giving an account." Reasons are offered and then examined. Upon examination we may find out that the reasons do not provide an adequate account. This is about as far as we can get with *Hidden*. That hardly means we have failed, only that we are still thinking. Or the reasons offered may rely on certain ideas that are themselves controversial or unclear, in which case those terms, too, need interpretation. I may think that I am acting in pursuit of justice, but after a little questioning I may decide that I need to investigate further what justice actually requires in this situation. I may conclude that I was wrong in my idea of justice, but still I may want to do justice. Or I may conclude that I simply offered the wrong interpretation of what it was I was doing. These questions and responses have no limit, apart from patience, time, and endurance. We decide for reasons, but the reasons are never exhaustive, and they never lead to just one possible outcome. If reasons were exhaustive, then one narrative would be correct and others wrong. Reasons in that case would be causes, and we would be back with the problem of freedom in a fully determined world. A free subject is one who can change his mind, not only about what he will do but about what he has done.

A fundamental, but deeply puzzling, fact about human nature is that our powers of creation far exceed our powers of planning.[9] Beauty captures something of this puzzle. I cannot decide to create beauty. Beauty does not follow from the application of an abstract concept or simply from excellence in instruction. The artist finds the possibility of beauty internal to the work. The work engages him; it pushes him in directions that arise as the creation comes to be. Imagine telling a story. As the story becomes more complex the possibilities simultaneously narrow and become richer. They are bearing more and more weight within the web of meanings that the story has already created. I must continue "this" story, not veer off into another.[10] Yet that hardly means that there is only one path forward. The artist does not figure this out in advance and then create the story as an application of his abstract thought. Rather, his reasoning is the following of certain lines of meaning that open up as he proceeds. The same is true of every creative work—from painting, to film, to the chapter that I am writing. Each brings forth a world; the actual creates the possible.

The artist creates in a dimension of meaning, and meaning is accessible only through interpretation. He must interrogate his own creation, which—like a child—has its own meaning as soon as it enters the world. The created stands apart from the artist because it is located in a symbolic order.[11] The artistic work is embedded in the larger world of the social imaginary and gains its meaning from the relationships it establishes and that seize it. There is no private act of artistic creation anymore than there is a private language. I may, for example, have thought that I would make some point in this text, but I discover that this is not what I said. I can always reject this text and start over. I cannot, however, control its meaning. It speaks to me, as well as to every other reader.

My text is not exactly writing itself, but neither is it the case that I am coming to the text with an established agenda that provides the words. There is a sense of its "truth" that is independent of me. I am reaching for the identity of this text. The artist feels a moral obligation of honesty; he subordinates himself to his text. For this reason the artist cannot tell you "how" he created his work, anymore than anyone can explain how a dialogue occurred. Causes will not explain the free act, including an act of writing. Once the work is done, the artist stands in relation to it in the same way as any other reader. He can do nothing more than offer his interpretation, with which we are free to disagree.[12] Indeed, often artists' explanations of their creations sound singularly banal, for they are not experts in the narrative form of interpretation.

Whatever our understanding of the free act, it must take into account this complex relationship between meaning and act that we see in artistic creation. If we cannot make sense of that relationship, we will be driven to a theory of nihilism, on the one hand, or of determinism, on the other. In the former the only free act is one that is completely my own, and all that is my own is the total denial of any meaning outside of myself.[13] In the latter the explanation of my act appeals to causes—whether internal or external. From neither of these perspectives does the human world of meaning appear.

REPRESENTATION AND IDENTITY

Interpretation is always a representation of something—for example, the found implement or the work of art. Without that reference representation is no longer interpretation. To enumerate possibilities is not to interpret. To offer definitions is not to interpret. To work out logical relationships or to make deductions is not to interpret. This relationship of representation to identity may be clearest to us when we think of ourselves as subjects about whom much can be said, but nothing that is said is ever commensurate with the person. There is always more to me than can be said; there is a surplus.[14] In every interpretation there is a kind of asymptotic relationship between representation and identity. Representation strives for, but never reaches, identity.

To describe interpretation as a relationship between identity and representation is not to make a metaphysical claim. Interpretation does not rely on a correspondence theory of truth. Indeed, I have been arguing that there is no fact of the matter against which we can check our representations. Identity does not precede representation. The relationship of representation to identity is internal to interpretation; that is, representation and identity are moments within interpretation. Of any representation, I can ask of what it is an interpretation. Because representation is bound by identity, judgment is possible: a representation can be true or false, better or worse. This does not mean that we agree on what makes a good interpretation. The contest of representations is built into the nature of interpretation. When we argue, we are posing different representations against each other. We do not escape the debate by "checking" the thing itself. We have no deliberate, conscious access to identity—to the object, person, or act—apart from the representation.

The character of interpretation is the same in fiction and nonfiction. We pursue an interpretation of King Lear, just as easily as we do of FDR. In neither case do we have access to a preinterpretive experience of identity: for one because he never existed, for the other because he is dead. Really, however, we are in no different position with respect to someone standing right next to us—or even to ourselves. Because identity emerges as a necessary aspect of interpretation, we can and do ask whether our interpretation of King Lear is correct. We compare representations, and we make judgments. It is not an answer to say that there is no King Lear and therefore any representation we make is "merely subjective" or that none can be better or worse than any other. Neither, however, can there be a definitive representation that simply displaces all others: the "truth" of King Lear's identity.[15]

Whenever we offer an interpretation, we understand that we might be wrong. We might think of our representations as only hypotheses to be confirmed as we learn more. This is no less true of King Lear than of President Obama. We, of course, have different methods of arriving at our representations as we study different sorts of subjects. I cannot read an interview of King Lear, let alone conduct one. When we read a good work of fiction, however, we may find the characters more compelling than when we read a poor biography. Tolstoy thought War and Peace a better interpretation of Napoleon's invasion of Russia than any historian's effort to explain Napoleon's actions.[16]

We cannot reduce identity to representation. We cannot say that there is nothing to King Lear apart from the content of our representations. That proposition is no more true than to say of President Obama that there is nothing to him beyond our representations. Identity is the moment of surplus, of the inexhaustible character of meaning. Identity pulls me into the world, which is always more than I can express; representation organizes by putting limits on that world.

The identity-representation relationship holds even when the person who is the object of interpretation is myself. I have an identity that is independent of, and greater than, any particular biographical representation made about me. It makes no difference if that representation is one that I express. My own representations will be judged as interpretations that must contend with those offered by other people who may know me well. I may have a lot to learn about myself. I may not have all that much self-awareness, I might not be very good at expressing myself, or I might have a reason to "misrepresent" myself. In short, I can do no more than offer a competing representation. The competition of representations is endless, not because we are inevitably in error but because identity always exceeds representation.

That which exceeds representation is necessarily a matter of faith.[17] Thus, I have a faith in my own identity. Similarly, I believe that my nation has an identity. I might believe that God has an identity. In no case, though, does the identity claim displace the need for representation. The point is just the opposite: I cannot formulate an interpretation—I cannot offer a representation—without simultaneously affirming the identity of the subject that is represented. Wherever I find the act of interpreting, I will find both an epistemic claim of representation and a symmetrical faith in identity. *Faith* is exactly the right word, for we are talking about a state of mind that can never be expressed in representation. It is the presupposition built into the possibility of interpretation.[18] Without faith we would fall into skepticism. The belief in a God that is beyond all representation expresses the intuition that faith is a necessary condition of our having a world at all.

A good deal follows from this relationship of representation to identity. A being incapable of representation has no identity to itself. Such a being, as the Greeks would have said, is either beneath or above humankind. Whatever identity my dog has, she has by virtue of my representation of her. She is not a subject to herself; she maintains no narrative of her life. Can we conceive of God engaging in an interpretive act of self-representation? Maybe the God of Abraham and Moses, but not the transcendent God, the creator of the universe. God's word is not representation but the creative source of the world itself. "In the beginning was the word" does not mean that first God represented the world—a kind of divine blueprint—and then built it according to the plan's specifications. Indeed, the inability to conceive of a space between God's word and God's being—between representation and identity— has driven much of Western theological speculation.

The deep split between the scholastic and the nominalist conceptions of the nature of God occupies this divide. If we attribute to God the perfection of reason, and understand reason as fully representable, then the identity of God threatens to collapse into representation. Where is the surplus of identity if we claim for reason all that is perfect? The possible and the actual collapse for such a God. There is no place for a will separate from reason. What, after all, is there to will apart from the perfection of reason? The scholastic's God retreats as reason literally fills the universe. A fully representable world is one in which God has no identity and in which there can be no miraculous intervention outside the laws of nature. Against this God of reason the nominalists opposed a God of will. This is a God with a surplus of identity that always threatens to negate our representations of him. Nothing adequate to his identity can be said of this God. Representation of the nominalist God, accordingly, is limited to what he is not. We "know" this God by negating every propositional claim that we might make of an individual. He is unlimited, but every representation expresses a limitation. We might think of this God as creating the world anew at every moment. Confronting the act of divine creation, which literally makes the world from nothing, we are always rendered speechless.

We seem to have to choose between a god of reason and a god of will. In each direction we are pushing to the limit—or beyond the limit—the twin elements of representation and identity that are constitutive of interpretation. This is the practical meaning of the felt sense that God is not a subject of interpretation. My point is not to investigate the consequences of the theological dispute for the history of Western thought.[19] Rather, it is to understand this dispute as itself an image of an antinomy that attaches to the work of the imagination wherever we take it up. Arguably, this entire theological debate has mistaken the structure of interpretation for a set of metaphysical propositions. Echoing Carl Schmitt, we can say that our political concepts reflect the theological, because both reflect the fundamental structure of the imagination.[20]

INTERPRETATION AND NARRATIVE

I want now to fill out my account of interpretation with several progressively more complex examples, ending with film. Interpretation is a process of dialogue in pursuit of a stable narrative. Narrative has the double quality of being bounded and unbounded, which in turn rests on the deeper structure relating identity to representation.

Consider what is entailed in meeting persons about whom one knows nothing. To respect them as persons is not to treat them simply as instances of a universal: humankind. Of course, I must see them as subjects with an equal claim to dignity, but to do only this would be to express no interest in them. Rather, I want to know who they are. I learn this by placing them in a network of relationships. I ask about family, friends, and professional colleagues. I am trying quickly to establish an orientation. In part I want to know how their world intersects with my own: do we have friends in common? But I am also genuinely interested in their world. I find out whether a person is married; I am curious about children. Do I see them as parents or as siblings? I move on to consider a variety of roles, professional and social. Do I see them as lawyers or laborers, as Christians or Jews? I want to know where they live and where they have been. More likely than not, the order of questions I ask reflects in rough measure the relationships and roles that are important in my own life at the moment of engagement. On a business trip I might begin with a question about work. At a sports event I might ask which team one favors. There is always the possibility of surprise. Indeed, the more I learn about them, the more likely I am to let my questions be guided not by my values and concerns but by their answers.

There is no simple checklist that I follow. There is no single right way to have this conversation: none of us would do it the same way twice. It is spontaneous but not arbitrary. Through my conversation I am trying to imagine the other person. As I learn more, the possibilities of representation become richer. Each answer leads to further questions. Unlike a game of Twenty Questions, however, there is no correct answer to be found. Rather, there are threads of meaning to be developed.

There is never a point at which I can say that I have learned all there is to know about a person. Nevertheless, at every point in this process I can offer a narrative that sets forth an account of what I have learned of the person. I don't simply list the information; rather, I try to provide a coherent account by organizing it along certain dimensions—for example, family, community, history, or profession. To construct the narrative, I must decide what to include from all that I have learned, what to emphasize, and how to set up relationships among different elements. Creating the narrative—imagining a life—I cut the world one way rather than another. This is always a free act; it will not happen without a decision. Philosophy's role is to examine the character and grounds of that decision, but that is nothing more than a further, more deliberate, step in the interpretive engagement. I cannot ground an interpretation on anything other than more interpretation. That ground is not the place from which I begin but the end toward which I reach.

What is true of the encounter with an individual is equally true of the encounter with a community. The community is not a "natural" actor, producing history. We don't know what the bearer of history is in the abstract. Is it the person, government, collective, local community, polity, those in geographical proximity, or those who share traits of gender or ethnicity? Is the subject of the narrative an intergenerational, collective subject—the nation or the people—or is it particular individuals? Are we trying to explain individual decisions or the patterns that we recognize in innumerable decisions? We cannot answer these questions by looking directly at the object of our inquiry any more than we could answer the question of the real by looking directly at things in the world—the problem of the atomists, with which I began. The object of historical inquiry only emerges after we have represented history one way rather than another. We answer the question, in other words, by writing a narrative. The narrative cuts the past one way rather than another. Until it is cut, it is not an available past at all.

Writing the narrative one way, I open up endless questions about whether that is the right way. Competing narratives emerge: political history competes with cultural history. Conventions emerge that govern how we write history. Those conventions can always be challenged; they change over time. They are not challenged by juxtaposing a real identity to the representation but by offering other representations. Which narrative, then, do I offer? I must decide, which means I must be convinced, just as I must convince others. Just as history refers simultaneously to acts and the account of the acts, it refers simultaneously to the freedom of the actors and of the historian.

Writing narrative is not something that we do only in the leisure of the academy. We are all composing these narratives constantly in order to make sense of our own lives and communities. We are subject to political claims, and we bring with us political expectations. These are based on a sense of who we are, and that sense only arises from the historical narratives that we maintain together. This is true of our relationship to the nation but also to those multiple collectives and institutions—church, town, family, union, corporation—within which we lead our lives. We always act with an understanding of the way the world is. We explain ourselves by appealing to, and thus supporting, narratives that give us a world. We don't do any of this alone. To live together, we must share a great deal in our ways of understanding. It is, moreover, exactly those shared understandings that make our disagreements possible. Even as we disagree, we try to persuade each other. We could not persuade if we spoke different languages. Similarly, we could not persuade if we cut the world entirely differently.

As we move from objects and people to aesthetic creations, the nature of interpretation does not fundamentally change. Let me start with a painting, since every reader can observe the picture, without relying on my description. The painting is Winslow Homer's *Veteran in a New Field*, painted in 1865.[21] Homer's painting locates us in a scene immediately after the Civil War, a war that was both awful and awesome, a combination of slaughter and sacrifice. The painting puts itself in dialogue with Lincoln's great effort to explain what this war, triggered by his own election, was about. His dedication of the cemetery at the Gettysburg battlefield is the beginning point of understanding: "Now we are engaged in a great civil war, testing whether that nation, or any nation so conceived and so dedicated, can long endure. We are met on a great battlefield. . . . We have come to dedicate a portion of that field, as a final resting place for those who here gave their lives that that nation might live."[22] The painting links the new field to the battlefield.

The veteran in the new field is the survivor of the earlier field of battle. The killing fields have returned to fields of wheat; life has again taken the place of death. The veteran literally lays aside the insignia of battle and picks up a scythe. There is a certain calmness in the scene: the battle is over. There is hope, and with hope there is the consolation of return. This much we might know, but this much would make the painting only one of any number of illustrations celebrating the end of the war. Winslow Homer's real accomplishment is to avoid such caricature. He has to accomplish a paradoxical task, showing us simultaneously grief and hope, desolation and consolation. He cannot do that by simply portraying the war as over and life going on. What Lincoln accomplished by speaking in the "now" of war and at the site of battle, Homer must do in a single frame. Indeed, the painting is more interesting when we begin not from hope but from loss.

The grief of war is first of all the grief of absence. Absence is the great thematic frame of this painting. Where is everybody? Dead. The veteran has stripped off the insignia of service. His jacket and his canteen lie on the ground, imitating the death of all those he fought with and against. There is the terrible isolation of survival. Maybe he is utterly alone—the last man standing. Maybe the wheat is so high because there is no one else. The connection with the "grim reaper" is obviously at play. Has he turned to the wheat, having finished with man?

The questions we ask stand in for the dialogue with the stranger I imagined above. The questions keep coming. Where is his family? Where is the farm? It is as if he has not yet returned home, or perhaps there is no longer a home to which to return. He was still in uniform, still carrying his canteen. Is this still soldier's work? There may be calm but there is no joy in this scene. He grips the scythe as if it were a gun. He cuts down the stalks as if they were men. What is this new field if not the battlefield flourishing now from the blood of the fallen soldiers? Is this why the wheat is so high? Is he actually reaping, or is he looking for what was lost on this field?

Absence is twice present here. It is not just that he is alone; we cannot see his face. Again, the comparison with the battlefield comes to mind: men charging at each other across a field look at each other full-on. Seeing the other can be as much an act of hatred as of love. We cannot be trusted to look on each other without hatred. As long as that is true, we are alone. The painting goes right up to the edge of desolation, of the failure of the word, and of the disappearance of the human. Can we connect to humankind if we cannot see the other's face? Humanity has brought itself to the edge of extinction.

Knowing of battle, we have become unfit to confront each other. Were we to do so, we would have to speak of what we saw, but that is wholly unspeakable. Speech may have to give way before the horror of human actions. There is no celebration here of the themes of liberty or union: the ideas for which the war was fought. Lincoln spoke of these directly, meaning he looked directly at an audience. But Lincoln, too, is now dead. We turn away from him and his words, for all of that is as nothing in the knowledge of human loss. Turning from the confrontation, giving up the rhetoric, picking up the tool, going to work—these are marks of shame. There has been an utter and complete failure of love on the old field. Until there is again the possibility of love, we cannot face each other.

Is there hope, then, that is not caricature: scythe for sword, wheat for death, labor for battle? Yes, but it lies outside the frame. By showing us only the back of the veteran, Homer reminds us that this scene is entirely his creation, that we are outside of it. It is a performance and a commentary. Homer was not drawn into the scene by the face of the veteran. Neither are we. We observe, without engaging the veteran. We do, however, engage the artist. He speaks and we respond. In a scene of loneliness and desolation there is a conversation. Homer forces on us the question: are human beings to be trusted, or are they only the instrument of their own destruction? Are we utterly alone because we would rather kill than love? But it is Homer that asks the question, and it is we who respond, either with hope or despair. We turn not to face the veteran but to face the artist, who shows more of himself in the painting than the veteran shows, with his back to us. We stand with Homer, looking on together, asking, and ultimately judging. To invite the question is to begin a conversation. The human is not entirely lost.

This is one possible interpretation. I have tried to offer a narrative with a certain unity. It does not, however, exclude other possibilities, which readily come to mind. Perhaps we are to think of the veteran as taking up the work of his farm even before he makes it back to his family home. He is late getting back from war, and there is work to be done. Perhaps we should imagine others starting in on the field from other directions, and all will meet face-to-face in the middle. Or perhaps we do not see his face because he is every man. Should we emphasize life and rebirth over death? the ordinary over the exceptional? Different people will have different interpretations, and together we have a conversation about what the painting means. Homer's views, were we able to discover them, would not be particularly privileged in this conversation. He might have failed to convey what he thought, or perhaps he conveyed much more than he thought.

All of these interpretations are situated in a political history, but other interpretations might free themselves from those circumstances. I could offer an interpretation that focused on the symbolism of wheat and reaping, placing the work in a much longer tradition. Or I could focus on the aesthetics of form alone, placing the work within a genre of artistic production that relates to other styles that preceded it and that influences what will come later. I could turn to a more specific history: how does the painting relate to the circumstances of Homer's own life?

Each of these interpretations is structured in a similar manner. First, we understand the painting itself as situated in a symbolic exchange. What, we ask, does the painting say about family, war, death, and community or about the nature of aesthetic representation? The painting is itself an intervention in a discursive universe. Symbolic structures are never fixed but only exist in and through their use. That use is always dynamic: propositions are formed, meanings are articulated. There is no use of language that cannot take itself as its own object. Accordingly, there is no way that any conversation can limit itself. Every proposition can become the object of a new proposition. Because a proposition gains its meaning from its connection to other propositions, even a simple repetition does not convey exactly the same meaning twice.[23] The conversation into which we enter with the painting cannot be, for that reason, the same one that Homer pursued. Indeed, some of the conversations in which we are interested may not have yet begun when he executed the painting. Nevertheless, we ask that the painting speak to the conversations that interest us. For example, I cannot focus on the apparent loneliness in the painting today without putting it in conversation with existentialism. I cannot speak of the absent face without putting the painting in touch with the work of Emmanuel Levinas.[24]

Second, the interpretation I offer enters its own symbolic exchange. My interpretation does not come from nowhere; it must consider a range of alternative meanings. I try to think through as many of the possibilities as I can. I try out various meanings and see how far I can push a conversation in that direction. I choose to emphasize one set of exchanges rather than another. I don't deny the presence of these other possibilities; I leave them for others to develop. In forming my interpretation, I am interrogating myself as much as the painting, for I am evaluating the possibilities in terms of what is compelling to me. I construct a narrative that I convey to others. I find myself in multiple conversations, some real and some imagined.

Third, the unity of the interpretation upon which I settle is located in its narrative structure. In the language I used before, the narrative cuts the world one way rather than another. Doing so requires an investment of resources, a decision, that tells us something about the character of the interpreter, as well as about the object interpreted. "Who" is as much at stake as "what." I can be asked to explain my choice; I must defend my interpretation. Homer will not do this work for me. I cannot say "just look" at the painting. Speaking, we are showing ourselves to others and to ourselves. We must take responsibility for the free act that is the interpretation. Just here, the inquiry into freedom in the last chapter and that of interpretation in this chapter coincide. We can approach the subject of meaning from either the perspective of action or of interpretation.

INTERPRETATION AND FILM

The basic character of interpretation is the same whether we are speaking of an implement, a person, a polity, a painting, or a film. Until I interpret the film, it has no unity. When I interpret it, I am making a judgment about the kind of unity it is—where its borders lie. Doing so, I am usually following a set of conventions that focus on plot and character. I might, however, come to the film as an economist, historian, cultural theorist, or biographer, finding a different narrative unity in each instance. Some of these narratives will take me far outside of the conventional limits of the film. In those instances I have cut the world differently.

Imagine someone who goes to a movie and is asked to report what he or she saw. This person offers descriptions of a series of individual scenes but can make no sense of the film. He or she would be like the character in *Memento*, who has a form of amnesia that prevents him from developing new memories.[25] For him every scene is a new beginning. He can only write notes and take Polaroids that he sends to his future self. The notes and photos, however, appear as if from nowhere, since he has no memory of the context that generated them. A film begins to have unity when we give an account of it. In *Memento* the audience achieves that narrative capacity only as we come to have the memories that the character lacks. The film literally makes us go through the process of recovery of memory by depicting scenes in reverse chronological order. We start where the protagonist does, without any memory—narrative—to understand an act of killing. For us, however, the messages he sends himself become clues that lead us backward.

The meanings that appear in an interpretation were not "absent" from the experience of viewing the film. The film was not "trying to say this." Rather, it was saying this. This is what it means to interpret; it expresses the necessary link of representation to identity. We build our interpretation by recalling different aspects of the film and relating them to each other. Recall is just what we are struggling to achieve in *Memento* with its reversal of time. Our interlocutors may have different views, choosing to emphasize other aspects or relating them in different ways. Interpretations are always plural in the same way that there is no single description of any event. No representation can terminate a conversation; every representation will invite a response.

The plurality of interpretations is held together by the identity of the object interpreted, not because that identity demarcates stable limits but because it is the common object of the representations. We are talking about the same thing, even as we argue about its meaning. Because interpretation is of something, we are compelled to argue with each other. We do not say that each of us has "his or her own film," as if the film were nothing apart from the plurality of individual experiences. Any such claim mistakes the social practice of interpretation with the psychology of individual experience. Interpretation binds us to a common world. Again, we find a compelling example in law. We might argue about the meaning of a precedent even as we agree that the case is authoritative.[26]

An interpretation of a film, even a philosophical interpretation, does not aim to displace our ordinary experience. Its inquiry is continuous with the sort of conversation we might have with friends after seeing a film. Engaging each other, we are not displacing our experience with theory; rather, we are focusing on exactly what it was that we experienced.

As we watch the film, we have constantly the problem of relating the parts to the whole, even though we have no access to the whole apart from the sequence of scenes. We cannot jump ahead to see the conclusion. We hold a kind of silent discourse with ourselves about the meaning of the film as it proceeds. At every moment we have the problem of making sense of the whole. The sequence of scenes plays out in the audience's time, but, as in *Memento*, it is not necessarily a representation of temporal sequence. We live with the film's temporality in the same way that we live with our own: we are constantly calling up our past and imagining our future as we struggle for narrative unity. As I experience more of the film, possibilities open and close. Surprise is possible, just as it is in our everyday life. But the dramatic unity fails if the surprise comes as if from nowhere. We may be pleasantly surprised if someone who seemed weak rises to an occasion of moral difficulty, or someone who seemed too proud suffers defeat. In short, even surprises must make sense.

A recent film, *The Box*, illustrates surprise as narrative failure.[27] A couple with a variety of financial difficulties is offered a choice: push a button on a box and they will gain one million dollars, but pushing this button will also cause someone they do not know to die. The dilemma seems strange, but it is an obvious representation of many of the ordinary dilemmas of life. We purchase inexpensive clothing, knowing that somewhere some child's life is being ruined in a sweatshop; we pursue our lifestyle of high energy consumption, knowing that climate change destroys the lives of those in developing countries. More directly, we choose to go to war for good reasons, and innocent people die. The film asks us to confront just exactly what we would do if we were to see the deadly consequences of our choices as clearly as we see the benefits.

As *The Box* proceeds, however, it resists the possibility of narrative unity. More and more surprising elements are added: unexplained aliens, strange zombielike behavior, movements beyond space and time, portals to the afterlife. Other things that we might have thought important at the start—for example, career frustrations—simply disappear. Haphazardness, however, is not the worst of it. The film portrays the couple in an entirely sympathetic light. She does push the button, not quite believing the choice it represents, but they immediately change their minds. Overwhelmingly, they are shown to have moral integrity. They learn; they fight to do the right thing. She shows a sympathetic love for those who have suffered, including the odd character threatening them. Finally, when she has to choose between her own life and the well-being of her child, she willingly sacrifices. None of this matters: the husband is forced to kill her to save the son. So what is the point? The film bears no narrative line that makes any sense. Despite the good idea from which it begins, the film falls apart.[28]

As I watched *The Box*, my surprise led simply to disorientation. But thinking back on it, I ask whether I can do better in my reflective interpretation than I could in the struggle to narrate the film as I watched it. Now, I pursue the thought that pushing the button can symbolize the decision for war. We speak of the president's having the option to "push the button." We may go to war for our own financial well-being at the cost of innocent lives abroad. We think of the oil in Iraq, we decide to act, some poor Iraqi dies. How does it all work? We don't know: the box, apart from the button, turns out to be empty. Yet perfectly well-meaning people seem to make this decision all the time: they gain; someone else dies. Political violence, we have constantly to relearn, does not have this simple, unidirectional line. There is no threatening the other without being threatened in return. A world in which we push the button is one in which others will push the button, and then *we* are dying for no apparent reason. We, too, are forced to kill our loved ones. Is that not one meaning of conscription? Each side thinks it will achieve the gain, but in the end each side suffers the loss. Worse, each side thinks it is acting for love, both when it seeks gain and when it sacrifices lives. Love is responsible for the best and the worst in us. The aliens want us "to stop pushing the button," meaning to live within our means in peace with one another.

This is a more coherent narrative, but it still leaves me with a puzzle of moral evaluation. The couple at the center of the film are virtuous; they become more so throughout the film. Why, then, is the "lesson" that none of this counts? Of course, the good and the bad die in war. One might think it a message of nihilism, but the film has no such feel to it. Since it is love that drives both the best and the worst—pushing the button and remorse—are we being asked to consider whether we would be better off in a world without love? Can we have love without sacrifice, or sacrifice without violence? These are real issues, but the film fails to assume responsibility to confront the questions it raises.

The point is not to evaluate the narrative unity of this particular film but to see the way in which the narrative that I develop while watching the film is continuous with the narrative I develop when I interpret the film. At the end of the film I had a sense that things had not worked out as they should have. Literally, the world fell apart, contrary to the moral intuitions on which the film relied. On reflection, I wonder if I can reach an interpretation that makes sense of my surprise and that deals in a more satisfactory way with the moral judgments that I made about the characters. I try out different interpretations. I may come to see the film differently, in which case I may come to be quite satisfied with its ending. My second reading of the film does not take me there, but it gets me a good deal closer. It is, for this reason, a better interpretation.

An essential quality of representation is that it can always take itself as its own object. We don't find language users who have only a first-order capacity to speak about the world and not about their representations of the world. The symbolic domain is either fully present or not at all present. Accordingly, films often take up the problem of film itself. Sometimes they offer interpretations of other films or self-consciously locate themselves in relationship to other films. *The Artist* was like this. They can also deliberately reflect on the character of representation that is itself at the heart of the experience of film. *Memento* was like this. Another recent film that approaches this subject is *The Other Man*.[29]

The Other Man involves a complex triangle of three characters—Peter, Ralph, and Lisa. Peter and Lisa are married, with a grown-up daughter. Lisa is a designer of high-fashion shoes; Peter is the head of a software company. We see them in a few quickly moving opening scenes, spanning public and private spaces, professional and intimate. We cannot quite get our bearings, for Lisa is obviously deeply troubled by something, but we don't know what. She questions Peter as to whether he has ever had an affair or wanted to have one. She speaks of the need to decide. Love is not something that happens to you but something for which you must decide. He is puzzled, telling her that he has loved only her. These opening scenes end with them in bed together and her saying she has to tell him something. We don't learn what. The next morning, she is off on a business trip, and then she is simply gone. We don't know where or why. We don't even know the time span between that departure and her desperate absence from Peter's life, which we experience in the next scene.

The rest of the film moves in two parallel dimensions: one involving Peter, the other involving us, the viewers. Peter discovers a file on his wife's computer labeled "love." The file, however, is protected by an unknown password. After much effort, he realizes Lisa left him a clue.

In the file he discovers pictures of his wife with another man, Ralph. They look very happy together. Why has she set this up, leaving the pictures and the clue to their discovery? He becomes obsessed with finding out who this other man is. Yet the real question for Peter is not so much who the other man is but who Lisa is. The pictures—representations—suggest an identity different from that which he thought he knew. She left them under the word, "love." Did she mean the love between Peter and herself, or was she referring to her love for the other man?

Lisa told Peter in one of the opening scenes, you must decide for love. Before he can decide, he must interpret the pictures. On the computer he sees Lisa as though she were the subject of a film. One easy interpretation would be that Lisa is simply coming clean by admitting betrayal. When we first see the pictures, we don't know what has happened to her, which makes us quite open to this interpretation. Her husband reacts with such rage that we think that the pictures are her way of inflicting injury. We think we understand Peter, when we interpret his obsession as resting on the belief that he will find Lisa with the other man. But this does not seem right, for we have been given no reason to think that she wants to injure him. Why would she want to wreck his life, given the tenderness we saw earlier?

Without this interpretation we are left as puzzled about her identity as Peter is. We stand in relation to Peter's relationship to his wife as he does to the relationship between his wife and Ralph. We, too, have access to that relationship only on the basis of a few pictures—his are on the computer; ours are the opening scenes of the film. In both dimensions the movie develops by juxtaposing contemporary scenes with flashbacks—more representations—offered as the imaginings of Peter. Sometimes he is remembering his wife; sometimes he is imagining her with Ralph. The latter imaginings are triggered by a photograph or a text message from Ralph. The flashbacks are his effort to construct a visual narrative, as if he were literally constructing a film by putting the pictures in motion. With all of these images we ask what is the relationship between representation and identity—just the question of the film itself.

Peter finds Ralph, and then finds him out. Ralph shows himself as a fashionably dressed "cosmopolitan"—a word he uses to describe himself. He has a passion for chess, romance, and grand stories of himself.

Peter befriends him, hoping to construct an opportunity for revenge. But he discovers that Ralph is not what he represents himself to be. In fact, he is the janitor in an expensive apartment building. He lives a kind of fantasy as he tries to make life more "beautiful." Peter's moment of revenge comes when he manipulates Ralph into believing that Lisa will rendezvous with him at the site of their old romance. Instead, Peter shows up, revealing both that she is dead and that he knows the truth about Ralph's identity.

By the end of the movie, however, Peter comes to see things the opposite way. Ralph, he tells his daughter, is quite "beautiful." Representation and identity have shifted places: that he is a janitor is not the truth of his identity; rather, his identity lies in the person he shows to the world. We are free to create ourselves. We must decide, which is exactly what Lisa told him early in the movie. To choose love is to choose for beauty.

And what of the identity of Lisa? We learn that she died of cancer. There is a suggestion that she died of breast cancer, and part of the reason may have been that she declined to have surgery. Is this a woman for whom appearance was reality? She was, after all, a designer of women's shoes. But there is something more, for there is also a suggestion that she intended the interaction between her two lovers after her death. At the very end of the film Peter thinks that the process of exposure, discovery, and reconciliation was something that she had wanted for him. That we can puzzle about this along with him demonstrates exactly the point of the relationship between representation and identity. Lisa, a fictional character, wants recognition of her own identity—an identity beyond representation. In this she is like everyone else.

The deeper point is about the emotional pathos that surrounds the relationship between representation and identity. We love the person, not a representation of the person. Yet we have no way to identity except through representation. There is no interpretation of the pictures Peter discovers that will make of them an affirmation of her love for him. We cannot love without accepting our own vulnerability. His love becomes an exercise in acceptance.

Lisa shows us interpretation as an act of decision. One must decide how to represent one's own identity. She decides for beauty. Peter shows us an inverse image of decision: vulnerability. Loving, we expose ourselves to the decision of the beloved. There are no guarantees; there is only the faith that we have in each other. I must trust that the decision for love will be a decision for me. When it is not, as hers was not for him, the question is what I will do. He moves from rage to acceptance, from hatred to love. That is a fair measure of the trajectory of all of us. We must move from rage at a world that inevitably disappoints our representations to acceptance of a world that is worthy of our love. We must, in the end, decide for a love that reaches beyond representation to identity. The word for that process is *faith*. Peter, we can say, recovers his faith.

A world of decision alone would be one in which we are each as changeable as the representations that we create. There would be nothing to love because there would be nothing in which we are fully invested. A world of faith alone would be the life of the monk in constant, silent prayer. It would be a world of denial of the self. We live our lives in the double world of decision and faith. This is as true of ourselves as it is of those whom we love. This double character of our imaginative life contains an echo of our sacred texts. Abraham had to decide and to have faith. He was vulnerable to the decision of his God; he had to accept in love what looked like betrayal. Out of his decision and faith we construct the founding narrative of the West. We are still writing that narrative. Sometimes we do it at the movies.[30]

Part II

FILM AND THE
SOCIAL IMAGINARY

I described in part 1 a democratic approach to philosophy, which takes as its object of inquiry the products of the social imaginary. I turn now to a direct examination of those products in the form of popular, contemporary films. Up to this point I have chosen particular films to illustrate my arguments. In this part my ambition is to create a sense that "any film will do." Our beliefs and practices are always on display—in successful as well as unsuccessful films. A particularly good film is not necessarily a better vehicle for critical reflection upon ourselves than a bad film. Nevertheless, this inquiry is not a survey but an interpretive exercise, and I have inevitably chosen films that are accessible resources for the themes I pursue. For the most part I focus on films that were popular at the time of my writing. I have deliberately stayed away from "classics" and from "experimental" films. The same form of interpretation could be pursued with these films, but neither qualifies as "ordinary," which is just what I am after.

Turning to particular films does not mean simply asking what it is that they have to say. I can no more expose myself as a sort of blank slate to the meaning of a film than I can to the meaning of a person or community. We come to a film with a store of experience and understandings. Without that we would not know how to put the pieces into a single narrative. Films are not cultural productions of an unknown time and place. Rather, we approach them ready to deploy an imagination that has already been fully formed. We have certain expectations, which the film confirms or challenges. Because we approach the film from a definite position, we can be surprised or disappointed.

In each of the inquiries of this part—on politics, love, and faith—I begin by setting forth a general sketch of the imaginative expectations with which I approach the topic. These sketches are themselves bound to be controversial. Support for them is not derived from abstract, normative theory. Just the opposite. In setting them out, I am relying on my general cultural sense—and my own past inquiries. I don't, however, expect the reader to accept those grounds or to consult my earlier books. Rather, the persuasive power of these sketches must be post hoc: it arises from the interpretations of the actual films that follow. Interpretation is inevitably such a reciprocal process of expectation and discovery. We must begin from somewhere and then see what we learn from the engagement with the actual work. The beginning is not a fixed point; confronting the particular work is not a form of application of an abstract paradigm. Interpretation is movement in both directions, making use of available imaginative resources to bring to awareness the world of the film, which is already our world.

The chapters of this part explore a number of important building blocks of the social imaginary. I take up topics with which I am familiar. I make no claim that these inquiries offer anything like a complete account of the particular films discussed, let alone of all films being produced today. If representation is without limit, no such claim could possibly be made. Nor do I claim that films, individually or collectively, somehow exhaust the possibilities of meaning on these subjects. Certain themes have been seized; others have been ignored. Popular films are, first of all, forms of entertainment. That does not mean that a film cannot be serious or even painful, but it does make it unlikely that certain topics will be considered. The topics I take up are *polity*, *family*, and *faith*. These are often at the core of popular films, in part because they are familiar to everyone. They have always been among the organizing themes of Western culture. That is reason enough to start with them.

While focusing on contemporary films, I bring an approach that is sensitive to this larger history. In particular, chapters 4 and 5 are loosely organized around a basic divide between Old and New Testament approaches to social meaning. The former asks us to focus on the experience of sacrifice and its place at the foundation of a political community organized by law. The latter asks us to focus on an experience of new beginnings, literally of rebirth through a kind of sacred innocence. Both of these elements remain central to the social imaginary: the possibility of sacrifice and the experience of natality. Both are expressions of love: paradigmatically, the love of Abraham for Isaac and the love of Christ for humanity. In one way or another love draws us into the world of film. How could we expect anything other, for it is love that draws us into the world.

CHAPTER 4

Violence and the State

Two great themes of film are violence and love. One could press even further and say that there is just one great theme, love. The violence that interests us most is sacrifice: the violent act done for the sake of love. Of the films that I have discussed so far, most have love at the center: *The Artist*, *The Sweet Hereafter*, *The Secret in Their Eyes*, *Crazy Heart*, *Elegy*, *The Box*, *The Other Man*. The exception is *The Hurt Locker*, but that exceptional quality is exactly what the film is about. The overwhelming presence of love and sacrifice in these products of popular culture tells us that we continue to live with a deeply Christian imagination.

A film, I have argued, must show us a world of meaning, and it can do so only by relying on common archetypes circulating among its audience. For us, a world of meaning is one in which there is love to be found or achieved, lost or recovered. Love gives us both comedy and tragedy. The former shows us love triumphant in reordering the world. The latter shows us not the failure of love but the demands of love in a world recalcitrant to love's ordering. Sometimes we are seized by the purity of a love that is innocent of all the sins of the world. Sometimes love will demand of us that we subject ourselves to the possibility of sacrifice. These great themes of innocence and sacrifice are the archetypes on which our narratives of love draw.

A meaningful world is not simply one in which individual desires are met. Nor is it one that is well ordered according to just rules. The world that actually claims us is that of family and polity. To be alone, as we saw in *The Artist*, is a sign of personal and social pathology. One of the characteristics of modernity has been the withdrawal of serious competitive claims of identity from a range of other groups—for example, church, union, professional association, and ethnic community. Of course, these continue to operate but more often as supplements to family and politics. We might, for example, participate in politics through a union or trade association; we don't oppose a professional identity to a political identity. Similarly, the church rarely challenges the state with a claim to authority over the individual, but individuals may find the church mediating their relationship to the state, just as it may help them in their relationship to family. One sign of an emerging postmodernity is the reappearance of competing identity claims, ranging from multiculturalism to fundamentalism. One way to gauge the significance of these trends is to look at their presence in—or absence from—popular films.

In family and state we find our identity in and through the relationships that bind us to the world. We are bound by a sense of care or, I would say, by love. With respect to these communities, small and large, individuals imagine the possibility of sacrifice. We do not condition these obligations of care on meeting a norm of justice. We do not ask of our children whether they deserve our sacrifice. Similarly, we do not choose our state on the basis of justice. It is rather the other way around: because we care about our children and state, we want them to be just.[1] Love comes before justice, sacrifice before law.

Love is not simply a matter of doing the right thing. Indeed, often in love we do the wrong thing. We cannot reason ourselves to love, and reason will not tell us what to do for the objects of our love. We sacrifice ourselves even as we recognize that the demand is unjust. What matters in love is not reason, not desire, but meaning. Love pulls us into the world of ultimate meaning. We often say that falling in love is like seeing the world anew. The point is deeper than the experience of romance. In Judeo-Christian thought God and humanity are bound to each other by love. God creates out of love, and humankind gives back that love to God. In the Old Testament this reciprocity of love produces law and sacrifice. The New Testament adds an idea of redemption and rebirth symbolized by the innocent child. Taking on the burden of Isaac's sacrifice, Christ promises to everyone the possibility of rebirth into innocence. One symbol of that rebirth is the overcoming of law. The covenant of law is transcended by rebirth in the body of Christ.

We cannot trace a direct route from the Old and New Testaments to the social imaginary that sustains the modern nation-state. In the language I used in chapter 2, the route has been one of reasons, not causes. It has been a matter of analogy and persuasion, not necessity. Nevertheless, these ideas of love and sacrifice, of law and grace, of innocence and rebirth are the elementary building blocks of the Western social imaginary. We find them wherever we look, including in films. They are the sources of our narratives of world creation and world maintenance. In our popular films these symbolic resources have been taken up and inflected through more specific narratives of the American experience.[2]

IMAGINING THE MODERN NATION-STATE: LAW AND SOVEREIGNTY

The American political experience unfolds within a twofold heritage of revolution and constitution. Revolution marks the appearance of the popular sovereign, while constitution is a representation of this original act of popular sovereignty. Law represents the now-withdrawn sovereign: it is the product of "We the People." The nation must be— revolution—and it must be something—constitution. Sovereignty captures the existential quality of the state; law captures its character as a distinct normative project. The popular sovereign is the nation conceived as an active unity: a transgenerational collective subject. The rule of law is the nation conceived as an order of representation. Sovereignty and law stand to each other as identity to representation. Seeing ourselves as members of the popular sovereign, we see law as the product of our own free act.[3]

Before the state can create itself as a project of law, there must be a coming into being of the sovereign entity: we the people. Revolution is that moment of popular, sovereign presence. This moment always has about it the character of the sacred—being and meaning coincide. It appears as if from nowhere, for no set of conditions "causes" a revolution. Not surprisingly, political scientists were not able to predict the revolutions of eastern Europe, or, more recently, the Arab spring. Trying to predict revolution is like trying to predict love. We cannot know in advance when and where revolution will erupt because it is not a natural event but a way of understanding self and community.

The popular sovereign succeeds the sacral monarch not as a rationalization of political power but as a relocation of the site of a political faith. The popular sovereign is no less mysterious than its predecessor. We are still enthralled by the mystical corpus. Thus, in the American political imagination popular sovereignty is the felt presence of an ultimate meaning in and through the collective experience of the sacrificial body.[4] The popular sovereign, accordingly, is no less dangerous than its predecessor.

There is no scale by which we can measure the value of the existence of the American popular sovereign. Can we answer the question of the point at which surrender is appropriate? We cannot because all political value begins with this singular event of the coming into being of the popular sovereign. There is no revolution without the expression of a willingness to sacrifice and no sacrifice without an experience of ultimate meaning. A claim of sovereignty is always a claim that politics can be a matter of life and death. For this reason the claim that we are entering a new, global, cosmopolitan order in which sovereignty no longer figures is always linked to the idea that war and sacrifice have been displaced by law and courts.

No proposition offered in justification of the revolutionary act is adequate to the meaning at stake. Americans claimed that their revolution was a response to British injustice; they claimed they were being treated as if they were slaves. But the colonists were slave owners, not slaves. They lived in what was arguably the freest political jurisdiction in the world. The fact that their words were not adequate to their experience hardly casts doubt on that experience.[5] We don't defeat a revolution by arguing that things are not so bad. We defeat it by showing that not the popular sovereign, but only a mob, is present.[6]

If revolution is the politics of the sacred, it will be as ephemeral as every other manifestation of sacred presence. Just as God gives Moses the law to function as a trace of the sacred presence even after God withdraws, the people give themselves the law as a trace of sovereign presence. We must pass from identity to representation: a revolution that fails to create a constitution fails as a revolution. We know that the revolution was an act of popular sovereignty only because of the law that it left behind. We must see through that law to the popular sovereign whose law it is. Law and sovereignty stand in a reciprocal relationship of truth: law is the truth of sovereignty, sovereignty the truth of law.

In the modern nation-state the popular sovereign wills the product of reason as its law. This is the founding myth of a state that is both democratic and enlightened. These two aspects are contingently related to each other: a sacral monarch could pursue enlightened laws; a popular sovereign can be unreasonable. The narrative of American political formation combines an experience of the sacred and a turn to reason, a violent act of sacrifice and a reasonable plan of order. As sovereign, the state is complete; as a project of reason, law is endlessly subject to reform. American law may have improved during the last two hundred years, but the popular sovereign was total, complete, and fully capable of demanding a life from the beginning. This dualism produces endless confusion and contestation between ideas of the political that emphasize law as a project of rational construction and ideas of the political as the expression of a transgenerational, collective subject whose history is the manifestation of its will. We cannot answer the question of whether law is the will of the sovereign or the expression of reason.[7] Which expresses the modern nation-state of the nineteenth and twentieth centuries: law or war? We believe that we go to war to protect law, but the equation can work the other way as well: law gives expression to the identity that will be defended in acts of sacrificial violence.

At stake in these categories of revolution and constitution is the relationship of legitimacy to justice, of sacrificial violence to individual well-being, and of identity to representation. We can align these terms in two groups: the popular sovereign shows itself through violent acts of sacrifice; it has will but not reason; and it grounds the legitimacy of the law in a collective experience of transgenerational identity. The rule of law puts at its center individual well-being, which includes dignity and material prosperity; it is an evolving product of reason working out a system of relationships between rights and duties; and its normative center is justice.

Accordingly, sovereignty and law together structure the state around competing but linked concepts of identity and representation. Sovereign presence is never a matter of representation but of identity. Finding ourselves, we acknowledge the power of the sovereign to demand a life. This is the violent, sacrificial act at the foundation of the state: it is the space within which we confront enemies. Every use of political violence in defense of the nation-state is an imaginative reiteration—a memory—of this revolutionary sacrifice. Constitution is the product of this sacrifice. Thus, law always points beyond itself to its source of authority.[8] No institution of government—not even lawmaking institutions—is itself the sovereign. Each claims to represent the sovereign. The criminal's violation of law is not a challenge to sovereignty because the sovereign is not present, but only represented, in law. For this reason the criminal is not the enemy; the enemy challenges state sovereignty, regardless of whether it challenges its law.[9]

The relationship of revolution (sovereign) to constitution (law) is the political form of the relationship of the sacred to a text: a god who leaves no text—written or unwritten—can have no historical existence. Thus, Christ announces both the end of law and the end of history. Conversely, without the experience of the sacred a religion might remain an intelligible system of representation constituting a moral order, but it would be stripped of its claim of ultimate value. The same is true of the state: without the experience of sovereign identity we will have rules without meaning. When we cannot see through law to the popular sovereign whose work it is, we face a crisis of identity, regardless of how just the law is. The popular sovereign is an endless source of meaning that overflows every attempt at legal representation. There is always more at stake in law than law itself can say.

The puzzle—or perhaps mystery—is the movement from sovereign to law (how does identity become representation?) and from law to sovereign (how do we see identity through representation?). At stake in maintaining transparency in both directions is our capacity to understand the political order as the realization of our own freedom and to understand that freedom as a matter of ultimate meaning. To join a legal order of well-being with a sovereign order of sacrifice describes exactly the social imaginary of the modern nation-state, which for two hundred years has brought us law and war, criminals and enemies, individual prosperity and destruction. Thus, we find the pledge of a life at the conclusion of a document—the Declaration of Independence—that tells us that the function of government is to provide for the "pursuit of happiness." For us, war has never been far from law.

These archetypes of political order are under considerable stress today. We find a fear that violence can no longer be read as sacrifice and a reciprocal fear that representation can no longer be linked to identity. Have word and flesh split apart, leaving behind the political imaginary of modernity? As evidence, we might cite the reappearance of torture in the war against terror. Torture was precisely the form of state violence characteristic of a premodern, sacral monarch. It treats the criminal as if he were the enemy. It emerges from a failure of separation of sovereignty from law.[10] At places like Guantanamo the conditions for law, and thus of representation, can never quite be achieved. We might also cite the emergence of an order of international law—human rights—that disavows any connection to sovereignty. This is representation without identity, law without sacrifice. Now enemies are to be treated as criminals: wars are to end with trials. Indeed, trials and law enforcement are entirely to displace war. In response to both of these forms of contemporary anxiety, we see a longing for the recovery of the traditional connection of representation and identity. When we turn to contemporary films, we find all of these themes; we find the anxiety of separation and the longing for recovery.

DEMOCRATIC SACRIFICE

Clint Eastwood's *Gran Torino* offers us a vivid example of the way in which these ideas of love, sacrifice, and law continue to operate in the social imaginary.[11] At the center of the film is a failure of representation that can only be overcome through a new act of sacrifice. That failure is seen in the inability of law to constrain violence and in the disappearance of language as a form of dialogue. Language has itself become a form of violence. A shattered working-class neighborhood of Detroit has returned to the state of nature, characterized by violence and loneliness.

Violence must be contained by law, but that cannot happen until the law, a shared system of representation, is refounded in love. Before there can be law or language, there must be faith. But in what? Where can we find a love adequate to ground the sacrificial act of faith?

Eastwood plays Walt Kowalski, a Korean War veteran now retired from his job on an automobile assembly line in Detroit. As the film opens, his wife has just died. He is attending her funeral at the local Catholic church. We quickly learn that he is a man without faith: he has little patience for the priest who tries to console him, as Kowalski's wife had asked him to do. Walt thinks the priest a child who knows nothing about the world. Walt is estranged from his own children as well, living alone in a house that he has occupied for decades. He speaks mostly to himself—and to his dog—in a language filled with racial slurs and insults. His anger at the world seems boundless; he is completely alone.

His isolation and anger result from more than the recent loss of his wife. A larger loss of community sets him apart. He no longer works at the assembly plant; his neighborhood is filling with Asian immigrants as the children of his generation move to the suburbs. There is, however, something even deeper that is driving his isolation: his experience in Korea. He is haunted by the memory of killing a young Korean soldier who was trying to surrender. He carries with him this secret, that he has killed the innocent. However little he may think of everyone else—family, neighbors, priest—he knows that he has killed unjustly. His memory of Korea is not of sacrifice but of murder. This is the fundamental disturbance at the center of his moral universe: he is not innocent. He is unable to find redemption or relief. He is a man without faith and, once his wife dies, without love.

He is the veteran haunted by the knowledge that he is a war criminal. The political has lost its foundation as a source of ultimate meaning. That absence of a transcendent identity now plays itself out as the collapse of the order of representation—of language and law. Having killed, he is now a sort of perpetual outsider inhabiting the edge, always looking in, for he knows a truth that can neither be spoken nor heard. He is exacting upon himself a form of punishment, retreating into the boundaries of his own small plot of land. This he will defend with deadly force; he sits on his porch with a loaded gun. He has become a nation of one, at war with everything beyond the edge of his plot.

Walt has lost the narrative of the state. Driven into himself, he has lost family, workplace, community, and church. None of these communities can offer him absolution for his act of murder. The church literally cannot fathom his sin, concerned more with sexual morality than political killing.[12] Late in the film, when Walt goes for a final confession after many decades of staying away, he admits to a wayward kiss but not to an act of murder. In the church's view he is a man hardly marked by sin at all. This church no longer speaks to the modern condition.

Walt's act of violent killing undermines the entire order of representation. When murder displaces sacrifice, the political order loses its foundation. The order of law—the political order—is failing in every dimension: crime, community decay, displacement. His neighborhood is filling with Hmong immigrants who have themselves suffered a similar collapse of their traditional community. They, too, are the victims of a political killing that was not a sacrifice. Just as Walt's children have gone to the suburbs to pursue the material values of the middle class, the children of his new neighbors are also pursuing material values but now in the form of crime and gang violence. In truth he shares most with the matriarch of the Hmong household next door—a person with whom he cannot even speak. Both of them look out on the world of violent decay from their front porches.

Despite his racial and ethnic prejudices, he is drawn to his Hmong neighbors who are trying to hold on to traditional family values. He is drawn in accidentally, when the young teenage boy who lives next door bungles a burglary of Walt's prized Gran Torino. The burglary was an initiation ritual into a gang that the boy does not really want to join. The Hmong family forces the would-be criminal to make amends for his attempted crime by helping Walt with various chores. Walt meets the articulate older daughter, who invites him over to share in a family celebration. He soon finds himself intervening to save her from her own poor judgment about a boy. Walt is, in short, becoming a father figure to both of these teenagers.

The movie develops through his growing attachment to this family. To them he is the outsider, who becomes the protector and savior from the surrounding violence.[13] He is armed and threatens the attacking gang. For this he is welcomed into the larger Hmong community. He finds there the meaningful world that had otherwise escaped him. The outside protector is a familiar anthropological figure, appearing in the myth of kingly origins, as well as in the myth of the savior god.[14] Walt, in the end, must act out the role of savior through an act of sacrifice that reestablishes the order of law. Roles have been reversed: the Polish, blue-collar worker is the outsider in his transformed neighborhood. He must recreate the possibility of the state. Doing so, he not only grounds the new community of law, but he redeems himself from a fallen world.

An uneducated man of deep racial prejudice, Walt elides the Korean youth he killed and the Hmong boy next door. He is determined to "save" the Hmong boy from the violence that threatens him. He wants to teach him "how to be a man," which for Walt means to be able to support and defend one's family. Walt must do more, however, for the community in which they live is quickly approaching the violent chaos of a state of nature. The gang attacks the neighbor's house and rapes the daughter. Self-possession and independence are not possible in the collapsing neighborhoods of Detroit. One cannot live with the threat of violence without the protection of law. What is required is the refounding of the state.

Recovery of political order is possible only with a successful act of sacrifice, which is exactly what we see. Walt stages what we expect to be an act of revenge against the gang members, but, in fact, he offers himself as a sacrifice. He confronts them without a weapon and invites their act of violence against him. He has, however, arranged for the police to arrive just as the killing occurs. There will be no problem of silenced witnesses this time. He literally suffers a violent, sacrificial death to secure again the foundations of law: the police arrest his killers who are also the violators of the children he had come to love. This is his act of atonement for the murder committed long ago. This sacrificial act brings forth the possibility of spoken memory, of familial love, and all of the other virtues of a community secure under law.

This figure who began the film as completely irreligious and alone becomes deeply religious and communal. He takes up the burden of giving himself in an act of sacrifice that founds an order of law. He has no otherworldly faith, only the faith that comes with love. Without this willingness to sacrifice, politics becomes mere violence, communities return to the state of nature, people lose their capacity to speak, and families dissolve. Before there can be law, there must be an original act of sacrifice. Not the violent elimination of the other, but the giving up of the self in an act of love founds the state. Absent that sacrificial origin, law is a weak force—so weak, in fact, that it makes no appearance in the film until that final moment.

Walt is the debris of the twentieth century, floating in a sea of violence without language. Church, family, and state no longer speak to him. But when we ask where is hope, we find the film appealing to the traditional structures of the social imaginary. There may be no place for the church, but the act of sacrifice remains the only source of a meaning capable of overcoming our finite condition. *Gran Torino* is a work of political theology for the twenty-first century. It reads our circumstances—including our anxieties—through the Western social imaginary with its archetypes of sacrifice, family, and law. What could more vividly express the sacred than Walt's act of sacrifice? He is the sacrificial offering. What is more familial than his love for these Hmong children? In the end the teenage boy inherits Walt's prized possession, the Gran Torino, which is itself a symbol of a lost era of community. The sacrificial gift of the self, followed by the gift of the car—an intergenerational transfer of a legal right to property—signal the transition from sacrifice to law. Walt is the father who will give the children a world by giving up himself. What could be more patriotic than his creation of the conditions under which law can protect us—an "us" constantly renewed by new immigrant groups?

There must be a movement from love to law. Without that movement sacrifice is only another killing, and killing—as Walt shows us—is the end of language and community. The polity is secured not simply by the justice of its law but by the knowledge that at stake in this order of representation is a meaningful world—a world founded in love. The film follows the deepest imaginative form that we have, from sacrifice to law, from identity to representation. This is a story that we know so deeply that we need only the barest indications in the film to understand that Walt is the modern sacrificial combatant who has taken on himself the task of reclaiming the world for love.[15]

Gran Torino offers us a democratic vision of the founding myth of political sacrifice. Walt is everyman as veteran. We find another version of this founding myth in *Taken*.[16] Again, the state is in need of a refounding in an act of sacrificial violence; again, there is the problematic relationship of law to love, of representation to identity. But now comedy has replaced tragedy. There remains the willingness to sacrifice the self, but in comedy it never comes to that: the killing of the enemy is enough to refound an order of love. This is the comedy of the superhero, who may not make us laugh but reassures us that all will be well.

That politics can be an order of freedom depends on maintaining the relationship between identity and representation. We must see law as an order of representation that we have given ourselves. We are, however, increasingly uncertain about how to do so. Sometimes our anxieties focus on violence that can no longer be imagined as sacrifice, sometimes on law that tells us what to do but not who we are. Meaningless violence is matched by meaningless law. *Taken* projects both forms of anxiety onto the relationship of the United States to France. Just as in the mid-twentieth century, France's failure adequately to defend itself results in a threat to the United States. Again, there is invasion; again, there is collaboration. The questionable political morality of the Europeans results in a defeat that calls for a response from the morally virtuous Americans. Now, however, not the German military but the Albanian Mafia are the enemy. This time the Americans come in the form of a lone combatant.

A teenage daughter on vacation in Paris is seized by Albanian criminals who traffic in innocent girls. The girls are drugged and sold into the sex-slave trade. They become mere bodies, without national or familial identity. Their value is as commodities sold to rich Arabs. This particular girl's father, however, is an ex-CIA operative. He recently retired in order to reconnect with his daughter. He has, as he puts it, a "very particular set of skills," learned through fighting the enemies of the state. Those skills are the administration of violent death, including torture.

Here we have all the basic elements of a modern political crisis of the failure of law. There has been an invasion by people—the Albanians—willing to deploy violence against the very heart of the domestic order—the virgin daughter. Their actions are formally criminal. Nevertheless, the instruments of ordinary law enforcement will no longer protect the family. The criminals have already bought off the French police, but one suspects the problem runs deeper. The police have no interest in risking their lives to defeat a criminal who threatens lethal violence. Policing has become just another job within a bureaucracy; it is not a site of sacrifice. If society is to be defended, this criminal must be seen for what he is: the enemy. If the police cannot see the enemy, they will see the virtuous combatant as a criminal. The father, accordingly, must fend off the police even as he attacks the enemy.[17] By the end of the movie every person involved in the attack on the daughter has been killed by her father. None are punished; all are killed. Those who attack the objects of our love are always enemies, not criminals.[18]

In the prehistory of the film, the father had acted out of love of country. He had given up his relationship to his own family in order to kill the state's enemies. He is the modern warrior. There seems, however, to have been no way to manage the relationship between the public and the private in his life. He had chosen to defend the state, but now he has given up that public role in order to try to recapture his private life. As a father he does not quite know what to do. Of what use are his special skills in seeking the love of a teenage daughter? Like his French counterpart—also an ex-agent—he turns those skills into a source of employment to provide for his family. Unlike the counterpart, he remains virtuous. He has the innocence of an American, searching for domestic virtues of love even within the materialistic world of pop culture. Like Walt he is an outsider to contemporary culture, and as with Walt the source of his estrangement is his killing for the state.[19]

His sense of displacement suggests a broader theme: mastery of violence is that upon which the state relies but that which it cannot admit. He cannot tell his family that he kills for the state. This silence makes him a stranger to their life. His wife leaves him; his daughter does not know him. Thus, he must choose between warrior and father. The failure of acknowledgment, moreover, threatens the entire political project: not just he, but his entire crew, has abandoned the state for private life, turning their skills to market ends.

The larger point is that contemporary states are turning from deployment of violence against their enemies to law enforcement against criminals. In the United States, where everything is privatized, the ex-warriors become private security guards; in France the ex-warrior becomes a policeman. This turn from enemy to criminal corresponds to a change in the character of the private from the familial as a site of love to the familial as a site of consumption. A world without enemies is strangely a world without love. The family is subject to the same tension of identity and representation that we find in the political. The criminals in the film are always represented as acting for money alone. Doing so, they destroy love. The merchant of sex tells the father, right before he is killed, that "there was nothing personal" in his business of selling the daughter. The father replies that for him "it is all personal."[20]

France represents the anxieties of what the United States might become. It no longer has enemies because it will not defend its borders. Paris is completely penetrated by others, from the Albanian Mafia to Arab princes who purchase the enslaved children of the virtuous. The borderless character of Paris is symbolized by Rue de Paradise, where the Albanians process the captured young girls. It is a place of family lost and of police corruption. It must become the place of battle, at which the American tortures and kills the enemy. The problem of not becoming France is simultaneously that of saving love of family and of refounding the state.

We might describe the narrative arc of the film as the effort to find a language for love that can manage the relationship of identity to representation. As the unrecognized warrior, the father performs that which cannot be spoken: the sacrificial killing and being killed that maintains the state. Coming back to his family, he is looking for a way to express his love. At the beginning of the film he is failing: he can do no more than purchase a gift (interestingly a karaoke machine) for his daughter, which is immediately displaced by a larger gift from her stepfather (himself a vaguely corrupt business man). When the father voices concern for his daughter's safety before her trip to Paris, he is not heard. Only after the violent performance of killing all who threaten his family is there recognition of the warrior's love. The fundamental point of this combat is to demonstrate the willingness to sacrifice the self for the sake of love. The family has now been refounded on the violent act of combat with the enemy. Saving his daughter from the enemy in a borderless Paris, the father returns with his daughter across the defended border of the United States.[21]

The end of the film shows us love triumphant, not only because he has saved his daughter but because the familial world can now acknowledge its dependence on the violence of killing and being killed. That which could not be said at the start of the film is now fully in view. Stepping back just slightly, we can see that sacrificial violence has been given a script, which is the film itself. A recognized sacrifice is violence given voice; it is identity founding representation. Now, we can move on to the normal order of representation—the world of law and family—without losing ourselves.

The father knows exactly who he is when he puts his own life at risk by engaging the enemy. He has always been the warrior for love. He has not changed, but his family can, at the end, acknowledge its own dependence on that violence. The film succeeds when the audience finds itself in the same position as the family: we read this act of violence as the refounding of the state. The enemy must be killed to refound the state in an act of love. Love unites the public and the private and teaches that both are dependent on a willingness to sacrifice. Law without sovereignty divides us from ourselves and, in the end, will not protect us from our enemies. It will not do so because it is blind to the fact that we have enemies.[22]

A very old political drama is being recreated in a democratic form here. The family that is now at the center of the state is not that of the king but of everyman. The sovereign actor is now the people. Before they can represent themselves through law, they must take up the burden of sacrificial violence. Only for love will we risk our own lives and kill others. To the action of love all opposition seems evil. We know just one thing: this threat must be destroyed. Only when love defeats evil, when the border is secured and the state of nature has been left behind, can we again have a world of representation.

Does it matter that the father survives, although injured, in his battle to save his daughter? Only as comedy stands to tragedy. Walt Kowalski is killed in a hail of bullets, but the father in *Taken* is never touched, no matter how many bullets are aimed at him. The modern comedy of violence is a form of magical realism. It constructs a hero with superhuman powers who cannot be killed by human hands. The point, however, is not funny at all. It is the willingness to die that creates the license to kill. Out of that reciprocity of sacrificial violence comes the modern nation-state. This reciprocal form of violence marks the domain of the political; to enter it is to take on the burden of founding the state. Indeed, survival can be more problematic than death for the veteran. This was exactly Walt's problem: he survived Korea and thus came to see himself as a murderer rather than a sacrificial combatant.[23]

A third film, *The Dark Knight* (a *Batman* remake), provides us a more explicit consideration of the mythical character of the act of sacrificial violence that founds the order of representation that is law.[24] Again, the film begins with a situation of violence that threatens the destruction of the legal order of the state. The objects of attack symbolize the promise of individual well-being made by modern law: the hospital and the family. Again, there is penetration from abroad; again, there is corruption of the police. Law enforcement is not sacrifice; the police are paid for their services. They are always subject to corruption because they do not act out of love. The police, accordingly, are never up to the task of protecting us from unrestrained violence. That is the point at which the criminal becomes the enemy, and the law does not protect us from enemies. This transition from criminal to enemy is marked in the film by the move from the criminal association—the mob—to the Joker as the source of the violent threat.

If the police will not protect us, the heroic combatant must come from outside, bringing again his special skills. The film presents this mythical theme in its comic-book form, but the point remains serious: a mythic exchange of violence—a willingness to kill and be killed—founds the order of law. When law collapses, there must be a refounding. That act must itself be grounded in love. Rather than the love between father and child, here we have a complex triad involving the figure of law—the DA—and the figure of the warrior—Batman—loving the same person, Rachel. There is only one way to resolve this competition in love: she must die as the sacrificial figure.[25]

As in the two other films I have discussed in this section, love marks the point of indistinction between the public and the private. State and family intersect at the point of unity that is the willingness to kill and be killed. Sacrifice does not distinguish between family and state as the object of love: one sacrifices for the state to protect the family. In a democratic society we know this as a kind of practical first principle: a necessary condition of a legitimate war is that the state convince the mothers to give up their children. This is a drama that we see acted out regularly with the return to the family of the body of the child who has made what we continue to call "the ultimate sacrifice."

The person against whom one sacrifices is the enemy. The Joker is the criminal who has become the enemy because he puts at risk family and state. The great choice he puts to Batman is whether to save the law—in the person of the DA—or love—in the person of Rachel. This is precisely an expression of evil for it splits apart what is supposed to be the single order of family and state.[26] Batman chooses love, but the evil genius anticipates this choice, reversing the location of the two potential victims.

Killing Rachel, murdering love, signifies the Joker's transition from criminal to enemy. Now, he literally announces that he will rule the city. To defeat the enemy, the citizens must offer themselves up in an act that expresses their own willingness to sacrifice. This point is expressed in a critical scene of two ferries, in which the people on each boat are told they can save themselves but only by destroying the other. Neither group acts. This is the appearance of the popular sovereign: a democratic taking on of sacrifice for the sake of the nation. Interestingly, one of the ferries is transporting criminals who had been serving time in the state's prisons. This is their redemptive moment. These criminals are not the enemy. They may have violated the law, but they remain a part of the popular sovereign.

The origin of the state rests in this willingness of citizens to sacrifice themselves. Sacrifice is always violence beyond law. *The Dark Knight* expresses this idea when we see the DA, the figure of law, literally go insane with the knowledge of the death of Rachel. He cannot translate loss of the beloved into a political narrative of sacrifice. He responds by trying to kill all those associated with her death, including those who tried, but failed, to save her. His violence is the senselessness of love lost. This is violence incapable of founding representation. Law does not have the capacity to found itself; it cannot look at its own origins without going insane.

Taken ends with us asking what happens next: can the moment of unity, of acknowledgment that ordinary life within the state requires the extraordinary act of sacrifice, actually sustain itself? *The Dark Knight* emphatically answers "no." After love is murdered and law goes insane, the question of the origin of the state is wide open. Again, the state must be protected by the special skills of the combatant: violence before law. This failure of law and turn to war cannot be recognized, however, without undermining the imaginative construction of the state. Law must win, meaning the originary act of violence must be suppressed from the imagination. Thus, the final act of the movie is one of sacrifice of the warrior for the law. The protector of the state, who acts outside of law for the sake of love, himself becomes the criminal. He is, in René Girard's terms, "the scapegoat."[27] Ironically, the comic-book film is far more tragic than *Taken*.

The legal order is a fiction that cannot see the truth of its own foundation. We must believe in law, if law is to have any chance of success, but the conditions of that belief include a denial of the place of violent sacrifice in sustaining the state. This is just where *Taken* begins; it is where *The Dark Knight* ends. There is a fear that clear vision would drive us all insane, for what the state demands of us is simply too much to live with. We are reminded of Walt's isolation in *Gran Torino*: he saw murder instead of sacrifice on the battlefield. The legal order of the state promises individual well-being—the protection of life and property—but the sovereign state also makes a claim on every life and all of the material resources within its jurisdiction. It will take the objects of our love: the children sacrificed in battle. Since the birth of the nuclear age, the threat of the state to destroy everything it promises to protect has been the background condition of the life of each of us. We cannot bear to look at this. Our films are not far from our philosophers on this point: "There is no document of civilization which is not at the same time a document of barbarism."[28]

The anxiety from which these films begin is the failure of law to protect us from violence. Each constructs an image of the enemy that threatens the order of love. They show us the reconstruction from below of an alignment of the private and public orders of love. This is the modern version of the premodern alignment of love and the state from above: the sacral monarch's love sustained the body of the state. His life was a drama of sacrificial death and rebirth, as he gave up the finite body and took on the mystical corpus of the state. The sacrificial warrior, whether modern or premodern, comes from outside of the law. He is not a figure of representation but rather the embodied presence of the sovereign. As such, he recovers that unity of being and meaning that is the mystical corpus of the state.

Not the royal family but the family of everyman has become the center of meaning of the state. Not commerce, not wealth, not even physical well-being—but love. The state must be defended by the action of love. These films suggest that only when we are willing to engage in sacrifice can the world sustain an ultimate meaning. If we lose faith in that meaning, then we will lose everything, for a world without faith is a world without love.

There is in all these films an aching for sovereign presence at the foundation of the world. The films, however, locate the retrieval of sovereign power at different points. In *Taken* the father as everyman must step directly into the place of the sacral monarch to reenact the primal killing that separates the domain of the political from the violence of the state of nature. That democratic vision is supplemented by *Gran Torino*'s displacement of the role of father onto the outsider. Walt is still acting out the democratic role of citizen taking up the burden of sacrifice, but now he is a kind of a "surrogate" father. In *The Dark Knight*, however, we see a different reading of sovereign presence. The sovereign power of foundation is no longer a common possession of us all. It is a mythical power for which we can only hope. Were such a power actually to appear, we could not be sure whether it was the power of foundations—Batman—or the power of destruction—the Joker. Both are beyond law. This is what makes claims of sovereign presence so dangerous. Terror is never far from revolution; murder is never far from sacrifice. Killing always pollutes, even when it is a sacrifice.

None of these films is about justice. It is not a requirement of justice that Walt give up his life; the crimes of the Albanians surely do not all merit the death penalty; Batman is the scapegoat to law. There is no justice in these acts of killing and being killed. Justice is a relationship within law; it begins only after the sovereign community has been brought into existence by an act of sacrifice. None of these films, however, is about the quality of law that follows on the refounding of the state. We do not need to wait until we learn of the character of justice in each political order to appreciate the significance of the actions we have witnessed. These are acts of sacrifice that gain their meaning from love. Law—and justice—must come later.

Love is not the answer to the question of justice. It is, however, a necessary condition of a state that would seek justice through law. Politics is not exhausted by the system of representation that is law. Before there is representation, there must be identity, and there is no identity without love. When we "know" that love is a matter of life and death, that love is not love unless it will support an act of sacrifice, we are as deep as we can be in the Western social imaginary. This is the lingering presence of the sacred. We see in these popular imaginative constructions a longing for unity, which is also a fear that without sacrificial renewal the double character of the modern state—identity and representation—will simply fall apart.

VIOLENCE BEYOND REPRESENTATION: NEITHER CRIMINAL NOR ENEMY

The act of sacrifice founds law but is beyond law. We can, as a matter of law, conscript citizens into the air force, but law cannot make them kamikaze pilots. Law can demand that citizens take risks, but it cannot demand that they literally give up their lives. Sacrifice is always a free act. Liberal theory puts the free act of consent—contract—at the origin of the state. That makes for a good normative theory of justice, but it offers a poor account of the phenomenology of the political. There, at the moment of origin, we find the free act of sacrifice, which is always a matter of love, not law. Our political imagination remains rooted in the Abrahamic faith that out of sacrifice will come a great nation. This faith may be wholly irrational, but that just tells us that we cannot explain ourselves in terms of reason alone.

Corresponding to this free act of sacrifice is a free act of interpretive reception: the political imagination must read the violent act in its sovereign, existential dimension. It cannot see only murder or senseless death; it cannot see what is beyond law as a violation of law. Because the sacrificial act is never the application of a rule, there is always a gap that the imagination must traverse to give sovereignty to law and law to sovereignty. We must see through the law to the sovereign whose law it is; we must attach law to the sacrificed body. At stake is our capacity to see in law a representation of our own identity. We must see the act of sacrifice as one in which we freely give the law to ourselves. When that faith fails, the gap cannot be crossed. We no longer see identity in these acts of violence. Instead, we see ourselves as murderers or victims. This is just how the veteran will read his own violence, if he loses faith in the sovereign enterprise of sacrifice.

Here we find an important source of contemporary political anxiety: can we still see violence as sacrifice? Sacrifice cut loose from text is simply violent destruction. The link between identity and representation is broken. The victim dies a "senseless death." That death is an act of murder, not sacrifice. We cannot give it meaning, beyond the privative meaning of the destruction of personal identity. The loss cannot be read politically; it is only mourned privately.[29] The failure of sacrifice, and the consequences of reading a political killing as murder, is just where *Gran Torino* begins.

The failure of political violence to signify anything beyond personal destruction is, of course, the theme of countless films. If the violent act fails as political sacrifice, then its meaning is limited to the personal narrative of suffering. The cinematic portrayal of the failed sacrifice can attach at the scene of violence, producing a picture of senseless—or insane—destruction; alternatively, it can attach subsequently, as the theme becomes that of personal recovery from destruction without meaning. Not surprisingly, the war in Vietnam gave us many examples of both. The first genre is represented by *Apocalypse Now*, the second by *Born on the Fourth of July*.[30] A more recent film that attempts to occupy this fracture between identity and representation is Quentin Tarantino's reimagining of World War II, *Inglourious Basterds*.[31]

Two ideas are central to Tarantino's movie: first, film—a system of representation—can speak only to other films; second, violence can only generate more violence. So deep is the divide Tarantino imagines between representation and identity that for film to become effective in the world, it must give up its character as representation and work instead as a flammable material. Films quite literally become the material for a bomb. Similarly, if representation is to breach the wall of fiction, it must be literally carved in the flesh. Thus, the most powerful moment in the film is the insistence on marking surviving Nazis with a swastika carved on their foreheads.

Two plotlines run through the movie, making contact but not intersecting in a single narrative. The first begins with the vicious killing of a Jewish family hiding in a farmhouse in France. Only the eldest daughter escapes. The movie will end when she has her revenge by burning down a Parisian cinema house that she has mysteriously come to own. She burns it down, using a large cache of films as an incendiary device, while it is hosting all of the Nazi leadership at the premiere of a propaganda film. The Nazis' violent act of destroying her family can lead only to the reciprocal violence of revenge. She herself will die simultaneously with the burning but now in a miniature subplot that again involves an exchange of violence: killing for killing.

The second plot casts the narrative of violence at a higher level. Germans are murdering Jews, so Jews (now Americans) will work their brutal revenge by killing Nazis. Atrocity can only lead to atrocity. Thus, the Americans counter the German high-tech genocide with a bizarre American Indian practice of scalping their victims. We cannot quite place these combatants within the ordinary representations of Americans: they are Jews, acting like Indians, at one point portraying themselves as mute Italians. They are "inglourious basterds." Who they are does not matter, for they are in the cycle of uncontrollable violence. Violence for violence is the message. These Americans also learn of the coming cinema event and separately plan to blow up the theater, killing the Nazi leadership. That plot, too, succeeds, such that at the end we have a double act of destruction: the theater is destroyed simultaneously by the daughter and the Americans.

Inglourious Basterds depicts violence as a force of nature following its own cycle of cause and effect. It is impossible, or nearly impossible, to direct the violence according to a narrative line, which means it is impossible to "read" the violence as the expression of some idea or set of ideas. The Nazis unleash horrendous violence against the Jews but become the victims of an equally primitive form of violence. They will be beaten to death with bats, and they will be scalped. They turn this group of Jews into Indians. Who would have imagined that possibility? But this is just the point: violence makes no sense apart from the act itself. Two separate narratives are introduced precisely to show that neither controls the violence. The relationship between representation and violence is simply arbitrary. There is a gap between word and act.

The film moves along on these cycles of violence, which mark the political domain as a part of nature as much as something man-made.[32] But the movie becomes much more interesting when we see that it is not simply a modern version of a Greek tragedy demonstrating the unlimited demand for revenge. There is a parallel theme moving through the movie, which has to do with the nature of representation. Because the film breaks any link between representation and identity—Hitler dies, and the war ends in the film's narrative—the film's meaning is constituted in a closed system of representation. In particular, the film refers endlessly to other films.[33] As representation it places itself not in relationship to a history of violence but in relationship to a network of other representations.

Violence leads only to more violence; representation leads only to more representation. There is a virtually unbridgeable gap between representation and identity. I say virtually because there is one point of contact: the swastikas that are literally the word become flesh. The hero—or is he an antihero?—explains that he carves the swastika on the forehead because he cannot "abide" the idea that these Nazis will take off their uniforms, as if they could remake themselves by adopting a new form of representation. Of course, this is exactly what the film does with history.

Short of the carved image in the flesh, we cannot attach representation to identity. Every history is a fiction. To see the groundlessness of representation is as intolerable as seeing the meaninglessness of violence. Thus, the desire—the need—to mark the flesh in an unalterable manner. To move from the presence of sovereign violence to a stable legal order, there must be a capacity to write the narrative in the flesh of the sacrificial victim. This was Lincoln's theme at Gettysburg: sacrifice for a proposition, identity become representation. Law must be read out of sacrifice if representation is to find its source in identity. Tarantino splits the world into parallel universes of violence and representation, bridged only by the sign carved in the flesh. This is the only firm point from which we can begin again after the war. Anything else that we might say would be false: a theme picked up internally in the movie by multiple failures of language.

Inglourious Basterds struggles with the postmodern condition of a failing relationship between identity and representation. In the film every narrative is false—from the largest narrative of the successful attack on Hitler and his cohort to false uniforms, to false eloquence. The insistence that the surviving Nazi bear the swastika is a desperate effort to stabilize a single true representation. With that mark we know who we confront. Here we can see the enemy. He is marked as Cain is marked at the moment of origins. From this stable point, where flesh and representation coincide, perhaps we can begin again. Cain went on to found cities. Tarantino is not so sanguine.

It does not take much imagination to see in *Inglourious Basterds* an approximation to the situation at Abu Ghraib or Guantanamo. Violence begets violence. Confronting the inhuman, we ourselves become inhuman: not Indians but torturers. Every representation offered turns out to be false, for we have lost control of the basic political narrative. We don't know what to do with the terrorist any more than the film knows what to do with the Nazi. If they survive, they fall into the zone of indistinction: neither criminals nor enemies. There is a desire to stabilize this, to affix a permanent representation that says this, at least, is true. So at Abu Ghraib we find ourselves not just torturing but photographing. We will make symbols out of their bodies: the flesh must become the word.

Guantanamo has the temporality of the exception: we make no progress, for nothing can happen to change the basic situation. Can any of this end? We have no reason to think that law will be able to resolve this situation. President Obama promised to close Guantanamo after one year. Still it remains open. We see the promise of law again failing before the fact of violence. The fictional character of film allows us to see the alternative: a refounding of the narrative of the state in an originary act of violence. This is precisely what is not available to us if we see the violence done on the body of the enemy as torture rather than sacrifice. Longing to recover a sacrificial violence in its place, we see repeated efforts to recall the Second World War and to compare the treatment of POWs then with that of the detainees today.

Inglourious Basterds offers a similar invocation of that earlier war. It rewrites the narrative of the Second World War to say something about our contemporary war on terror. An earlier generation struggled with much the same problem in interpreting the violence of the Vietnam War. Here we can take an older film, *Forrest Gump*, as an example.[34] Gump has the ubiquity of the popular sovereign. He is present at every decisive moment in the nation's recent history; he stands with presidents and with protestors; he fights in Vietnam and runs a small business. He is symbolically everywhere. He is the nation, pure but also senseless. The extent of his capacity to represent is drawn figuratively in the happy face and expressed in his singular insight, "Shit happens."

Precisely because he is an innocent, he can be filled by the meaning of the sovereign. Gump is always exactly what he seems; he is America as presence, not instrument to some other end. For Gump representation and identity coincide. What he does, he does without ambiguity or doubt. Without intelligence Gump is of the body—as athlete and soldier. Political identity, too, attaches directly to the body.

If Gump expresses the wholeness of sovereign presence, all those around him are experiencing the failure of representation. For them the violence of the state is without meaning. They are killed or injured for no reason. An unbridgeable gap has opened between identity and representation. That gap is Vietnam, which is both a place and an era. Violence has been detached from any representational claim.[35] Without a discernible political purpose it results only in destruction. Instead of a readable politics of sacrifice, we see a counterpolitics in the huge demonstrations on the mall. Who now embodies the sovereign—protestors or soldiers? That counterpolitics fails to become a revolution, however, for it fails to produce a stable representation of itself. Without that, popular political mobilization falls apart as individuals succumb to the pathologies of sex, drugs, alcohol, and eventually AIDS.

Our choices seem stark. The politics of identity, on the one hand, is a tale told by an idiot. A politics of representation, on the other hand, is transparently false. No representational claims can justify Vietnam. Government has become a reckless instrument of our own destruction. Political violence has been unleashed from any plausible representative claim, but still it comes. The uncontrollable character of violence makes a political project that links sovereignty to law, identity to representation, impossible. This is a critical element in the imaginative deconstruction of the modern nation-state: violence has been stripped of its representational significance. What proposition are we defending once the Gulf of Tonkin Resolution is seen as a misrepresentation? False claims construct a false sacrifice—there is only the violence. That Resolution stands to that era as the Yoo torture memoranda stand to our own: misrepresentations covering over a world of violence begetting more violence. One has to be an idiot to see it otherwise.

Gump knows one thing: love. He loves his childhood friend, Jenny; he loves his mother; he loves his comrades from Vietnam. Love is at the foundation of community. Gump will sacrifice completely for the objects of his love. One does not need representational intelligence to succeed in love. Indeed, just the opposite. Thinking too much, we may question love. Can faith survive philosophy? Can sovereignty survive jurisprudence?

Gump is never potential; he is always actual. As such, he is the living force in the world. His presence drives history forward. He runs. But Gump cannot give an account. He can speak the name of the beloved, "Jenny," and he can speak his own name, "here am I." Is that enough? Not for the survival of the nation-state. Out of Gump's love there must come a new narrative if the community is to be born again. This is his child: a new Gump who is raised in love but has the intelligence Gump lacks. The dark vision of state in the 1960s gives way to a new hope.

If violence can no longer support representation, then the modern nation-state is a failed project. That state depended on the capacity of the political imagination to suture identity to representation through sacrifice. But *Forrest Gump* and the other Vietnam films suggest that violence can no longer bear a political meaning. The political choice for violence ends with destruction, not creation. Violence that cannot be sacrifice exists in a world in which we have no enemies—or at least have no way of determining who they are. If we cannot be sure who our enemies are, then we cannot be sure that the government is not itself criminal. Who is the criminal at Abu Ghraib?[36]

A History of Violence takes up directly the question of whether violence can have a human, or only a natural, history.[37] The human history of violence is the political narrative of the nation. A history of violence stripped of the connection to the political is only a series of causes and effects—the same as any other natural force. If violence is a force of nature that cannot be turned to human purposes, it can only destroy, not create. The history of violence at stake in the film is a natural, not a human, history. The human life of the protagonist only begins with the turn away from violence to the familial virtues of small-town life. The narrative does not extend back before that turn.

In questioning the capacity of violence to suture identity to representation, *A History of Violence* is in many ways the opposite of *Taken*. In both films a father has turned to the familial, giving up his special skills in the administration of violence. In both, violence invades the familial, and those special skills must be retrieved to secure the family. But there is no celebration of unity through sacrifice in *A History of Violence*. There is no recognition of a founding act of sacrifice. There is only the relentless message that violence can destroy but cannot create. Violence produces only more violence. The history of violence is the invasion of a natural force, like a virus destroying members of the family.

The movie begins with a small-town restaurateur defending his business from an intrusion by criminals. His excellence at killing brings him an unwanted notoriety. With that, figures from a hidden past invade his life. It turns out he had a prior life as a Mafia hit man. He gave that life up and remade himself over the past twenty years as a father, husband, and neighbor. Past violence pursues him, however, seeking revenge for killings about which we know nothing more than that they happened. In the end he must return to the place of violence and kill all those with a memory of his past. After a night of violence in the city he returns to his family and joins them at the family table. The past is dead, not recovered. It is silenced, not given voice. It is literally eliminated in an act of violence—or so we hope, for we have reason to fear that it may already have infected his son.

The history of violence is not to be celebrated; it is not to be imagined in a narrative of sacrifice. It is history that is best left dead—unrecovered and unseen. Violence cannot enter into the human world of discourse without destroying that world.[38] Thus, the protagonist has lived twenty years without speaking of this past. No one suspects anything, for there is no deficiency here. He has a full life, not one that lacks meaning. He is secure in family and community. Violence invades from outside, but this invasion cannot be represented as the threat of the enemy. There is no enemy to be defeated; there is only a disruption caused by the natural consequences of his own past violence.

This world of violence that can only destroy meaning is one in which the categories of criminal and enemy are completely unhinged. The invaders from the past are criminals, but so is the protagonist. We might also consider them enemies, since they threaten the family. Yet it turns out that they are all directed by the protagonist's brother. Which side of the line is family on? Violence is destructive of every possible representation. It is world destroying, not world creating. Criminal and enemy cannot frame the imaginary at work in the film because no one can speak about violence at all.

Despite its nonpolitical framing, this is a relentlessly political movie. Violence begets violence, and all violence destroys meaning. The protagonist's history of violence founded nothing. It was, instead, the original sin that might still destroy all that he constructs. Violence has a past, but it is to have no future. The protagonist is not far from the veteran trying to flee the memory of his violent past. That he worked for a criminal organization—the Mafia—does not differentiate him from the Vietnam veteran who believes that he killed for no reason at all or, for that matter, from Walt Kowalski, who believed that Korea made him a murderer. The question for us is whether we still believe in the possibility of the redemptive act of sacrifice that founds and refounds the nation. Can violence any longer be harnessed to a representational end? Can it have meaning? This is not just a question for the narrative of contemporary films but has been deeply a part of our politics for the last decade.

On September 11, 2001, the nation suffered a perfect sacrificial moment. The attacks showed us the ubiquitous character of popular sovereignty today: anyone can be killed because of their political identity at any time. Finding ourselves in the wrong building or on the wrong plane, we can be asked to kill and to die for the nation. Sacrifice is unregulated by law. This experience of politics as a practice of ultimate meaning, of transcendence of life itself, must be incorporated in the national narrative: identity and representation must be brought together. Politics may be founded in sacrifice, but it dies absent an ever-renewed connection to representation. The silent sacrifice must become the object of political narrative. The narrative succeeds when it persuades us to see ourselves and our community one way rather than another. Then, we know who we are; we know our way forward.

Arguably, the war on terror has failed in this dimension of representation. What is the narrative at this point? Instead of linking sacrificial violence to constitution, violence at places like Abu Ghraib and Guantanamo was linked to pornographic representation. Applying the criminal law to these acts of violence, we hope for a normalization that will dismiss the incidents of torture as "without meaning"—a story of the criminal pathology of a few "bad apples." But we do this knowing that torture was not aberrational and was not random.[39] The torturer threatens to become a symbol of the combatant in the war on terror: we don't know whether to script our own political violence as murder or sacrifice.

Similarly, we do not know how to speak of the Guantanamo detainees. They were to be without representation in the double sense of stripped of words and lawyers. Thus, they were to be literally senseless: deaf and dumb, unseen and unclaimed. If they spoke at all, it would be a scripted speech produced by torture. Words produced by violence are without epistemic force, but words produced for violence, as in the Yoo memos, may equally be without epistemic force. In the world of violence, words—theirs and ours—no longer mean what they say.

We literally do not know what to make of the detainees. We cannot see in their bodies a representation of any sort of law. We can attach no text to them. A better term for them would have been the "alawful." Understood as pure violence—senseless violence—they become the object of senseless violence. Is this the criminal or the enemy? How could we begin to answer that question? They are the speechless and the unspoken. They occupy the same position as the "disappeared" in other wars on terror. Their recovery has been a matter of trying again to give them voice by giving them representation within the law. The black hole of Guantanamo is to be illuminated by the extension of a legal regime. But law as a system of representation keeps crashing against their bodies. Thus, they can be tried, but they will not be released.[40]

The detainees are a product of a world in which the relationship of representation and identity can no longer be managed. In that world we go silent in the face of violence. This is the politics of the disappeared and the tortured. Because we cannot speak what is actually happening, they will be held beyond the gaze of law. We will have a political crisis whenever there is a penetration of that sovereign violence by the legal imaginary. That may be the best way to characterize the last decade of experience of the American political imaginary.

We are close to a fictional narrative in all of this. Tarantino is our modern chronicler of the state. With him we wonder whether violence can be controlled to advance an articulable political end. Are narrative and violence no longer capable of supporting each other? We find ourselves again in a "quagmire" that can only be sustained by deception or naive innocence. Cheney was our agent of deception. Was Bush our Forrest Gump?

When sacrifice can no longer link representation to identity, politics becomes a world of words without referents, on the one hand, and uncontrolled violence, on the other. We have claims that we are threatened by Iraqi weapons of mass destruction, but there are no weapons. We have denials of what everyone knows and affirmations of what no one believes. No one is invested in any particular representational claim because no one believes in the truth of what is said. Words are spoken for their effect, not their truth. Political speech is always on the verge of being exposed as falsehood. Actions taken become the immediate object of regret, for we believe we were not truly ourselves at the moment that we were persuaded. Thus, America goes to war in Iraq in what comes rapidly to be seen as an act of bad faith. We want to affirm the meaning of the combatant's death as an act of sacrifice, but we cannot actually say for what he died. It was "the wrong war," but we are not sure we can find the right one.

All of this should remind us of the nuclear dilemma with which we have been living for decades. Nuclear weapons announce the sacrificial character of the sovereign: for the sake of sovereignty, we will give up life itself—all of it and everyone. But we can make no representational sense of these weapons. They advance no one's interests; they can be directed at no articulate purpose. We are literally in a world of "strange love," for what kind of love is it that will destroy not just the self but the beloved in an act of sacrificial violence? These weapons of absolute destruction express the inarticulateness of ultimate meanings, but that which cannot be said has become absurd. This is precisely our anxiety: we want to affirm the sacrificial meaning of the sovereign, but we cannot justify the act. We cannot attach text to act. At that point the violent act becomes merely destructive.

THE CRIMINAL IS (NOT) THE ENEMY OF HUMANKIND

The modern nation-state managed a complex relationship between identity and representation by and through its capacity to control the meaning of violence. The act of sacrifice is the moment of sovereign presence; that moment must be read as the foundation of the political narrative. Identity and representation—sovereignty and law—meet at that point. If narrative cannot claim the sacrificial act, we will find ourselves outside of law in one of two ways: sovereign presence without voice or senseless death. These, of course, have a way of turning into each other. Contemporary forms of anxiety, however, are less about the resurgence of revolutionary terror (sovereign presence) than about the failure of violence to register a public meaning at all (senseless death).

There is nothing new in this. The law of the state has long been a script read off the body of the citizen-soldier. Lincoln spoke of this in his famous Lyceum speech, when he linked law to revolution through the body of the Revolutionary War veteran. Those bodies provided "a history bearing the indubitable testimonies of its own authenticity, in the limbs mangled, in the scars of wounds received, in the midst of the very scenes related—a history, too, that could be read and understood alike by all, the wise and the ignorant, the learned and the unlearned."[41] A state that can no longer read law off the wounded body is one that can no longer call on its citizens to sacrifice. Lincoln worried that we cannot have reverence for law without the willingness to sacrifice. His own life and death became a test of this proposition linking identity and representation.

Today, our Lincolnesque worries are not presented in formal lectures at the local lyceum but in the imaginative production of film. The longing for the unity of sacrifice as the point of intersection of identity and representation was my first topic in this chapter. It provides the archetype upon which a film like *Gran Torino* relies. The failure of sacrifice when violence resists representation was my second. This produced the anxiety of senseless violence, that is, a violence that could not be read. This is the archetype we find in a film like *Inglourious Basterds*. A similar anxiety arises from the other direction, when representation cannot attach to identity. Now, representation closes in on itself; it becomes a symbolic system in which the elements point only to other elements in the system. It has then the closed character of a code. The code knows only itself; it offers no answer to the question "Who am I?" This generates a Kafkaesque anxiety of representation entirely displacing identity. This is a situation in which identity can get no purchase, for it is always outside the borders of representation. If law is a code, how can it be a domain of freedom? The citizen must see through the representational order of the state—law—to the popular sovereign. If the citizen can never see beyond the code, if law leads only to more law, then politics will no longer be an expression of freedom.[42]

The imaginative linking of representation to identity does not just create the possibility of political freedom; it is the exercise of that freedom. In our ordinary political life we realize this freedom in the task of interpretation—a theme I developed in part 1. Because identity is an unlimited source of meaning, while law is a finite system of representation, the gap between the two can never be eliminated, only temporarily bridged. We can never close off the debate over the meaning of law because it always stands in relation to that inexhaustible source of meaning that is the popular sovereign. When we argue over the meaning of a constitutional norm, we are taking up the task of interpreting who we are. Interpretation is an endless effort to cross the gap between representation and identity. There is no "right" interpretation; there are only more or less persuasive interpretations. To take up this task of persuading and being persuaded is to exercise political freedom.[43]

Closure of the system of representation would sever the link to popular sovereignty. It would undermine the claim that law is the product of freedom. Here we have the origin of the "democracy deficit" attributed to European Union law: we have law—endless law—but we have no sense that it is *our* law. The code manages itself as if it were the product of disembodied reason. Technicians of the law constantly adjust the elements of the law to each other through proportionality review.[44] This law no longer creates history; instead, it manages the present. Interpretation is no longer a free act of rhetorical persuasion building the connection between the transcendent value of sovereign presence and legal representation. A law that is pure representation, we might say, represents no one at all. The more complete the code, the more we gaze upon it from the outside. A law that represents no one can be a global rule, at which point the distinction of inside and outside loses any sense. Such a law would apply to everyone but belong to no one.

The fictional response to this displacement of identity through the closure of representation is to go to war with the code. Violence becomes a performance of human freedom. We are again imagining the refoundation of the political order in an act of sacrifice that will link identity to representation. Thus, the anxiety of code is a reverse image of the anxiety of violence described in the last section.

When the legal realists argued that those who believe in law as a formal system are speaking "transcendental nonsense," they were saying that a closed system of representation can make no contact with the real forces that determine political practice.[45] Law closed in on itself is blind and therefore without any force. This is the benign form of a closed code: a fiction that cannot do the work of social regulation. More common is the anxiety that a closed system of representation is authoritarian. This was Kafka's charge, and it continues today. This perfect system of representation tends toward a specific signature in film: representation becomes code, and code becomes machine. The dystopian vision matches human against machine.

The supercomputer HAL, in *2001: A Space Odyssey*, was an early expression of this symbolic equation of machine, code, and authority.[46] The more complete the order of representation, the more complete the denial of freedom. A computer that can operate by itself will dispense with human beings entirely. The struggle against the computer is, accordingly, a struggle to maintain control over human destiny. The film explicitly draws the connection between representation and tool. The capacity to use tools relies on the same epistemic conditions as the capacity to form a proposition. Human beings arrive on the evolutionary scene with the capacity to work with tools, which is inseparable from the capacity to talk. Language and tools evolve together such that the final tool is the computer. We fear that we will lose control of our lives to what had been brought into being only as a means. The story line is no different from that in which money—another tool of representation—comes to be an end in itself. Computers, money, law—all systems of representation—threaten this inversion in which humanity becomes the victim of its own free creations.[47]

Contemporary films deepen the anxiety over this dystopian vision as the net has increasingly become a part of our everyday life. Is the net a tool for realizing our freedom, or is it creating a closed code? A perfectly ordered representational world is one in which machines govern. They do not govern through violence but through controlling representation. We are in the dystopia of *The Matrix*. The machine no longer has just a "mind of its own." Rather, it makes our mind its own: representation grasps us so deeply that identity is no longer even imagined as a free act of self-creation. We are caught within the web and cannot get out.

The Matrix shows us a world in which representation is wholly detached from identity and thus is completely closed to interpretation.

The matrix is a perfect system of representation, on the one hand, and a completely illusory world, on the other. Representation is coherent (or nearly so). Every proposition is linked to every other. There is a logic—the code—that guarantees coherence. Nevertheless, there is nothing on the other side of the representational propositions—not identity but illusion. We might find ourselves arguing about events and their significance within the matrix, but we are arguing about nothing. At stake in this argument is never who we are, because we are not there at all. In the end the argument itself is nothing more than a further twist of the code.

To see the closed character of the code is to discover that the freedom one thought one had was only an illusion, for everything we have done has been determined—a thought that already troubled Descartes almost four hundred years ago.[48] He, however, had to imagine the closed system of code as a sort of dream induced by an evil genius. We have the net. Genuine freedom of the will requires a violent act set against the code. Identity begins with the willingness to sacrifice—an act that cannot be explained by the code. Identity is reconnected to representation through the act that places the body, the real body, at risk. The body must take on a meaning to ground representation in identity. Thus, the point of connection between the representational world of the matrix and the reality of identity is death: to die in the matrix is really to die.

The sacrificial body is always an expression of love, which is exactly the experience of the unity of identity and representation. Morpheus, the leader of the free subjects, explains the unity of death to Neo, the would-be savior of humanity: "the body cannot live without the mind." The deeper point, however, is about the unity of body and mind, or identity and representation, in love. Love refounds the world. In the film love not only supports sacrifice; it conquers death: Neo is brought back to life by the woman he loves, Trinity. Within the matrix, identity and representation can never be brought together. Love, accordingly, will always fight code.

We might take *The Matrix* as a dramatization of Kant's transcendental philosophy. Kant believed that our phenomenal experience constitutes the limits of what we can know. We can speak of what must be true for us within this phenomenal world, but we are never in a position to speak of a truth beyond our possible experience. Of the thing-in-itself we simply can say nothing. Experience is structured according to a set of categories. Most importantly, everything we experience is causally related to some prior event. The phenomenal world, accordingly, is a complete system of representation that allows no space for freedom. Thus, Kant faces the problem of explaining the possibility of freedom. He tries to answer that question by explaining the relationship between identity and representation. We live, he argues, in an epistemic world of representation and a moral world of freely formed identity. We can no more give up our concept of ourselves as free than we can give up the concept of causation. We know ourselves in this double aspect, even if we cannot explain it.

In the cinematic version the noumenal world of the thing-in-itself is not just other than the phenomenal world of the matrix. That world—the "real world"—begins with humans as batteries to the machines. Humankind must first create itself in a free act of self-appropriation; it must disestablish its link to the machine. Only then can human beings attack the closed world of representation. What then would success look like? It would be a world in which identity and representation are held together, such that we see ourselves in and through the ordered system of representations. In Kant's terms it would be a world in which we freely give the law to ourselves. In political terms constitution follows revolution. Kant is speaking of morality, not politics, but the point is the same.

If we push the point one step further, we see the structure of the film turn in on itself in much the way that Kant's transcendental philosophy does. What exactly would the world given by humankind to itself in an act of free self-creation look like? We have no reason to think it would be different from the representational world of the matrix. That world, created by artificial intelligence, may be the best that intelligence can do. It is not without reason that Cipher, one of the free members of the crew, chooses representation—the matrix—over identity. To get there, however, he must betray his comrades—that is, betray love. Better never to have to face this choice, which means to exist securely in the world of the matrix.

This, too, is where Kant ended up: the phenomenal world is our only world. Moreover, who is to say that the occupants of the matrix don't have their own religious beliefs? Like Kant they can hold to the belief in a greater truth—the truly real—as a possibility beyond this life. The point is that the entire imaginative structure of identity and representation is always seen from a particular position. There is not some transcendent truth from which we literally build the world anew. It is always our world that we recreate in the free act. We are studying the social imaginary, not doing metaphysics.

This same fear of a dystopia in which the computer has turned against humanity is the theme of *The Terminator*.[49] Where *The Matrix* constructs the tension between freedom and representation in spatial terms—the free space is under the earth—*The Terminator* uses a temporal frame. Kant is again the essential reference: space and time are fundamental categories establishing the field of representation. *The Terminator* begins with the effort of the machines to restructure the past in order to control the present. Causation becomes a malleable representation in the world of code. This thought, too, is very Kantian: if time and space are simply categories of representation, then there is no essential reason why they cannot be altered. A perfect world of representation is no more one thing than another; it is literally plastic, as we see in those scenes of *The Matrix* in which those who completely master the code can change shape, defying cause and effect.[50]

To defeat the machines, in *The Terminator*, man will have to create himself: the child must become father of the man. We are back to the drama of freedom as self-creation, which is now cast against the complete control, including temporal control, of a closed system of representation. To open up that system is to preserve the possibility of freedom. As in *The Matrix*, only through a willingness to sacrifice does one seize control of the meaning of one's own life. To succeed is to link identity and representation. A system of representation—a machine—does not know sacrifice; it does not know love.[51]

In the closed system of representation that is this dystopia, there are no enemies, only criminals. There cannot be enemies until there is a free man. In *The Matrix* Neo's birth into freedom is also his transition from criminal to enemy. He becomes "the One." He is Christ, prosecuted as a criminal but proclaiming that the truth is not of this world. It is not code but love. What seemed life had been death, while true life is found only through death. The free man literally creates himself, which is just what we find in *The Terminator* as well. As in *The Matrix*, we are left to puzzle about the world that the free man gives himself. Having seen the future, we already know exactly what that world will be. Freedom for the political imagination always threatens to fall into a kind of apologetics.

We would not be far off to think of the contemporary international law of human rights as an image of the matrix. It, too, is a perfectly ordered system of representation: a code that governs every possible proposition. It claims the completeness of every system of law, capable of pronouncing any act legal or illegal. Its home is in the net and in networks.[52] It purports to be a complete system of ordering a political space that is now global. The completeness of this code, however, is quite independent of its capacity to actually order the world. It is representation turned in on itself. For example, the Torture Convention comes into force in 1987 but has little relationship to state practices. The relationship it actually has may be the opposite of what it purports to command.[53] The law of human rights flourishes as code in the last decades of the Cold War, but there is virtually no effort to enforce this code. The conditions of its creation were the separation of law from actual political practice.[54] A law that is not taken seriously as a prescription for behavior is a law that can develop according to its own internal logic. We can talk endlessly about human rights; we can hold endless conferences and draft legal rights to respond to every need. We can do so because nothing happens beyond the talk itself.

Alongside these cinematic representations of a complete code, then, we should place the drama of the indictment of Sudan's President Bashir by the International Criminal Court. Once again, we have the self-contained code that constructs a world detached from identity. It is a world of networks and NGOs that is actually nowhere because it purports to be everywhere. Despite its claim to omnipresence, we find ourselves outside of it. We cannot see through it to ourselves. The code would reconstruct in its own propositional logic the political acts of Bashir. He, however, has no reason to enter this matrix. To him the code is a fiction. This will remain true until there is some political community that takes possession of the code as an expression of its own identity.

Under international law Bashir is allegedly a criminal. He is a criminal because he is the "enemy of mankind." But the enemy of mankind is not the enemy of any particular political community. None see in him an existential threat to their own community—except, of course, those fighting an actual civil war in the Sudan, who would kill him if they could. Bashir is enemy to the rest of us in name only: no one will sacrifice his or her life to defeat this enemy.

At the turn of the millennium we had a complete system of representation—a code—but we could not answer the question of identity: whose law is this? We could describe acts as unlawful, but in the absence of enforcement we could not know what that meant. We could not enforce this law because no political actor would claim possession of it as a matter of citizen identity. Purporting to be everyone's law, it was actually no one's law. We might be for justice and human rights, but we are not willing to sacrifice ourselves—or demand of our fellow citizens that they sacrifice themselves or their children—to assure those rights to others.

The Universal Declaration of Human Rights did not create a single state. No one can look through the various conventions on human rights and see a sovereign act of self-creation. Just the opposite. There is nothing to see because this law is not the product of a free political act. It is "mere words." As a closed system of representation, it announces the irrelevance of sovereignty to law. We now hear claims that under this law the individual, not the state, is sovereign.[55] But that is just another way of saying that politics is no longer a domain of freedom. No one believes that this law is given by the citizen to himself. Rather, it is given to him as if a gift, but from whom? Coming from nowhere, it has no foundation. It is not brought back from the mountain by a modern Moses. It comes from a network that has no place, no time, and no identity.

A code that strips representation from identity will verge on comedy, for surely it expresses a kind of comic hubris to think that we can so easily speak a world into being. A code that will not be defended is only words. We speak a language, but we are not speaking about anything. Like Shakespeare's comic dramas, it is as if the entire affair is a dream: until we wake up, we think we are acting in the world, but we are not.

CONCLUSION: IMAGINING OURSELVES

The imagination always works through the particular; it is concrete, not abstract. It constructs a narrative; it does not apply a rule. The philosopher's burden is to bring self-conscious reflection to bear on this process of imaginative construction. He or she must interpret the particular work, with the ambition of bringing to deliberate awareness those archetypes by which we understand ourselves and our communities. The work of the imagination, I have tried to show in this chapter, is not so very different wherever it appears. The distance between the drama of life and death in film and our political drama of life and death is no distance at all. For we ask the same questions when we read the newspaper as when we go to the movies: who are we, and what are we doing?

In this chapter I have argued that we find ourselves in a politically anxious age. The source of that anxiety is a destabilization in the relationship of identity to representation. The nation-state managed that relationship through its control of the narrative of sacrificial violence. If we cannot attach a meaning to violence, then the relationship of identity to representation will fail. Anxiety over this possibility produces the three responses I have tracked: a longing for recovery of the unity of love (*Gran Torino*), a fear that political violence cannot be stabilized in law (*Inglourious Basterds*), and a fear that an all-too-stable code will preclude a free politics of identity (*The Matrix*).

Interpretation is not prediction. We cannot say in which of these directions we will go individually or collectively. We can only say that there are today substantial stresses on the relationship of identity and representation. At stake is the possibility of understanding politics as a domain of freedom. We do not occupy a position from which we can make a normative judgment on this formation of the political imaginary. We cannot say whether the nation-state is good or evil, or whether its demise would be good or evil. We can only say that it has been our world for both good and evil and that whatever imaginative products succeed it, they will again create a field in which we will struggle to link identity and representation. Here we will find love and interpretation. But here, too, we are likely to find violence and evil.[56]

CHAPTER 5

Love, Romance, and Pornography

The previous chapter revealed a puzzling gap between political theory and the political imagination. Political theory today is dominated by a liberal approach to the fundamental structures of the state. In this view the measure of a legitimate political organization is whether it can be understood as the result—direct or indirect—of a hypothetical contract among the individuals who constitute the community. An individual will join a political order that appears to contribute to his or her long-term advantage. That is not likely to be so unless the basic framework, the constitution, respects fundamental rights—no one wants to be abused or to lack basic freedoms. In addition, the political order must provide opportunities for individual well-being, for everyone wants to satisfy his or her needs and at least some desires. The reason for the state to exist at all is to serve the interests of individual citizens. It is generally up to each citizen to decide what those interests are. Accordingly, the state must be neutral regarding different life plans, respecting individual autonomy and treating each person with equal dignity and respect. Different liberal theorists explore different aspects of this paradigm, but they all accept its basic terms. When we look at the imagination of the political in film, however, this is not what we find.

FROM POLITY TO FAMILY

Liberal theory begins from an idea of the state of nature. For everything else, nature may be a model of order, but for human beings it represents the threat of disorder: in nature people would have a life that is "nasty, brutish and short."[1] Contemporary theories of the state of nature are less likely to use the Hobbesian language of a war of all against all than the language of social choice theory, speaking, for example, of the failure of collective action. The point, however, remains the same. The problem of state creation is that of bringing individuals into an ordered arrangement, without requiring that they change their nature. Each wants to advance his or her own ideas of the good life. The state is to serve these individuals; they are not to serve it. Contract theory remains an apt description of the liberal approach not because there is any actual bargaining but because the premise is that the political order serves each individual's interests. A reasonable person, accordingly, would agree to this.

Liberal theory imagines the founding of the polity as an exercise of practical reason working on a clean slate—as if we start from nowhere and build the basic order of the state using reason alone. Philosophers, whether Rawls or Habermas, would still be kings.[2] They imagine themselves as fundamentally rational, asking what it would take to get them to agree to enter a political organization. The organization would have to advance their interests; it would have to have mechanisms to assure that everyone was subject to the same fair rules—thus, the emergence of the rule of law protecting rights, property, and contracts. Short of this, one would only agree to participate in a political order because of coercion. What I do solely from fear, however, is not a measure of justice.

But where is love and sacrifice? Where is history and destiny? Where is the revolutionary violence that has been so tied to our political history? Where, one wants to ask, are the families and children for the sake of which we live our lives? These may not appear in political theory, but they are just what we find when we examine the way in which the political order is imagined in film. It is not enough to say that these are matters of merely individual interest, that is, matters of individual life choices. Only if one accepts the starting point of liberal political theory would one think this. That is surely not the way we live our lives.

Hobbes thought that fear of death was the primary motivating factor that moves the individual from nature to polity.[3] A rational actor, in that case, would not enter a political arrangement that demanded his life. How could he, if the entire point of the agreement is to advance individual interests by securing life? But we would be hard pressed to say that the purpose of the state, as we have known it, is to secure life over death. The development of the Western nation-state has been deeply intertwined with war. The United States has been at war or preparing for war for more than half of its national life.[4] This is not just bad luck or the working out of a progressive path to what the state "really is."

Is it all a matter of risk management? Would a rational actor enter into an arrangement that imposed a risk to his life if that risk were less than that which he faced in the state of nature? That seems rational, but it is the wrong question. What has to be answered is why he would stick to his contract once the risk materialized. If the choice is between breaking the contract—flight—and death, why would I choose the contract? There is no argument that compliance advances my current and future interests. The answer cannot be the moral force of the promise alone. The question of why be moral is the same question as why maintain the social contract at the risk of one's life. Hobbes's answer tended toward coercion—the sovereign has the power to enforce the contract. But that answer assumes that we would and should violate the contract if we can get away with it.

The answer we find in film to the Hobbesian conundrum is that we sacrifice for love. We freely give ourselves to the violence of the state as an act of love. The films I discussed in the previous chapter reveal liberal theory to be a literal failure of the imagination. That theory fails to capture the way the social imaginary works in our political narratives. We are not each of us a hero, but neither are we the rational actors that liberal theory imagines. In both cases, film and theory, we use ideal types to express how we imagine political experience.

We know what we are to do in the extraordinary moment, just as we know what we are to do when a loved one becomes gravely ill. We don't recalculate our interests; we give of ourselves. Think of the national response to 9/11. We did not calculate individual interests, and we did not rely on the coercive power of the sovereign. The passengers on United Flight 93 knew just what it was they had to do when they found themselves suddenly on the front line of a battle for which they had not previously volunteered. The line between fact and fiction is crossed just at that moment, for it is the imagination that sustains meaning in both.

None of this suggests that we are personally confident in how we might act in moments of crisis. Just the opposite: having imagined so often the narrative of sacrifice, of killing and being killed for the state, we cannot help but have a kind of performance anxiety. Nor does it mean that we seek out situations of sacrificial violence, any more than we seek out tragedy in our relationships of personal love. These are possibilities maintained by the imagination. They establish the background conditions against which we live our day-to-day lives. We hope things will go for the best for our families and our communities. But that has always been true; it is true even as nations send their children off to war. The interest in individual well-being did not arrive with the economists who thought they could make of it a comprehensive science of the social. Politics is a field in which the ordinary is bound by the imagination of the extraordinary—life by sacrifice.

If a liberal theory of politics fails to capture the richness of the political imagination, is the appropriate response simply to turn to conservatism? Classic conservatism was certainly skeptical about the capacity of reason to reconstruct the state from first principles applied in an imagined state of nature; it certainly defended family values over abstract rights. However, it was never the object of a popular democratic politics. It could not be so because the protection of tradition appeared as a class-based project of protecting social hierarchy. Conservatives defended the family as a center of male authority; they defended tradition as the source of unequal distributions of wealth; and they defended the church as a source of moral norms that could discipline the masses. Together, family, state, and church defined a class-structured society in which wealth, public power, and moral authority all worked to subordinate some groups while empowering others. Arguably, conservatism was more about exploitation than it was about sacrifice. Its concern for tradition had less to do with the grounds of love and more to do with the sources of privilege. This is not what we find in the popular democratic representation of politics in film.

Of course, we do know an antiliberal populism. Political order seen through the lens of various forms of corporatism has been a central feature of fascism over the last century. The centrality of the nation-state as a source of transcendent political value marks fascism as no less a modern political movement than our own constitutional republican-ism. Fascism sought to normalize an extraordinary politics of originary violence. It could find little support in the American tradition, because here there must be a movement from act to law, from revolution to constitution, from identity to representation. Permanent revolution—whether of the right or the left—has no appeal to a political imaginary that links revelation to text.

Films take up the exception but continue to recognize it as the exception. The conclusion is almost always the return, or the promise of return, to the normal. The father and daughter come back from abroad; law is refounded as the enemy is defeated. Film does not seek to displace the ordinary by the extraordinary but to call forth again a memory of the extraordinary. Films offer us not a critique of our political narrative of sovereignty and law but rather a constant re-presentation of this narrative.

Liberal theory imagines that we can speak the state into existence. But the origin of the modern state is in the act (revolution), not in the word (constitution). The state emerges out of a violent act by which it creates itself. That moment of political creation is also a moment of political destruction because it occurs not in a state of nature but in a world already organized politically. A new state comes into being by destroying an old state. The modern nation state, accordingly, had not only to create itself but to maintain itself against existential threats. About this originary violence the liberal theorist speaks not a word. Indeed, there is a great silence at the core of liberal theory. This is ironic because the theory is so often modeled on an imagined discourse. Per-haps that is just the problem. The liberal theorist skips the revolution and moves directly to the constitution, just as he or she ignores war and moves directly to adjudication. Film fills the silent void of liberal theory. It focuses on the act, not the word.

The narrative of the film brings into view the identity that cannot be spoken in political theory. This violent truth of politics can be spoken only after it has been linked to familial love. This is the exact point of contrast with liberal political theory: not the individual but the family occupies the center of our political imaginary. What connects family and state is that both rest on love, not reason. And all forms of love, as Plato wrote in the *Symposium*, are bound to each other.

A politics of the deed is a politics of sacrifice. The suicide bomber reminds us of this today. Because he deploys against us our own deepest archetype of the foundation of politics, he is perceived as an existential threat. The imagination of that threat far outpaces the actual harm done. His threat exceeds his grasp because an enemy willing to sacrifice himself imagines no limits on his willingness to use force. This is a deep truth we know about ourselves. There is an easy move from the lone suicide bomber using the weapons he has at hand to the use of weapons of mass destruction. This is why we so easily imagine the terrorist threat as one that involves nuclear weapons and why we are so fascinated today with the ticking-time-bomb hypothetical.[5] That hypothetical was itself recently rendered in the film *Unthinkable*.[6]

In this film the terrorist bomber willingly gives himself up to what he knows will be torture: he must sacrifice himself. The bomb—actually multiple bombs in his case—that is ticking away is nuclear. That threat poses the question: "What will we do?" Will the figure of law enforcement, a woman FBI agent, give way to the figure of the torturer—a shadowy figure who operates outside of formal, legal recognition? The film answers: "Of course we will torture." Against the terrorist's political commitments the interrogating agent of the state—the torturer—poses love of family. The torturer goes so far as to murder the terrorist's wife in front of him. He threatens to do the same to his children. He poses this question to the terrorist: Will he sacrifice his children for his politics, or will he sacrifice his politics for his children? He chooses politics over family.[7] With that we are left only to wait for the nuclear explosion.

A politics that is not tempered by the love of family is exactly our image of a fanatical politics. It is the point at which faith and nihilism intersect—the end point of all millennial religions. Despite the film's effort to create a gap between the familial and the political, we know that the families of suicide bombers often honor their acts no less than families of our own sacrificial soldiers honor their children's acts. For both, family and state align under the sign of the sacred. To portray the terrorist as evil, and not just the enemy, there must be a violation of this order of the family. It is not the terrorist's sacrifice that we find shocking. It is his resistance in the face of the murder of his wife and the threat to his children. This is what we find "unthinkable," although that hardly means "unimaginable." Indeed, the film ends with the figure of law—the FBI agent—who constantly resists and then gives in to the torturer, walking out holding the hands of the terrorist's young children. We know where they belong; law will protect the children. Law, however, we also know has no power to resist the coming explosion.

If *Unthinkable* is about the moment before the catastrophe, then *The Road* is about life after the explosion.[8] In the opening scenes of the movie some global catastrophe occurs that destroys animal and vegetative life on the planet, leaving only a few humans wandering around looking for food. We are back in the state of nature, and it is a very inhospitable nature. The movie is about a father and his young son, born shortly after the catastrophe. The mother cannot bear the idea of living in this world. She would follow other families in an act of collective suicide. The father insists on hope, finding in his son a "warrant" to continue to live. The mother wanders off into the woods to die. The father and son try to make it to the coast, avoiding threats from other survivors who have become cannibals searching desperately for food.

This is as stark a picture of the state of nature as one can imagine. The father believes he must endure for the young son. His child is called an "angel" and his "god." There is nothing metaphysical about these claims, only the endless power of love. The father will do anything, kill anyone, to protect his son. He tells his son to treat everyone as a threat, although the son's natural inclination is to help whoever he comes across. Ultimately, the father dies at the edge of the sea, leaving the son alone—but not for long. It turns out that a family—mother, father, son, and daughter—have been following them out of concern for the child's well-being. When his father dies, they quickly step in to adopt him.

That moment of adoption is the original political act. It answers the question of how a community might emerge in the state of nature. Until this moment everyone they meet is literally a threat. Sometimes that threat is of murder and cannibalism. Other times it is simply the threat of taking up scarce resources and thus hastening their starvation. There is only one thing that is powerful enough to overcome self-interest in this state of utmost scarcity: children. The child is the warrant not just for the father's endurance and sacrifice but also for a community of intergenerational sacrifice. Without children there is not only the literal end of the world, but there is, before that, the end of the political.[9] As an old man, whom they run into in their travels, says, God has long ago turned his back on humans. God will not save humanity, for the only god is the child.[10]

Only for love will we kill and be killed. It is not the killing, but the sacrifice, that marks the origin of the state. This is origin in the double sense of starting point—as in *The Road*—and foundation—as in *Unthinkable*. Only here do we learn who we are, just as others learn the truth of our identity. Thus, in *Unthinkable* the terrorist gives himself over to be tortured as a test of himself and proof of who he is. Willing to kill, he must be willing to die. Sacrifice can be paid in only one currency: identity. In *The Road* we learn that the father loves his child and that for him he will sacrifice himself. Both stories are easily recognized by us, for there is a direct line from these films to the Old Testament story of Abraham and Isaac. The terrorist reminds us of what Abraham was prepared to do: sacrifice his son to his god. The father reminds us that God did intervene and that family and state worship the same god.

The terrorist is constructed in an image close enough to our own imagination of sacred violence that he appears to us as an existential threat to the state. Law is imagined as too weak a force to counter the terrorist. Apart from torture, which is nothing more than a test of the martyrdom sought out by the terrorist, there is only love of family to pose against him. One form of love can only be countered by another. But we cannot know in advance whether the terrorist will choose god over family or family over god. Who could know what Abraham would do until the moment he raised the knife? The nation-state of the twentieth century was well aware that, when it chose war, it put at risk its own children. Indeed, Europe destroyed a generation of its children in the First World War and then suffered the even greater loss of young and old in the tactics of urban destruction, ethnic cleansing, and genocide in the Second World War. Still, it chose war.

Torture and terror answer in the most brutal way possible the question of who I am. The terrorist who gives himself over to be tortured in *Unthinkable*, no less than the torturer who operates completely outside of law, are both expressions of identity over representation. They exist in the world of the deed. If the torturer defeats the victim, forcing him to talk, that is the speech that refounds the state as an order of representation.[11] It is not contract, but confession, that puts off a world destroying violence.

It is no accident that the political response to torturing regimes is often a "truth and reconciliation" commission. We might better call these "confession and forgiveness" commissions. They operate with a religious aura at the point of a new foundation.[12] Whether truth can actually lead to reconciliation is a difficult empirical question, but that politics must be founded on giving voice—representation—to violent sacrifice is central to the construction of political narrative in fact and fiction.

Sacrifice at these moments of foundation is always complex, involving multiple actors in intersecting narratives. Those killed by the prior regime are now read as martyrs. Their loved ones sacrifice their moral entitlement to revenge: reconciliation is their sacrifice for the foundation of the state. The victimizer, too, must show that his violence was no less in thrall to a political narrative. He does not confess to personal pathology. This is the confession of the defeated. They must sacrifice their prior political identity. If a new political order is to emerge, truth must be linked to sacrifice on both sides of the conflict. This makes reconciliation—forgiveness—possible. This is the faith that founds the polity by moving from violence to word, from identity to representation.

The politics of identity represented in these films is that of the extraordinary moment, not that of ordinary life. The satisfaction of ordinary personal interests always comes later. It is that which we can achieve only after the threat has been removed, the sacrifice performed. Representation succeeds identity; the ordinary requires an extraordinary foundation. What is distinctly not at issue is the ordinary political confrontation between those who identify themselves as liberal, on the one hand, and as conservative, on the other. These are matched political positions battling over a different question: what are the norms that should be pursued in and through the laws and customs of the polity? Film cannot take up the ordinary disputes between our political parties without becoming narrowly didactic.[13] In contrast, I have been speaking of the archetypes that inform the political imagination, whether of Democrats or Republicans. Family is not a value unique to conservatives;

sacrifice is not avoided by the liberal. The issue here is not party politics but the fundamental structures of the imagination within which that politics operates.

THE FAMILIAL STATE

One important point of contrast between liberal political theory and the political imaginary at work in popular film is the central role of the individual in the former and of the family in the latter. So far, I have been speaking of the tragic demand of politics on family: the creation of meaning through sacrifice. Sacrifice is the action of love, but love grounds comedy as well as tragedy. We often find films exploring the relationship between the political and the familial in its comic form. The theme is the same as with tragedy: familial love provides the necessary condition of a successful politics. The point is well made in a popular film from a few years back, *The American President*.[14]

This is a romantic comedy, not a drama of life and death—although even here there is a necessity in imagining that the president orders the death of someone, somewhere. This power of life and death is what marks him as the president.[15] This is not a matter of legal process but of the presidential decision to kill for the state. There is always something of the torturer of *Unthinkable* in the image of the president. This sets him apart whether or not he is personally charismatic. The point of the film, however, lies elsewhere. It shows us again the inescapable intertwining of the familial and the political in the national narrative. Indeed, nowhere is this intertwining more evident than in the symbolism of the "first family."

Residence in the White House continues to carry the same sort of symbolic weight as that of a royal family. We see the democratic version of the king's two bodies: the finite character of particular presidential families rotating through the permanent institutional expression of the presidency. The Oval Office is matched by the residence, with the president literally moving daily between his embodiment of the world-destroying power of the American empire and the scenes of ordinary domesticity upstairs.[16] In the film state dinners are matched with "meatloaf night" in the residence.

The president, Andrew Shepherd, comes into office as a recent widower, with a daughter who is about twelve years old. The movie is the love story between Shepherd and a lobbyist, Sydney Ellen Wade. Wade has to see through the office to the man, while Shepherd must constantly insist that the office has nothing to do with his feelings for her. Trying to be ordinary while the rest of the world watches—and reports—proves to be more or less impossible. The president cannot find a private space in which to pursue the loving family; instead, the resolution is to turn familial love into a source of political strength.

Family, however, cannot just become a means to political ends. That moral pathology is glimpsed when Shepherd asks his chief of staff if he would have won the election had his wife lived. Was her death turned to political advantage? That would be as unacceptable as making politics a means to familial ends. Shepherd must avoid using the power of the presidency as a means to win over Wade. But it turns out that the residence cannot be a merely private space. The bedroom is constantly penetrated by the public's desire to see and the president's need to act, just as royal monarchs were always on display. He cannot "leave his work at the office," which means he can never be a merely private person in his relationship with Wade.

The president occupies both the residence and the Oval Office without subordinating one to the other. They are instead in a relationship of mutual support—ultimately, the two bodies of the nation. We see both the positive and negative side of this reciprocity. He is attacked by his political opponents for morally corrupting the office because his affair with Wade must be bad for his daughter. That alleged domestic scandal is linked to political scandal: early in her political career, Wade was photographed burning an American flag. This is the conservative attack: aligning a corruption of family morality with an allegation of un-American, political immorality. On the other side we see the romantic harmony of familial life—including the daughter—which can only survive if it is aligned with a renewed political vision. The triumph of love occurs at the end, not when love is successfully separated from the political but when it gives new force and vigor to the political. Only when Shepherd gives up legislative compromises and defends his core political values does their love fully succeed.

The deep structure of the narrative is the necessity for familial completion as a predicate to political power. This necessity operates quite independently of the particular political values that Shepherd pursues. Those values happen to be liberal: gun control, protection of the environment, and support of the ACLU. His opponent is the political conservative. These positions, however, could be reversed. At issue is the repair of a family; the president's family must be made whole. His daughter needs a mother as much as he needs a spouse. The maintenance of the state requires the completeness of love. Thus, only when family and politics are aligned can we be confident that the president will win reelection. Until the first family has been repaired and defended, the nation is in peril. That peril is represented as an openness to unfounded fear. Love, quite literally, grounds the security of the state.

This same narrative operates in a variety of forms in our actual politics: some banal, some hypocritical, some romantic. Consider, for example, the recountings of the narrative of Edward Kennedy's life that circulated in the media after his death in 2009. Often, the narrative was presented as a moral narrative of sin and recovery.[17] Recovery begins with a renewal of familial love. Only when he was happily remarried could he become the master of the Senate—someone above partisanship, for he now represented the nation as a whole. A banal variation is found in the countless rhetorical performances of the withdrawal from politics "in order to spend more time with my family." Here the suggestion is that politics has taken a pathological form by undermining family. The politician announces that he is giving up a life of one sort of love—political—for that of another—familial. This is a career-ending speech, for the task of the politician is to model the unity, not the separation, of these forms of love.

The American President is romantic comedy taking up the same question of the origin of the state as the narratives of sacrificial violence in the last chapter. Film places itself in the exceptional situation, which is not just the point of origin but also the point of renewal. Political and familial renewal are one and the same. The state is in constant need of renewal in part because it exists in a world of threats but also in part because the extraordinary gives meaning to the ordinary. The retreat at the end of the day to the family residence in the White House is the entry point for the power of love to renew the ordinary politics of party confrontation.

The cinema's role here is not so different from the traditional role of the church. What were those countless narratives—verbal and visual—of Christ, if not reminders that the normal depends on the exceptional? Entering the church, we are to suspend the ordinary and reflect upon beginnings and ends, on the sources of ultimate meanings for ourselves and our entire world. Entering the theater, we are engaged in a similar suspension of the ordinary. We want to hear again the narrative of beginnings and ends, of ultimate meanings and extraordinary actions. The value of the exceptional is always that of love, whether we look to church, state, or family. Love in any of these forms of expression can lead to pain or to pleasure, to well-being or to suffering. Indeed, pain is inextricably tied to happiness, for within these communities we experience the death and suffering of those we love.

It should be no surprise, therefore, that when we turn from theory to imagination, we find little concern with individuals and the social contract. We find in film something closer to classical political theory than to modern theory: the polity, Aristotle thought, emerges naturally from the coming together of families.[18] This idea of familial origins, however, is no longer seen as transformed by the coming into being of the polity. Instead, political and familial order are both linked to a thoroughly Christian idea of meaning coming into the world through sacrifice for love. We find a secularized, political version of John 3:16: "For God so loved the world, that He gave His only begotten Son, that whoever believes in Him shall not perish, but have eternal life." Love, sacrifice, and faith are the elements of the political narrative we want to see again and again.

What fascinates is not the use of the state to provide a space for an economy of material interests but rather the image of the state as an economy of love. Films create for us a narrative of the willingness to sacrifice. This is the burden of love. Meaning begins not from the satisfaction of need but from the possibility of sacrifice. It begins in the act that cannot be derived from argument. We "fall" in love; we do not reason ourselves to love. The same is true of our relationship to the state. We do not choose our state from a list of existing states. We do not have the option of "none of the above." We find ourselves already grasped by a political community. Its history is our history; its future is our burden.

Just here, we find the answer to the question of why the family appears so central to the political drama despite the absence of the family from political theory. These films are fundamentally about the action of love. The bringing of meaning into the world through sacrifice—real or metaphoric—is the archetype at issue. The point is not that politics is founded on families rather than individuals—both are theoretical abstractions—but rather that love collapses distinctions. Distinctions are maintained in an order of representation. Love reaches beyond representation to identity. We see this most immediately in the biblical expression of unity made possible through the creation of Eve: "two become one" in the connection of man and woman. Identity beyond difference is always the meaning of love. This giving up of difference and becoming one with the object of our love is given existential expression in sacrifice.

The point is not that film is simply making use of politics to tell a story of love. Just the opposite. The modern nation-state has been a construction of the erotic imagination before it has been a construction of reason.[19] In political terms we must have sovereignty before law. Sovereignty is the point beyond distinctions, the point of identity that founds an order of representation.

Liberal theory is simply not prepared to deal with love as a creative force—a force that was already central in Plato's understanding and that is at the center of Christianity. When these films show us the inseparability of the familial and the political, they are taking up this world-creating power of love.[20] They place the family at the center because family has become for us the sign and signature of love. We associate the familial with the transcendent claims of love. This is especially true today in the relationship between parent and child. We find in the innocence of childhood the absolute and unconditional claim of love. As the father in *The Road* explains, the child is his god. Nothing really competes with this as a symbol of the power of love to take us beyond our concern for protection of our rights and satisfaction of our interests.

INNOCENCE AND THE SACRED

A common theme of film is the competition between one's love of family and one's professional role. Is the political narrative of the familial simply another version of this story? Not quite. The general theme has profession giving way to love. There is a reordering of values such that the protagonist sees that professional life or social role in the absence of familial love is empty.[21] The resolution is the turn away from this role to the reality of love. This story appears in the rhetoric of the ruined politician who "wants" to spend more time with family—a rhetoric I have described as banal. The strong form of the political narrative is quite different: the resolution is not in the turning away from the professional role but in the alignment of family and politics. The first family is not an alternative to the political; it is the supplement, the foundation, the necessary condition of the political.

To qualify for a professional role is to possess a body of knowledge. The exercise of the role is the application of that expertise. This is especially so in a service economy in which the ends for which that expertise is applied come from outside of the actor. The lawyer and the businessperson—paradigms of professional roles—serve others. The reason deployed in such a role is thoroughly instrumental. One consequence is a gap between role and identity. That gap is portrayed in film as the absence of love. We know in advance in which direction the trade-off will be made: no one gives up love for role without suffering the trauma of existential loss. This is the modern version of "the deal with the devil": professional success is purchased at the cost of one's eternal soul. The narrative in film is of recovery and repair; it puts role in its place, finding identity in love.

Political participation, in contrast, is not a role; rather, it is an expression of identity. The demands of citizenship are themselves demands of love. Love must be protected from role, so politics must be kept pure of role. Thus, the endless demand for "honest" politicians. This is only another way of saying that for love there is an absence of distinction between the familial and the political. This is our oldest story of sacrifice. Abraham was promised that if he were to sacrifice his only legitimate son, he would become father of a great nation. Nation is family and polity.[22]

The romantic family of the contemporary social imaginary derives its power overwhelmingly from the innocent child. Isaac, too, was the innocent child. Jesus, of course, becomes the sacrificial offering in place of Isaac. There is a particular fascination with the innocence of the infant Jesus in Christian art—carried forward even today in our endless imagery of Christmas. This idea of the innocent child has always been available, but modern historians tell us it was in retreat until quite recently. They argue that the concept of childhood as something other than a privative form of adulthood is a recent innovation.[23] Morally, the child represented the lack of discipline that opens a space for sin. Economically, childhood was a state of need to be traversed quickly in order for the child to become a productive resource for the family. This early modern child had to be controlled by the authority of the parent, or the child would be lost spiritually and fail economically.[24]

Whether this historical claim is correct or not, clearly it is not the case today that childhood is seen as a time of threat or danger. We find quite the opposite: the innocent child instructs the parent. The parent who has allowed him- or herself to be corrupted by the world needs to be saved.[25] He or she occupies a role that fails to connect with personal identity. The child is the purity of identity before representation. We have countless films deploying this archetype. Sometimes the child appears in the adult's life through some sort of accidental death of the parents;[26] sometimes it is the parentless child of the orphanage or the abandoned child who is the source of innocence;[27] sometimes the child is the product of an accidental pregnancy.[28]

The child has no role apart from being him- or herself. The infant shows forth its meaning in its very presence. This coincidence of being and meaning is the quality of the sacred—a point I made with respect to revolution in the last chapter. The child is always the world made new and has, therefore, an innocence that must be protected and preserved. In the presence of the child we want to linger as long as possible. An adult who fails to respond to the presence of the innocent child is irredeemably lost.

The murder of a child—or even the loss of a child—presents the deepest tragedy imaginable in a film. It leaves in its wake broken adults who can never fully recover. An older film in this genre is *Don't Look Now*, in which there is not even sanity left for the parents of a child who accidentally drowned.[29] A more recent film, *I've Loved You So Long*, takes the tragedy one step further.[30] A woman has spent fifteen years in jail for murdering her six-year-old son. She has been released and has temporarily moved in with her younger sister's family. She wants mostly to be left alone, resisting contact with others. Only toward the end do we learn what seems to have been hidden from everyone everywhere, including at the trial. The killing had been a "mercy killing." She was a doctor and had "kidnaped" her own son, when she realized he was dying of a disease that would cause excruciating pain. Doing the act out of love, she gave herself over to endless punishment. The loss of a child, she tells us at the end, is the worst form of prison, one from which you are never released.[31]

Here, too, we find comedy tracking the same themes as tragedy. *Juno* was such an endearing film because of the way in which it established a kind of double relationship to the innocence of the child. This is the story of a precocious high school student who becomes pregnant and decides not to have an abortion, electing instead to go about finding suitable parents for her child. Juno is herself still a child. We like her in part because she knows this about herself. She seems incapable of dishonesty, of playing any role other than herself. She says at one point, when asked by her father what she has been doing, that she has been dealing with issues way above her "maturity level." She has about her the innocence of a child, which makes her presence a source of love for others.

Pregnant, Juno also has the power to give this gift of innocence to another. She can redeem an adult from the meaninglessness of his or her role. The couple she finds to adopt the child, however, is not quite ready for redemption. The would-be mother is, but the father, who still fantasizes himself as an adolescent, is not. Indeed, meeting Juno encourages this fantasy on his part. He wants to be of the world that Juno occupies—a world without the responsibilities of adulthood—rather than to be the parent who cultivates that innocence in another. The adoptive couple shows us this double response to the burdens of their role: she would be a mother; he would be an adolescent. The parent can find redemption from the meaninglessness of her or his role through the innocence of the child, but this is quite different from becoming a child again.

The resolution of the film brings the world back into the proper relationship of innocence and responsibility. Juno's infant goes to the adoptive mother, while the would-be father leaves to live out a fantasy. Juno picks up her own life within the protective aura of the love of her own family. She is again matched with her boyfriend in a scene of entirely innocent adolescent love. From the child all meaning flows.

Juno is not a political film, but it does help us to understand the link of the political and familial. We find films locating the possibility of the political in the familial because we find there the expression of love. We do not need instruction on the meaning of the family and the world-renewing power of the innocent child. It is not that the political needs the familial to offer a convincing narrative; rather, it needs the love that is on offer in the family. For this reason it is difficult to think of films that represent the drama of the political without locating it simultaneously within a drama of the familial. Not even friendship is enough of a ground for the narrative. The love at issue must always point beyond the political to that ideal of domesticity, which is the two-become-one of love.

One exception is the Secret Service agent who fascinates us precisely because he will "take a bullet for the president." This person is in some ways the living dead; therefore, he can have no family. His only source of meaning is the president himself. Consider, for example, *In the Line of Fire* or *The Sentinel*.[32] In the former the agent is haunted by his failure to take the bullet for President Kennedy. He can have no ordinary life—no family—until he redeems himself through sacrifice for a president some thirty years later. The latter is interesting because it includes an affair between the First Lady and the agent, as if they both confuse the president with the agent whose identity is defined by the president's life. The plot may be silly, but the idea of the two-become-one makes a kind of mythic sense.

Film has hold of a powerful strain of democratic legitimacy in linking familial love to political violence. One symbolic measure of the legitimacy of political violence is whether the state has convinced its mothers to give up their children. A democratic state that cannot sustain the support of the mothers when it asks their children to kill and be killed has no legitimate claim to make war. This is the lived experience of the Kantian idea that a democratic state will be reluctant to go to war, for it risks rejection in the polls if the people do not support its demand for sacrifice.[33] The mothers will not sacrifice their children for the sake of an abstract idea of justice. They are not likely to accept the sacrifice of their children to prevent other people from behaving poorly toward each other. The love of family must be aligned with the love of nation. Today, the ticking time bomb must be nuclear, and it must be aimed at us. This was, of course, the logic behind the apparently false rhetoric of the American invasion of Iraq in 2003, which spoke of a threat from weapons of mass destruction. If this threat is false, there is no backup argument to be made about bringing justice to Iraq. That is not worth my child's life.

What is the value of a child's life is directly at issue in one of the most successful of recent movies, *Saving Private Ryan*. Here the question is not whether the sacrifice of the child is something we can ask of the mother but rather how many such sacrifices can we ask of her. The film begins with the death of three of the four children of Mrs. Ryan on the battlefields of the Second World War. On a single day she receives notices of all of their deaths. She has one remaining son fighting, and the question is "Has she given enough for her country?" The military command decides that she has and sets about trying to find and save the remaining Private Ryan, who is fighting behind enemy lines in Europe. After much bloody travail they find him. He will not, however, abandon his unit, which is about to be assaulted by the Germans.

We might think of this as a conflict between the mother's love of her son and the son's love of his fellow combatants. But that is not quite right. There is no conflict because there is no limit to the sacrifices that will be made for love. That his brothers died is not a reason for him to save his life—just the opposite. The military command applied the wrong metric. Private Ryan is not violating his mother's love; and she would not condemn his willingness to sacrifice. State and family are inextricably bound to each other. Of course, the movie assures us that all is right in the order of sacrifice. Private Ryan lives, although those who came to save him die. A useless mission? Not exactly, for the only measure of all such actions is the willingness to sacrifice out of love, which is never a means to an end. What survives out of sacrifice is that intersection of familial and political love that is Private Ryan.

The drama of the state is the drama of familial love because there is no sacrifice for the state that is not experienced as the sacrifice of a family member. *Brothers* is another example of a recent film that works at this connection between the familial and the political.[34] The film opens with a contrast of two brothers. The older, Sam, is successful at everything: school, sports, and family. He is married, with two young daughters. He is also a captain in the marines. The younger, Tommy, is a failure at everything. He has just been released from prison after an unsuccessful attempt at bank robbery. Sam is about to leave his family and return to Afghanistan for a second tour of duty. Tommy returns to a place that offers no home. He is at odds with his father; he tends toward irresponsibility, anger, and drunkenness.

In Afghanistan Sam's helicopter is shot down. His family is told that he died in the crash. Actually, he is taken prisoner, tortured, and ultimately made to perform the unspeakable act of shooting his fellow prisoner. Tommy increasingly steps into the familial place, bonding deeply with Sam's two young daughters, falling in love with his wife, and taking on the role of supporting the domestic household. Had this been some other culture, the younger brother would literally have inherited the family of the older brother. The problem is that Sam is not dead. He eventually returns home, suffering now the psychological consequences of his murderous act of betrayal. He is cold and distant. He cannot speak of what he did. He is able to speak and to think of just one thing: the suspicion that his wife and his brother have been sleeping together— they have not.

He has become a stranger to his children, who want nothing to do with him; they want their loving uncle. His wife knows something happened, but since he will not speak, she cannot help. The family falls apart, dragging in a pathological older father who, it turns out, had raised his children, Sam and Tommy, in the shadow of his own experience in Vietnam. He, too, had been unable to speak of his war experience, an inability that led him to drink and abuse. The result was two sons, each reflecting one side of his split personality: one son is a leader, the other a criminal. By the end of the movie these roles have been reversed: we are not sure which son is the criminal and which the hero. Or maybe neither is criminal or hero. Both are only victims, one of the family and one of the state, but there is no line separating these.

Family, law, and political violence are all at issue here. Sam, who goes to war, must be able to read his act as the sacrifice that makes possible the innocence of familial love. When his violence cannot be read as sacrifice but only as murder, the result is a corruption of the family. If he is a murderer, then he can neither love nor be loved (remember Walt Kowalski from *Gran Torino*). A murderer cannot be the father of the innocent child. That innocence cannot redeem his act of murder. His moral corruption sends him out of their presence, as he turns to drink and violence. Figuratively, the children banish their father in favor of their uncle, Tommy, who may have committed a crime but, having "served his time," has nothing to hide. Indeed, his participation in the innocence of family gives him the strength to go to the victim of his crime and offer an apology. His voice contrasts sharply with his brother's silence. Sam says at one point that he did what he did for the sake of love: only by killing his companion could he get home. But he says this as an accusation against his wife: "I did this, while you betrayed me." The problem, however, is that he does not really believe this. He believes that he has murdered, not that he has sacrificed. He comes home polluted, and that pollution prevents his reentry into the family.

The two brothers are images of each other, just as each was a partial image of their suffering father. Both are capable of crime. Both love the same family. Only the love of family can save each of them from the consequences of their crime. The soldier cannot save the family; rather, only the family can save him. Before it can do so, however, he must put himself in a position to receive that grace. He must confess: there must be truth before there can be redemption. This, too, is an extremely old theme. The redemptive process was no different for Tommy, the younger brother: to receive the grace of the innocent, he had to confess to his victim. Until and unless Sam can speak the truth of his sin, he cannot be a part of the family. Thus, after an explosion of violence in the family home, he is sent for therapy. The modern form of the talking cure is to accomplish the traditional work of the confession.

The truth that cannot be uttered is that which reveals the sacrificial foundation of the state to be nothing more than an act of murder. Their Vietnam-veteran father refused to confess, and this led to the pathology of his family. Sam, the good son, shows us the brutal reality of the state beyond the myth of sacrifice: it is a killing and being killed, and that is all there is to it. It is not an order that succeeds the state of nature; it is the state of nature itself. On the field of battle there is only the murder of the other in order to save oneself. There is nothing heroic about this. We might think that we are only killing the enemy, but we are killing men. If we are willing to kill the enemy to save ourselves, we are willing to kill our companions to save ourselves. We want to live, and we will do whatever is required to do so.

If the truth of battle is murder, then the truth of love is sex. As long as Sam cannot speak the truth he lived, he can see his wife and brother only as sexual partners. The failed sacrifice, his act of betrayal, makes him less than human. Family and state both retreat before the brutality of the body alone. Thus, failed sacrifice is the end of family because it is the end of love. The veteran who believes he should have died believes that everything is without meaning—more or less what the younger son, Tommy, believed before he was redeemed by familial love.

The thought that there is nothing beyond the coming together and coming apart of bodies is unbearable. To learn this lesson at war, rather than the lesson of Private Ryan, is the end of politics and the end of family, for it is the end of love. There is nothing more dangerous to the state than the veteran who returns and speaks of war as murder, not sacrifice. Today these veterans are seen through the framework of pathology. Thus, Sam ends up in the psychology ward of a veterans' hospital—the same place that many of those who threatened political dissidence in the Soviet Union ended up.

Defiance, another recent film about two brothers in war, makes a similar point but in far more conventional terms.[35] The film concerns a Polish Jewish family caught up in the German genocide. They flee the advancing Germans but in different directions. One brother escapes into the woods and creates there a nonpolitical space of assistance to homeless Jews. A kind of enclave is created in which all live as an extended family. The other brother joins the Red Army and becomes a leader in the fight. The film traces their movement back to each other. The brother who seeks a secure place for familial love learns that he cannot avoid the violent political act of defense. The other brother learns that without family there is nothing worth defending. The brothers ultimately join together, bringing back the necessary alignment of family and state, of love and sacrifice.[36] We can read the film as a search for a middle ground between the bourgeois values of the West and the loveless communism of the Soviets. But it is more compelling as an inquiry not into political forms but into the structure of the imagination. There cannot be love without sacrifice; there cannot be politics without love. Familial identity must ground political representation.

The stable point of meaning, the source from which all meaning flows, is the family: the innocence of children, the loving spouse, the love between brothers. An unsuccessful war is one that cannot link political violence to the protection of the family. The family can extend its reach to the criminal, but it cannot save the soldier who has learned the singular truth that war is murder and that in the extreme situation all men will kill rather than be killed. The failure of sacrifice is literally the end of a meaningful world. Sam had to choose, just as the Christian martyrs had to choose: life or death? If he chose death, the world would be saved for a kind of innocence. But he chose life, and with that he banished innocence from the world. Choosing, he proved Hobbes right: nothing is of more value than life. The problem, however, is that this is a truth with which he cannot live.

Exploring the narrative of the political in film is necessarily an exploration of the familial, for these are the double sources of a single national narrative: family and country as a unified order of love. The pathology of one necessarily corrupts the other. A failure of sacrifice will undermine the family, but will a failure in the family undermine the order of political violence? This is a much harder theme for film to take up because of its unrelenting message of failure. One has to wonder, however, whether our long controversy over the serving of gays in the military is not related at least in part to this felt relationship between the familial and the political. More often in film, we see a compensatory response to this worry about the political consequences of familial failure: the military provides a community of value sufficient to overcome the familial deficiency. A classic expression is *An Officer and a Gentleman*.[37] The film plots the struggle for the erotic core of the child of a broken family who "wants to fly jets." It must displace the failed father with the father figure of the drill sergeant: tough love for no love. Learning the virtues of the officer remakes the possibility of the familial. He is "reborn" as both an officer and a gentleman.

In film the borders separating the private and the public continually disappear in the representation of the sacrifice for love. The innocence of children and the world-creating character of the coming together of two individuals to form a family are very much at the center of the imagination of the political.[38] There is no liberal individual on the field of battle or in the familial order, for each is a domain of life and death rather than of the pursuit of interests.

FAMILIAL LOVE AND CONTEMPORARY THREATS: COMEDY, HORROR, AND PORNOGRAPHY

I have been exploring one of the oldest metaphors that we have: the nation as family. God, we read in the Old Testament, is married to Israel. The metaphor shifts from spouse to children when Israel is seen as the patrimony of Abraham. It takes yet another form with the appearance of Christianity. Christ is the son of God, and the church is the body of Christ. All these images are variations on what the Genesis story of creation describes as the "two become one" of love. Unity must overcome difference. Without that we fear we will be condemned to an unbearable, existential loneliness. Death is the symbol of that loneliness, while love is always the symbol of rebirth.[39]

These deeply entrenched ways of thinking about self and others, about the meaning of life and death, remain the archetypes of order even in our modern, secular age. We can no more think of politics as a product of contract than we can think of marriage as a contractual relationship. More precisely, we can think it, but we cannot imagine it. For the imagination it is not contract but covenant in both cases. A covenant bears remnants of sacred presence—we covenant with or before God—and of new beginnings. The pressure in the modern wedding ceremony, in which the couple writes their own vows, is not to displace the language of God with that of contract but rather with the language of love. Love is enough: with love we don't need God.

Of course, there are many loveless marriages, just as there are many states that fail as communities of meaning. Contract or quasi contract may survive in both cases. We know of prenuptial agreements in which contract precedes and sets the boundaries of marriage. Such agreements are usually directed at what will happen to property if the marriage fails. Historically, many states refused to recognize prenuptial contracts precisely because they seemed inconsistent with the meaning of marriage: they plan for its dissolution rather than its success. Some states would recognize such agreements only until the point at which the couple has a child. Family, they seem to be saying, cannot be a matter of contract. Neither is the state a matter of contract.

In the end a prenuptial agreement cannot tell us the meaning of marriage, for it is written in anticipation of failure. Similarly, a failed state cannot tell us the meaning of the political, for it occupies precisely the situation in which the political fails to take hold. We cannot learn the meaning of God from an atheist.[40] This is not to say that film cannot explore the failure of family, state, and faith. We understand these situations as failure, however, only when we understand what has been lost. That is indeed a serious question for all of us.

Coming to the familial from the political emphasizes the family as the site of love and the source of sacrifice. The child, I have argued, is at the center of our imaginative construction of the family and of the state. All of these ideas and images have had a very long presence in the West. Twenty-five hundred years ago Plato was already speaking of the creative power of love and investigating the relationship between family and polity. Christianity offers the image of a sacrificial community founded on love. While the circumstances of application have changed in modern films, there has been no radical challenge to these archetypes. The same is true of another idea central to the Western imagination of love: the association of love and innocence. The child is innocent. The promise of the child is that he or she will refound the world on that innocence and thus bring meaning back to a world that has fallen into the meaninglessness of the ordinary. Paradigmatically, this is the story of Isaac coming as a blessing to the elderly and childless Abraham and Sara. Sara's laugh on hearing of what was to be is the recognition of the marvelous.

The child as father of the man is a common archetype of film. With respect to this idea we must ask the same questions that structured the previous chapter: how is origin represented, and from what directions do we see contemporary threats to this ideal of meaning? At issue in the familial is the same structural relationship of identity to representation. There are, accordingly, familial parallels to the forms of anxiety investigated in the last chapter. Contract threatens covenant in the same way that a closed code threatened identity, and just as a meaningless violence threatened sacrifice, the materiality of sex threatens love. The former threat appears in a contemporary form in horror films, the latter in pornography. These are the double threats to romantic comedy, which is the cinematic home of the loving family.

ROMANCE AND THE AUTOCHTHONY OF LOVE

We do not necessarily see the natural as innocent. There is nothing innocent about Hobbes's state of nature. Similarly, we might think of childhood as a dangerous moment in which the moral character of the person is not yet formed. Against both of these ideas of the dangerous beginning lies the idea of innocence. The innocent child has both a negative and a positive sense. He is not yet corrupted by our communal and individual compromises; his hands are not yet dirtied. More than that, however, he is pure and as such a source of meaning that can never be fully captured by representation. The child need not justify himself; he need not speak at all. We are speechless before the newborn infant. Presence is reduced to naming. Without need of justification the infant is that for the sake of whom everything else is done.[41]

In politics the innocent point of origin is the founding; in religion it is revelation. Both of these ideas of beginnings borrow from the experience of natality: the coming into being of the person, which is always the start of a new world.[42] For this reason human beginnings are never caused; they are never explained merely by their location in a sequence of events as if they were the product of a slowly changing pattern of DNA. A biography is a history, not an account of the chemistry of DNA.[43] No child—and no state or faith—is simply one among many. The child, even before she says her first word, is never a fungible commodity: we are not indifferent to which child we take home from the hospital. We will not trade. The same is true of nations and faiths: ours is always unique; each is incommensurable with others.

At stake in the idea of beginnings without cause is a distinct idea of human freedom: to be free is to be capable of beginning again. This is the promise of "rebirth" in Christianity. It is also the promise of "naturalization" for the immigrant. The child, too, is not the made product of the parents, as if he or she were simply an aggregation of preexisting parts. The Nicene Creed says of Jesus what is true of every child: "He is begotten not made."[44] In myth the beginning of the person is the arrival of the soul to the body. If we ask of the origin of the soul, we are told it is without beginning.

Innocence captures all of these ideas of natality, origins, exception—of an identity outside of representation but the point from which all representation flows and to which it must refer back. The sacred always has this quality of innocence. It has it even when it terrifies. Thus, in both politics and religion the idea of innocence easily becomes an idea of violent destruction: the Terror is the moment of innocence destroying corruption. Lincoln's Gettysburg Address, with its appeal to a "a new birth of freedom," accomplishes the same identification of innocence with violent destruction. In religion the millennial wish to return to the purity of origins is often associated with a vision of destruction of this all-too-compromised world. In film the connection of innocence and terror can be much more vivid, as the child becomes the source of horrific destruction.

Because I love my child, one might be inclined to think that I create a world for her. But this is no more correct than thinking that love is an interior experience. It makes just as much sense to say that the child creates a world of meaning for me. The child brings me into the world as much as I bring her into the world. If I try unilaterally to give my child a world, I am suffering a pathology of narcissism. This double relationship of world creation—of parent creating child and child creating parent—is the theme of countless romantic comedies in which the child takes on the burden of creating or completing the family. These children never seem to be threatened by the entry of a possible competitor for their single parent's love. Rather, they see the need to create a world that is whole and complete. These films are always comedies, for what could be more pathetic than to see such an effort fail?

The innocent child as the origin of the family has a distinct cinematic signature. This is the child who finds a spouse for the father or mother and thus finds, as well, the missing parent for himself or herself. A well-known example is *Sleepless in Seattle*, in which a young adolescent acts in response to his father's overwhelming grief at the loss of the spouse/mother.[45] Such films are often appealing to children, precisely because they are about child empowerment in response to the threat of parental failure. Think of *The Parent Trap*, made first in 1961 and then again in 1998.[46] It offers a theme that is always timely: identical twins secretly changing places and successfully plotting to reunite their divorced parents. The empowerment of the child is a powerful reassurance in the face of the fear that comes from recognition of the fragility of self and family. A world in need of repair must return to the origin: the innocent love of the child. The message to the child is the same as to the adult: love creates a world. The world that matters in the first instance is the family.

Recently, in *The Kids Are All Right*, these themes were given a contemporary twist in casting the family as one with two moms.[47] This is otherwise an ordinary, suburban family with an eighteen-year-old daughter and a fifteen-year-old son. The kids could not be more typical: a shy but bright daughter about to leave home for college; an athletic but confused son who is easily impressed by the wrong people. Even the parents are ordinary in their daily struggles with children, home, and careers: one is a successful doctor, the other a stay-at-home mom looking for a new career now that the kids are older. This family does, however, have a unique feature in its explicit acknowledgment that the children owe their biological origin to contract. The moms contracted for the services of an unknown donor through a sperm bank—the same donor for both children. What, then, is a father?

As teenagers the kids want to take responsibility for their own existence. At eighteen, the daughter is legally allowed to inquire of the sperm bank for information regarding the donor—her father—but he must agree to its release. He does, and then begins the unfolding of a new set of relationships to their father, who has remained unmarried. The kids want to bring him into their lives and into their home. He enthusiastically embraces them as "family." So much so that he finds himself having a brief affair with one of the moms and fantasizing about her and the kids moving in with him. That would be the moment at which the children had successfully created their own family—the moment in which contractual creation is displaced by the necessity of love.

Of course, it does not work out that way, for these children already have a family. Families are not simply on offer. The father is, as described by the other mom, an "interloper." Biology gives him no more of a claim than does contract. The origin of these children was not in contract or in biology but in love. In the end he is not welcome in this family because it was not in need of repair, only of a little therapy. We, along with the kids, are left to puzzle about what exactly he is: father or sperm donor? In a reflection of the archetype, he learns this lesson of love from the kids: no longer content to be the sperm donor, he wants a family. It will not, however, be this one.

There is no absent parent in this family. That the children are fine is an affirmation of the completeness of this family, with its two moms. They were not lacking a necessary member but only suffering the ordinary problems of teenage angst and middle-age crisis. Love, we are told in the climactic scene, is work. The work of love, we might say, is to bring representation in touch with identity. Each member pursues his or her career or education—the comings and goings of daily life—but all must renew contact with the singular source of meaning that is familial love. The film ends with everyone dropping the daughter off at her new college dorm. The distance of separation is a metaphor for the problem of representation in general. No longer secure in the home, she can only represent herself to others. She will have to answer the question of who she is. She can now sustain this burden of representation because the family has been repaired after the trauma of intervention. The family has found within itself the whole of what it needs.

One image of the world-creating power of love is in the children's ability to create their own parents. The same power of renewal is at stake in the parental longing to return to contact with the child. The conventional world of representation finds its limits in the existential loneliness of old age and then death. The aging parent, no longer employed, losing health, friends, and then even the capacity for speech, is a familiar image. This literal meaninglessness must be met by the necessity of love. One version of this idea appears in the political narrative of sacrifice that I traced in the last chapter. There is a gentler side of this idea that appears within the ordinary family drama. A movie on this theme came out at the same time as *The Kids Are All Right* and with a similar title, *Everybody's Fine*.[48] Robert De Niro plays a recent widower planning a reunion for his grown children at the family home. He is retired and living alone; he seems to be without any significant friendships. He is overwhelmingly lonely. His career had been in making cable for telecommunications. One has the sense that he had not been much involved with the interior life of the home as his children were growing up. He was, instead, a technician of representation, leaving love and identity to his spouse.[49]

When all the children cancel, he sets off to visit each of them around the country, despite warnings of danger from his doctor. What the doctor's prescriptions cannot provide, however, is the presence of love in the now-empty family home. As he moves from child to child, he finds that each is hiding something. Some truths cannot be spoken. No one wants him to linger; each passes him off to the next. None is capable of sharing the bad news in his or her life with him. The ultimate bad news is that his oldest son, a New York artist, has just died of a drug overdose in a Mexican jail. The father is aware of the multiple deceptions, but he is uncertain about what is really going on. He suffers a heart attack on the plane trip home.

When he awakes in the hospital, his children are there. He insists on the truth and learns of his son's death. He also learns that his older daughter, although a business success, has separated from her husband, that his other daughter is a single mom and not much of a success as a dancer, and that his remaining son is not a successful conductor but a minor member of a regional orchestra. His children had identified love of the family with their now dead mother. Their father, they thought, was concerned only with their professional success. As things fell apart for each of them, they could not bear to tell him the news.

The movie, however, ends with the redemptive power of familial love. The final scenes are of a reunion at the familial home. The film concludes with its longed-for beginning. That gathering has now been freed of expectations about order and success. Under these conditions the truth can be spoken, for it cannot touch the identity of love. We see, most especially, the new figures of love. The infant grandchild is there, along with the mom's lesbian lover. Similarly, the older daughter is there with her son but also with her new partner. The extended family had been suffering the burdens of death, professional failure, and divorce. All of this is overcome—everybody is fine—once we can see through to the power of the child's love. Fittingly, it is Christmas: the traditional point of renewal through the love that comes into the world with the new child.

At stake in both of these films is the world-creating power of familial love. Love is not a private feeling but a way of being in a world. Every family, happy or unhappy, is its own world. We feel this even with our closest friends: we cannot quite imagine life within their families. There is always something that eludes us. In this sense love is private, not because it is interior but because it is so complete. Thus, even a biological father can be called an "interloper." Both of these films associate the remaking power of love with truth, but it is not the truth of representation. Representation might see a father as a sperm donor or be disappointed in a child's professional failure. The truth of love is the truth of an unconditional acceptance that depends on neither contract nor success.

If we think of truth as a quality of representation—as an accurate representation of the facts of the matter—we will miss the point of these films. The family home, in both films, stands for the site of movement from representation to identity. In love there is no place for roles, only for identity. We are not "supposed" to be anything within the home. Love, in each of these families, is an exercise in acceptance. We accept the other because in and through love he or she is always innocent: everything else falls away. This is why love always appears as a sort of renewal. It is also why we find the world-creating power of familial love frustrated in the teenager and renewed in the infant. The teenager is concerned with his or her role and confused over identity. He or she becomes lost in a world of representation. The infant, however, has no capacity to represent and is, accordingly, pure identity.

If love always exceeds representation, then we can never quite understand why others love each other. We can't see what they find so compelling in each other. We can never give an account adequate to the fact because we can never see the world that they create. We know this about ourselves as well. There is something opaque or mysterious about relationships of love that have been lost. We can never remember how it was that we were in love with that person. Love lost seems rather never to have been. It is easier to understand it as mistake or illusion than to try to understand how there could have been a world that is now gone and not retrievable. Thus, the figure of the "ex" in film generally has one of two qualities: either love remains, in which case the parties will get back together, or there is only intolerance, with no sympathy for what was once there.[50]

The opacity of love to the outsider seems universally true, whatever the locus of love. We can't quite imagine what other people find compelling about their own countries, when we have no attachment. Similarly, we can't imagine the authenticity of their faith, when what they believe seems bizarre or archaic. "Who could believe that?" we wonder, while worshiping our own God-turned-man.

What cannot be expressed is the experience of an ultimate or transcendent meaning. Translation is not possible across these experiences because they are beyond or before representation. Films are notoriously immoral in their expression of the exclusivity of the world-creating power of love. We see this most obviously in those endless portrayals of the faceless enemy who are nothing but bodies to be destroyed. Enemies rarely have a subjectivity rooted in a world of love. They are seen only as the threat of negation to our world, not as the affirmation of their own world. Enemies are destroyed with reckless disregard for the fact that they, too, are persons. The idea of the "extra" captures this rather precisely. The extra is literally expendable. He or she has no voice and makes no claim to identity. There is a deep immorality suggested by the extra: he or she is the person emptied of personhood. Whether literally killed or simply cast into the background as part of the scenery for the central drama, the extra is, in Hannah Arendt's words, denied "the right to have rights."[51] There is a relatively short step from the ethos of the extra to the ethos of the zombie. The extra who has a life that is not life—the living dead—is the zombie.[52]

The world that emerges from love is a necessary world. This necessity does not arise from a relationship of cause and effect but rather from its characteristic exclusivity. It is necessary because it is not bound to anything else. Finding myself in love, I find myself in a world that places demands upon me. I don't ask whether these demands are just or whether they are a means to some other end. They are simply the way the world is. Love is, in this sense, like death: necessary but without reason.

The redemptive power of the child is very much at issue in *The Burning Plain*.[53] The trick of the film is that we don't realize until deep into the movie that two sets of characters, who seem quite different, are actually the same people at two different points in their lives. When we do make the connection, we experience literally the effort to move from representation to identity. The problem of the film is to question whether this identity can be achieved after so much separation. The answer is that it can be achieved but only through the redemptive love of the child.

We see the main characters, Santiago and Mariana, falling in love as teenagers; we see them years later living very separate lives. Santiago is now a crop duster in Mexico with a twelve-year-old daughter. Mariana runs a fancy restaurant in Seattle. The film cuts back and forth between these two different sets of circumstances without giving clues sufficient—at least for me—to pick up the fact that there is a difference in time and thus the possibility that these are the same people. We wonder for a very long time what is the connection between the characters in Mexico and those in Seattle. He is a devoted father; she is engaged in a destructive series of brief sexual affairs with random men. Once we realize that we are seeing two different moments in the lives of a single couple, we reach the more serious question: not what is the connection between different people, but what is the identity of a single person through time?

The film does not unfold in continuous time, but its narrative nevertheless has a structured beginning, middle, and end. The beginning is in an affair between two middle-aged people, with families of their own. We know nothing of the origin of this affair, which crosses lines of ethnicity (he is Mexican) in a rural area of the Southwest. We never learn much about him. We do learn that she is recovering from breast cancer. Her husband seems impotent, and we suspect it is because he cannot deal with her illness and mastectomy. We see the adulterous couple creating their own world; they are happy meeting in a trailer in an empty plain, halfway between the two towns in which they live. We also see, in the very first scene, the trailer exploding in a ball of fire with them inside.

The movie is not about them but about their children, Santiago and Mariana, who see each other for the first time at the funeral of the father. The husband of the adulterous wife has brought her children to heckle the Mexican American family as they leave the grave site. Santiago, the teenage son who lost his father, sees Mariana, the teenage daughter, standing with her father. Santiago, in turn, goes to watch the funeral of Mariana's mother and then follows Mariana home. The two of them are drawn to each other, at first because each is curious to learn about the parent's lover. They quickly step into the roles of their respective parents, making love to each other in their parents' beds, keeping their relationship secret from their families, creating their own private world. They engage in a significant act of representation, both burning scars on their arms by which they are to remember their time together. They also engage in symbolic acts of familial life: eating a meal together and sleeping together. As Santiago rescues her from a raging father, who has just found them out, Mariana tells him that she is pregnant.

That was twelve years ago. Now, each is leading a remarkably different and separate life. She lives under a different name, Sylvie, in a distant place. She is materially successful but spiritually empty. She has fled her past but seems unable to find anything meaningful in her present. We don't know why she is so troubled, in part because we don't know that she is Mariana. Having random affairs with men whose names she does not remember, she treats her body as something that deserves to be abused. We see her cutting herself, not as an act of symbolic representation but as an act of self-inflicted pain. It is as if she is looking for some feeling, some response to life. She contemplates suicide, as she moves without purpose among men who would treat her as a body to be used.

In contrast, Santiago is a person with immense enthusiasm for life. He is deeply attached to his twelve-year-old daughter. There is no separation between them; each understands life in terms of the other. He also has a male friend who is deeply bound to him and to his daughter. Santiago flies his crop-dusting plane with a zeal for the beauty of flight but even more as an affirmation of the beauty of life itself. He has the love of an innocent child; Mariana/Sylvie has nothing.

Santiago has a serious accident flying and ends up in the hospital. He sends his friend and daughter off to find her mother in Seattle. She rejects them at first, refusing even to admit who she is. In the end she embraces the daughter. Before she can come back into the familial order, however, the daughter must accept her, which she does. We learn that Mariana had abandoned her daughter and Santiago just days after the birth. She did so because she "did not deserve" the child. How can you not deserve a child? Is there a moral qualification for parenthood?

Only toward the very end do we learn that her undeserving is rooted in the fact that she set the fire that caused the explosion of the trailer and death of her mother and Santiago's father. She had not meant to kill them, only to drive them into the open. But this act, which could not be spoken, was that for which she had to do penance by giving up love, by offering herself to the world as an object to be used, by cutting herself.

She must speak this truth about herself before she can see herself as worthy of love. She confesses to an anesthetized Santiago in his hospital room, but perhaps that is enough, for she has already been forgiven by the innocent child. The child's act of grace creates the possibility of her directly speaking her past. Wholeness cannot be recovered by acts of penance in this world—even by acts of self-destruction—but only by the innocence of the child.

There are a number of elements at work here. First, we see the sheer contingency of love. The relationship of Santiago and Mariana begins with a chance sighting in what is supposed to be a scene of acrimonious confrontation. This is one of the oldest archetypes we have: love crosses borders. Its character as foundation means that it creates new communities in disregard of established lines. This is what makes love so politically dangerous. A recent, futuristic retelling of this tale was offered in the hugely successful *Avatar*.[54] Whether that new foundation succeeds or not, we recognize the stakes. In *The Burning Plain* the young couple are driven out by her father's rage; in *Avatar* the crossing of borders makes possible successful rebellion of the colonized against the colonizer.

Second, we see again the concern with stabilizing identity in representation. The self-inflicted scar is to mark the permanence of their love. This is reminiscent of the scarring in *Inglourious Basterds*.[55] There, the swastika was carved on the forehead so no one could forget or be mistaken about who these people are. Here, the scar is self-imposed so that they will not forget who they are. Their daughter, the twelve-year-old, reads the similarly placed scars on each of her parents as a sign of their unity. Of course, this is exactly what she embodies: the expression of their unity. She is the singular product of their love, and thus the point of intersection of representation and identity.

Third, the presence of the child confronts the moral failing of the mother. Mariana is undeserving, for she has murdered her mother and Santiago's father. Murder always undermines love. In *Brothers* the act of murder by the brother while a prisoner of war undermined his capacity to recapture love of family. Cain murders his brother and is marked; Mariana murders her mother and must bear that self-knowledge. Not surprisingly, we see her cutting herself later on. This mark of Cain must compete on her body with the shared mark of love.

Mariana is a kind of Oedipus figure—now as a teenage girl. Oedipus steps into the place of his father, Mariana into the place of her mother. Neither is morally entitled to that place because each murdered the parent. Both are exiled from love. When Oedipus learns that he murdered his father, he puts out his eyes and flees from his family. Mariana does not put out her eyes, but she too flees, and she refuses to let herself be seen. She, like Oedipus, casts herself into a space that is nowhere. Oedipus, however, has been touched by the gods and is ultimately recognized as a kind of sacred figure, the object of a competition between Thebes and Athens for his dying body. We don't have those gods available to us, but we do have the child. Instead of Thebes sending an emissary to recover her for the city, we have Santiago's friend and the twelve-year-old Maria setting out on a mission of recovery. There are no gods to forgive Mariana, but there is her daughter.[56]

The lovers in the film always seem to live in a complete moment that excludes everything and everyone else. For this reason their actions can seem reckless to outsiders: they respond only to an internal dynamic. This was already true of the parents of Santiago and Mariana, who created a separate life in the trailer. For Mariana's mother neither her marriage nor the responsibilities of motherhood offered any resistance to the possibility of love. Staying away seemed literally impossible. Similarly, Santiago's father loves her as she is, not as she once was or might become. He tells her she is beautiful and that she should not have breast reconstructive surgery. This completeness could lead to nowhere but death; as soon as the world penetrates, they are dead. The children who take up a parallel relationship are also impervious to all the risks, threats, and claims of familial opposition. Love simply must be. It is, as Santiago says repeatedly, no one else's business; it is their world, into which no one else can enter. Their self-imposed scars speak a language no one else can read—until their daughter matches the markings on each.

In love we say we find ourselves, but what we actually find is a world. This is why we cannot explain love as a personal feeling or an interior state. We come to that world by giving up the self alone. This is just the movement of the film: Santiago and Mariana, like their parents, create a world. If that world closes in on itself, if it resists representation, insisting on a constant presence, then it will appear not only impenetrable but dangerous to everyone else. It will be like a state of permanent revolution, in which creation is inseparable from destruction. The impossibility of such a world is seen, in one form, in the parents' death. The threat of such a world is seen in another form in the familial horror films I discuss below.

In family, as in state, identity must give way to representation; extraordinary, ultimate meaning must ground the ordinary. That, we have seen, is the narrative of romantic comedy. In *The Burning Plain* the problem to be resolved begins with Mariana's flight from the objects of her love: her family. She exiles herself, creating an unbearable loneliness no matter how well she succeeds in her new role as restaurateur. Santiago, in contrast, raises their daughter and thus stays within the sanctified boundaries of familial love. His enthusiasm for his daughter is no less an enthrallment with the entire world that he receives through her.

Creating a world, we expose ourselves to the vulnerability of that world. Thus, the parents die horrific, even if accidental, deaths. Their closed-in world cannot survive in a larger imaginative space. Love no more promises happiness than unhappiness. One hopes that extraordinary sacrifice will not be required, that the world will come around to its proper ordering all by itself. Nevertheless, one knows that the demand for sacrifice can always surface. Every parent knows this: the hope that one's family will express itself as romantic comedy, and the fear that the family will be a tragic site of sacrifice. It is not really up to us, whether we find ourselves living comedy or tragedy. Loving, we open ourselves to the contingency of circumstances. I can no more wish the pain of my child away than I can wish away the nation's enemies. A world of love is one in which we are in desperate need of good fortune, for we are not prepared to be stoics in the face of harm to the beloved. We do not measure this pain as if we could make a choice of other possibilities, for love gives us the world and this one happens to be ours.

CONCLUDING COUNTERPOINT:
HORROR AND PORNOGRAPHY

We find in contemporary films a localization of love and a displacement of the sacred onto the family. The family begins with the erotic bond between a couple but drives toward a material embodiment in the child.

The innocence of the child is the moment of identity stripped of, or prior to, representation. It is a commonplace of modern life that a role is never commensurate with identity. The felt origin of this idea is, for many people, the presence of the infant. This democratic infant—the infant as a part of every family—has displaced the infant Jesus as the point of sacred origin: not contract, but presence; not role, but identity. This is why liberal theory, as well as a liberal legal order, has such a hard time with familial relationships. There is an inability to decide whether the family is a domain of privacy into which the state should not intrude or a concentrated form of power into which the state must intrude to protect the child or spouse. What is the unit that liberalism would protect—the individual or the family?[57]

Just as the sacral monarch has been replaced by the everyman of the popular sovereign, the sacral infant has been replaced by the innocent infant of every family. The familial order provides in microcosm the same rhythm that we saw in the political order: the movement from identity to representation. We must secure the erotic foundation, the truth of subjecthood, before we can take up the burden of representation. As the existentialists say, "existence before essence." That moment of origin remains the foundation toward which representation always points. "Who are you?" we ask of others, just as we ask it of ourselves. We answer with a yearning for the truth of the subject revealed in familial love. This is the question asked and the answer offered in *The Burning Plain*, *Everybody's Fine*, and *The Kids Are All Right*—the list could continue indefinitely. Home is the place to which we return to find ourselves. We find ourselves there because home is wherever we find love.

We find ourselves in a meaningful world that is the product of our own imaginative construction. We don't, however, occupy this world unreflectively, as if it were simply a changeless natural order. Nor do we occupy it as in a dream, as if we can give no account of how or why we are there. Rather, we occupy it as subjects: we take ourselves and our world as objects of thought. We take up the elements of our imaginative construction, asking questions and expressing doubt about each or about the entirety. There is no faith without doubt, no love without anxiety. Home is the place to which we return and the place from which we flee. Freud taught us that we so love the father that we would kill him, if we could. Families, accordingly, can be the source of a world-informing love or of a world-destroying hatred.

This capacity for anxious self-reflection, for doubt, is true of our individual experience but also of our collective reflections on the nature of our imagined world. We entertain the possibility that our fundamental premises are wrong. Indeed, it is safe to say that no philosophical claim is ever put forward that is not doubted or denied. Just as politics is characterized by plurality, so is philosophy. Philosophy's origins are in the conversation in which the appropriate first response to any proposition is, "Really?" Philosophical claims of truth are met by skeptics, just as religious claims are met by agnostics. Every religion spawns its heretics, every narrative a counternarrative. Just as in the previous chapter I explored the way films express widespread anxieties about the viability of the imaginative structure of our political world, here I want to turn to film's examination of familial anxieties. The stress lines are analogous, for the same imaginative structures of representation and identity inform both family and state. Thus, we find again an anxiety that the body cannot support any meaning beyond itself and a parallel worry that representation closes in on itself. The contemporary loci of expression of these anxieties are porn and horror films.

I have focused on the role of natality in politics and family, drawing an analogy between the revolutionary coming into being of a people and the appearance of the infant as the source of identity beyond representation. In politics there has always been a counterrevolutionary response to this idea, associating revolution not with revelation but with mobs, terror, and destruction. Just as Donoso Cortes and Joseph de Maistre saw a kind of Satanic terror in the French Revolution, we have films locating evil and terror in the infant. Instead of innocence infusing the meaning of family through the infant, we have the infant as the object of Satanic possession.

These responses mimic an earlier fear of the displacement of religious orthodoxy from the place of ultimate meaning. For the counterrevolutionaries, the good news of transcendent meaning has already occupied the world in the body of Christ. If so, a claim that the infant can be a new source of ultimate meaning only expresses a demonic threat of deception. That deception may promise renewal, but it can only bring death. As a social movement this sort of fear of the child is difficult to find in our secular age, but it has a familiar presence in film: the inversion of the moral valence of the infant—not innocent but Satanic. A culture that attaches such power to the infant may end up in thrall to the infantile, and from there it is only a small step to the fear of destruction by that which is worshiped. Films remind us that in our fears and anxieties we may not be as modern as we think.

Films in this devil-child genre include *Rosemary's Baby*, *The Omen*, *Children of the Corn*, and *The Exorcist*.[58] Sometimes, the child is literally the progeny of Satan; sometimes, Satan has possessed the child. There is a fear that the child will not renew but capture the parent, that it will not redeem but murder. The point of renewal at which everything is possible is also the point at which everything is at risk. Sacrifice loses its meaning before a murderous child. We turn to the infant for love but find only murder. This idea that a child who kills its parent is tainted by evil is precisely the concept of "undeserving" at work in *The Burning Plain*. That we might not be able to tell which is the innocent and which is the evil child is a theme at least as old as *King Lear*.

The sacred has always had this double character of redemption and threat, of creation and destruction. If the child appears outside of the ordered domain of representation, then we cannot be sure whether he or she is good or evil, whether we will experience renewal or death. To stand too close to God was always as dangerous as it was promising. The child for whom we will sacrifice ourselves is not so far from the child who would murder us. The difference between sacrifice and murder can come to no more than a difference in belief. We can change our minds; we can come to doubt.[59]

Horror films in this genre play on the fear that the turn to a redemptive child, the hope for meaning from natality, will be met by rejection, denial, and destruction. That which promises redemption is necessarily also that which threatens irredeemable loss. Not surprisingly, corresponding to these films of infantile threat are teenage horror films focusing on a moral, rather than a redemptive, message. When the child appears as a threat, the parental response will itself be murderous. In these films, if the teenager engages in illicit activity—specifically drugs or sex—then he or she will suffer a horrendous death. Think of the earlier *Rebel Without a Cause*, *Halloween*, or *Hell Night*.[60] This line of films is itself acknowledged in *Scream* when one of the characters summarizes a rule of horror: "sex means death."[61]

With the failure of love the family breaks into a competition between the murderous threat of the child, on the one hand, and the murderous threat against the rebellious teenager, on the other.[62] Both threats suggest the same vision: not innocence and renewal but violence and destruction. The interesting point is the reciprocal vulnerability of parent to child and child to parent. Where exactly does evil lie in the family? Just as in politics, there is no threat that does not draw forth a counterthreat. In both domains the line between sacrifice and murder may be no line at all.

What exactly is the familial anxiety that leads to these double visions of murderous intent? One suspects that it involves a kind of psychological "dirty hands." No one is so pure of heart that he does not feel that he, too, is fallen. Every person is aware of his mixed relationship to his own parents. He knows that he was hardly innocent, that he did not fulfill this redemptive role. Freud taught us this much. Reciprocally, facing one's own children, one suspects oneself of using them. Is redemption on offer, or is it a demand imposed? We fear that we want from them for our own sake, not theirs.[63] This juxtaposition of the sense of sin and the hope of redemption can turn into a fear. We fear we will get what we deserve, and we know that we are not deserving. The relationship of sin to grace is so complex that it had to be mediated by the ritual formalities of confession and forgiveness in the church. Unleashed from convention, it can be an open sore of psychological trauma. Here hope and fear intersect. The result of that intersection can be love or murder.

The parent who fears his or her own undeserving will experience the child's rejection as an act of spiritual murder. In film it becomes an actual murder. The reciprocal threat is felt by the child who fears that he has failed his parents. A child can easily feel the parent's concern as a form of intrusion, an effort to deny his own subjecthood. It can appear to him as a kind of murder. What did Isaac think on the altar: love or murder? Must not Abraham have feared that Isaac would grab the knife and turn it on him? Is it not possible that he thought he deserved no less, for perhaps he was wrong in his faith? If we can no longer make sense of the family as a site of sacrifice, then we are likely to see it as a site of murder. Is the child sent off to war sacrificed out of love or murdered out of selfishness? The move from sacrifice to murder is traced by the disappearance of love. The horror film that "ends well" is one that allows for the recovery of love. The horror film that ends in murderous destruction has exiled love.

In contemporary slasher films these themes have become thoroughly ironic. These films operate with a self-reflective humor, mocking our fears. They can do so because we are acutely aware of the constructed character of representation in these films. The classic instance of this is *Scream*, which incorporates self-reference to earlier horror films in its plot.[64] Film has become a topic of film, and the audience is in on the joke.[65] There is nothing to fear in evil, for there is nothing to fear in film. That which has been constructed as evil can just as easily be inverted. We can dispose of the threat by rewriting the script.

Of course, we could always do so. But now the film does not let the audience's awareness of itself as audience lapse. We are making fun of ourselves as speechless spectators when we see zombies on the screen.[66] In the same way, we make fun of the moralizing impulse of the classic teenage films that linked premarital sex to destruction. *Reefer Madness*, a film originally made for educational purposes, becomes a cult classic, as does *The Texas Chainsaw Massacre*.[67] Irony is in the cast of mind with which we approach these traditional tropes. This is a position we can take only from deep within a world of representation: it is a representation of representation. No irony is possible in the experience of identity.

The contemporary slasher film is a self-referential, representational order that invites the audience into a kind of ritualized participation.[68] There is no longer any question of doing battle with code. The possibility of freedom is now located in irony, not sacrifice. Identity is never at issue: it is all role playing and self-mocking. We see this same sort of self-mocking institutionalized in the carnivalesque showings of *The Rocky Horror Picture Show* or *The Sound of Music*.[69] In the contemporary slasher film, acts of horrendous destruction do not have the moral weight of murder in a political narrative, let alone in the conventional social order, for there is never a moment in which the intended audience does not understand that it is participating in a film. Someone unaware of the conventions will be repulsed by these films: he or she will flee the theater because the films violate all the ordinary conventions of representation. The representation of violence has been severed from the production of any meaning outside of the production of more violent representations. It is as if the point of the film is only to produce its own sequel.[70]

Horror in these films is a practice of self-referential representation. It is another form of the code turned in on itself—now as the object of an adolescent anxiety that beyond representation there is no identity to be found.[71] We are reminded of the figure of Cipher in *The Matrix*: Cipher chose to return to the self-enclosed world of the matrix. Youth, in these contemporary slasher films, has little to do with innocence and everything to do with victimhood. Representation without identity is experienced as a threat of death. For example, entering the adult world of business, travel, and sex, the teenage characters in *Hostel* discover that their only function is to be hunted and tortured.[72] They are the commodities of a business that sells to the wealthy an opportunity to engage in the hunting and torture of youth. A symbolic order of exchange—whether of money or sex—comes to this: without identity we are simply objects to be used, and used up, by those who have more money.[73] When political identity does show itself, it does so only as an element of exchange value: it costs more to purchase an American for torture. Whether rebellion is successful or not is actually irrelevant, for the conditions will always repeat themselves absent the refoundation of an order of love in both family and state. In a world of representation shorn of identity, however, that is exactly what is not possible.[74]

The point of the contemporary slasher film with its endless gore is to convert murder into nothing more than a vehicle of symbolic exchange. The characters are stylized, acting according to the rules of the genre.[75] To look for sex is still to find death but not because the film teaches a lesson in conventional morality. The good and the bad will be slaughtered alike, for the fundamental normative character of a closed-in world of representation is indifference.[76] There is no good or bad, which is why slaughter has no particular moral effect—only an aesthetic affect. The films create suspense—when will the inevitable death occur?—but that suspense is no longer in the source of any imagined form of politics.

Thus, even vampires are no longer representations of evil. There is only a kind of mocking, ironic representation of representation: we can make of the vampire whatever we wish, for this is an entirely plastic world. There is nothing beyond the ironic representation of the traditional morality of film. The same is true of the traditional adolescent exploration of the world: the symbolic journey. The trip always leads to death, not because one ought to stay home—death will seek you out there as well—but because the film is mocking the character of representation itself.[77] If previously the trip stood for the movement of self-discovery, it will now be shown up as heading to nowhere but death.

The strain on the imaginative structure of family is no longer religious or moral but self-referential and symbolic. These contemporary horror films pick up the theme of the threat of code, of representation detached from identity, that we saw in chapter 4. The child who knows he or she is not innocent, who knows he or she has no redemptive love to offer, is captured by representations that have no meaning beyond death, which is to say they have no meaning at all. The audience of these films is no longer reading *through* the narrative, as if there is a world that is represented in the film. Rather, viewing the film is better understood as a form of ironic self-representation. Thus, *Dawn of the Dead*, which features zombies invading a shopping mall, "has become a midnight favorite at shopping malls all over the United States."[78] In this world symbols can refer only to other symbols. The films literally refer to each other; representation reproduces itself.

The reappearance of zombies in horror films supports this same line of interpretation. The zombie, which has no language, is the signifier stripped of the signified. Zombies are the force of language that remains even after communication fails. They are nothing but the violence of the word, once the word has lost its capacity to express meaning. Any symbolic system let loose upon the world, but no longer communicating any meaning, will tend toward meaningless destruction: money, sex, violence. What Shakespeare wrote of a tale told by an idiot, full of sound and fury but signifying nothing, is today expressed in the zombie horde full of fury but signifying nothing.[79] From the perspective of a lost identity, every symbolic system can threaten to appear as a horde of zombies. The zombie looks human—indeed it looks familiar as friend or relative—but identity no longer holds. It is the walking dead: all that remains when we no longer have an identity beyond representation.

The locus of the horror film remains the family. Its general motion is to displace sacrifice by murder, love by evil. It does so by severing representation from identity. The natural home for this movement is the family, beginning with the innocent infant and moving to the teenager on the brink of finding romantic love, which is the moment of regeneration of a new family. Politics does not threaten the familial order; one order of love does not threaten another. Rather, the symbolic burden is to align the orders of love. What threatens the family is the same thing that threatens the polity: representation turned in on itself and stripped of identity.

Sometimes the threat of the horrific comes not from a division within the family but from an entire family. The murderous family characterizes *The Texas Chainsaw Massacre, House of 1000 Corpses,* and *Deliverance.*[80] Each of these films shows us a family literally turned in on itself, that is, one occupying an otherwise empty space of the rural American landscape. These families can see no meaning in the outsiders. In this they are like the adulterous parents in *The Burning Plain.* Cut off from the possibility of representation, those parents must die. The symmetrical move in horror is to murder outsiders, which includes an imagined threat to the audience. The exchange between inside and outside is always death.

A world of representation turned in on itself, in which representation is literally of nothing, is a world in which individuals are fungible because they are nothing more than placeholders in a system of representation. In *The Matrix* individuals are either representations in the code or batteries for machines. In the horror film they are literally deconstructed: either they are dismembered or they become zombies. Either way they may as well be dead. If there is to be a victory, it must come from a recovery of love. But part of the message of this genre is that no such victory is ever really possible. Representation can always turn in on itself. We continue to live on the edge. So, unlike the political narrative, there is no compulsion that these movies end with the positive affirmation of love.

Seen as the inversion of the archetype of familial sacrifice, horror films have a good deal in common with pornography.[81] Both genres stand in opposition to the identity-representation structure of the romantic family and the modern nation-state. Horror displaces sacrifice with murder; pornography displaces love with sex.[82] In both, truth is immediate and of the body, whether of pleasure or pain.[83] In horror we have speech without meaning, for every representation can lead only to death. In pornography words become mere sounds. There is only physical pleasure and its absence, sex or repression. Every other representation must be penetrated to reveal the mute truth of sex.

Sex that fails to generate representation is sex that has been stripped of its connection to reproduction. Materially, the pornographic coming together of bodies produces no children. Symbolically, it produces nothing at all—except, of course, more of itself. The pornographic moment, like the horror film murder, is only capable of repetition, not narrative representation. It is an iterated, repeated pleasure, never transcending the act by founding a human world of representation.

We might offer a narrative of a porn movie, but it would be little more than description of what has occurred. If surprise is the sign of freedom in discourse, porn contains no surprises. The narrative is more like a soundtrack. It tells a single story: pleasure (usually female) has become a problem, but that problem is resolved only by an unrestrained/unlimited sexual act. For this reason there can be a vast enterprise of privately created, amateur pornography on the web. It bears no burden of representation, of narrative. We need know nothing about characters or plot, for the meaning of the act is the act itself. This collapse of meaning and act is the scandal of the pornographic, for it is a sort of inverse image of the sacred, which also collapses being and meaning. There is, of course, a long tradition of their intersection in the practice of individual penitents. Representation and identity collapse in pornography because the act of watching—voyeurism—is simultaneously an act of sexual pleasure.

The pornographic always offers itself as an alternative to the differentiated human world of role and representation. It pulls into its blunt materiality the occupant of every conceivable role from priest to politician, from housewife to businessman. These people are not literally dead, but a world that is reduced to the sexual act is not so far from the world of the zombie. Language has no place in either world, and without language there is no history. There is only endless repetition.[84] If pornography is without language or narrative, discussion of a particular pornographic film is a problem—not just the problem that I cannot assume any familiarity with particular films but a problem that goes to the nature of the genre, which resists narrative particularity. For this reason, unlike other discussions in this book, I speak of pornography as a genre. The narrative form of pornography is closer to the medical than to the historical or familial. Sex is a "cure" for the problem of the incompleteness of the body itself—usually but not always represented as a female lack or absence.

Pornography today literally fills the interstices of electronic media. Pornography is present already in the still picture. It needs no narrative that places the image in time or space.[85] A pornographic film aggregates multiple pornographic moments. We can turn off the volume and still understand the film. A film that tries to supplement the pornographic with a narrative line will likely appeal to a banal story of familial love. It does so because we cannot make the pornographic speak without changing its nature. Language in pornography is always at the point of dissolving into directions—and groans.

The pornographic literally strips the world of any meaning beyond the act. There is no before or after, for the act does not place itself within any narrative beyond that of coming to the act. Thus, the moment of sex can occur anywhere and anytime. It is free floating, unattached: a kind of antisignifier. The pornographic moment is the diversion that makes a claim to being all the truth that there is. It inverts the world, casting everything else as a flight from the singular hard fact of bodies and sex. Strip away role, stop the speaking, and all that we find is an endless desire for more of the same: physical pleasure.

Horror and porn trade on the same ideas and anxieties, but they do not take the same attitude toward these common sources. The former is ironic; the latter has a curious kind of seriousness to it. Irony signals the presence of a representative community that is self-conscious. Thus, horror films easily lend themselves to collective, ritualized practices that are self-mocking. The horror film is always on the verge of moving from disgusting to funny. Humor is a collective experience: the wholly private joke is hard to imagine. Pornography, on the other hand, presents itself as deeply antisocial. Of course, there is some social viewing of pornography that adopts the mocking tone, but it is far less certain of itself and fit only for the college campus. These films are fundamentally to be seen alone. They cut off communication in their insistence on the limits of the body. It is not an accident that the spectacular growth of pornography is associated with the computer and private cable access; both are means of viewing alone. It is hard to imagine the growth of an online community of pornography viewers.[86] What might they say to each other? Online porn sites solicit comments, but those comments do not constitute reciprocal discourse among the viewers. Rather, they are participatory expressions of the voyeur; they are often the sort of words we expect to hear on the screen. The spectacular growth of the horror film, in contrast, is associated with the multiplex cinema as a gathering place for young people.

Because pornography is serious in a way that horror is not, it must generally be embedded in a deeper morality tale in which the pornographic moment is succeeded by the reaffirmation of the conventional order of family and role. No one is ever trapped in the pornographic—never a kind of zombie of sex. Rather, the pornographic experience remains what the film itself promises, a diversion that enables return—not a return to the redemptive moment of innocence but a return to the ordinary pursuits of the everyday. Thus, the pornography on ordinary cable television offers a narrative of itself as a kind of "aid to marriage." Normal people pursue the pornographic as an occasional diversion that promises to put them in touch with the truth of the body but all in service of the ordinary.[87] When pornography does not end in the affirmation of convention—most importantly family—it crosses over into horror.[88]

If childhood is not innocence, then family is not the site of identity. If love is not identity, then it is only sex. Horror and porn are so popular with teenagers because they know themselves not to be innocent and suspect that they are not capable of love. Porn and horror together represent the splitting apart of the familial order of love as one that links identity and representation. Because porn and horror both have their origin in the familial, they can elide into each other. Nevertheless, analytically we need to maintain the distinction. The horror film turns the body into an empty signifier, while pornography claims that the body is itself the limit of whatever meaning there is. Pornography occupies the place of identity, horror that of representation. Pornography suggests that we are already complete in ourselves and need only withdraw from convention to find this enduring truth. It is a secular form of the ecstatic, which requires no speech.[89] The horror film suggests that the absence of meaningful speech leaves the body as only an object for destruction. Without speech we are zombies.

Each of these genres replicates a form of anxiety identified in the last chapter. The zombie is machinelike, the signature of a complete code that precludes the possibility of freedom. In political films the subject must go to war against code, just as he or she must go to war against the zombie. Of course, in the political film love and freedom triumph over machine and code. The horror film does not press the narrative of freedom on to the anxiety of symbolic closure. Instead, it confronts that anxiety with irony.

Similarly, the pornographic expresses again the fear that the body cannot support a system of representation. Political films express this in the idea of an uncontrollable violence that cannot be read as sacrifice. Similarly, the pornographic body cannot be the sacrificial body. Indeed, just the opposite: the timeless, repeated sexual act is a denial of death itself. Sacrifice and pornography take diametrically opposite views of the body: one is a giving up of the body for an idea; the other is a denial that any idea can or need take on the material reality of the body.

Pornography is often accused of encouraging a form of violence.[90] In fact, our politics is a celebration of violence in the form of the sacrificial act, while pornography is a taking back of the body from the domain of sacrifice. It is a form of political heresy precisely because it denies the metaphysics of sacrifice. Horror films, too, are accused of a kind of celebration of violence. That accusation not only misses the irony of the genre but fails to see that the mutilated body has already been stripped of identity and rendered an empty signifier. In both cases we can say that the violence of our political life needs no support from horror or porn. The celebration of the foundation of the state brings sacrifice deeply into our imaginative lives, and that may be all the violence that we can stand.[91]

Conclusion

Film, Faith, and Love

In the end we watch movies for many of the same reasons people have traditionally gone to church. Before there were movies coming from Hollywood, there were itinerant preachers who would bring the community together in revival meetings to hear the good news brought from afar. Indeed, the modern movie theater resembles a church—especially those large evangelical churches with enormous parking lots. Not surprisingly, there is a convergence of aspects of the "entertainment" industry across faith and film. Both combine text, image, and music in a spectacle. Today, we even have drive-in churches. Arguably, the calendar of the saints has been replaced by the calendar of the movie industry, from summer blockbusters to Oscar season. If we expand our view of film to include television, we find that media has organized the weekly calendar just as the church once did.

Technology has made the physical space in which we accomplish our collective imagining less important. This is true not just of film, in which much of our collective experience now occurs in what are called "home theaters," but also of the practice of faith. The cable channels are full of evangelical preachers and even the Catholic Church has a regular broadcast. This is even more true of that third form of modern, collective imagining that has a place alongside church and theater: sports. Here, too, we find an organization of the calendar around our engagement with an organized spectacle; here, too, we move easily between the actual stadium and the televised viewing of the event. Indeed, at the modern stadium we are likely to find ourselves viewing a large screen projection of what is happening right in front of us.

It is a commonplace that sports competitions increasingly serve as a locus of sovereign identity. This is most evident at moments of international competition. The obscure Olympic sport that we only learn of once every four years, but suddenly embrace for the sake of our national team, stands in the place once held by the small war. The sustained competitions, particularly in soccer, stand in place of the endless wars of European balance of power politics. These national sports competitions trace their modern origins to the same sites and forums that produced national armies—both experienced the great democratization of the late nineteenth and twentieth centuries. The importance of national identity in these sports competitions is assumed: we don't often find citizens favoring some other nation's team over their own. Here, citizenship continues to matter.

Church, sports, and cinema all have the odd character of the public-private. In our legal imagination they are squarely within the private order. In our social imagination, however, these are among the most public activities in which we engage. Together, they are largely constitutive of an American civil society. They are social practices outside of the domains of politics and markets—although all three are deeply connected with business and politics. If we take politics in its broadest sense as the construction of a community that expresses a set of values, that sustains a particular narrative of itself, and that reproduces itself over time, then all three are at the foundation of our political life. Each helps to shape the social imaginary; each passes on the set of values, the substantive narrative, and the historical project that is the community.

All three are deeply connected to each other as well: the sports drama always has about it an air of the religious ritual, as well as a faith in divine providence. There are, of course, endless iterations of the sports movie. We learn in such films of the emptiness of the self alone, of the need to sacrifice for the team, and of the success that will come with faith, even when confronted with what seems an impossible task. These are all virtues that we want to teach our children. They are not different from the political virtues for which they are not exactly placeholders but are rather further iterations. As with the political representation of these virtues, the sports drama is also likely to shade into the familial drama, for team and polity stand in a similar relationship to the familial order of love.

The intersection of family, sports, faith, and the political were all prominently on display in the film *The Blind Side*, which is about the transformation of an impoverished and abandoned black teenager into a successful football player.[1] Homeless, he is taken into a prominent, white, Christian family, whose love transforms his life from one of sadness and loss to fullness and care. Without love he can no more be a good football player than a good citizen. Success in sports depends on success in family, and this family is a site for the practice of Christian faith and charity. There simply is no line to be drawn between family and team, any more than between family and faith. Indeed, the teenager is a failure at football until his adopted mother tells him to protect the other members of the team as if they were part of his family. All of these elements are set alongside a political message of racial harmony within a larger collective identity. Collegiate football at Old Miss becomes the center of an intergenerational, familial-political community that overcomes difference through love.[2]

It is often noted that the rest of the world forms an image of America through the films that we export. It is less often noted that this is true internally as well: we know ourselves through films. For many, the normative center of civil society is no longer church but film. For our adolescents and young adults, films are taking on the critical role of forming the social imaginary. Going to the movies is an extended rite of passage. The teenagers gathering in the lobby of the multiplex on Friday nights are the distant progeny of those earlier Americans who would gather together as a community once a week at the local church. Even for adults, watching a movie is often a way of renewing contact with the fundamental narrative structures—the archetypes—of the social imaginary. These structures are on full display in a film like *The Blind Side*, which ties together familial love, faith, and politics. Indeed, it may not be too much to say that while some of the violence of a sacrificial politics has been displaced onto the violence of football, the story of love and sacrifice remains what it has always been.

Both cinema and church require trust, for both require that we suspend disbelief. Doing so, we expose ourselves to the possibility of a dangerous disorder. In both settings we give up control. We are literally in someone else's hands. Ordinary roles no longer count. This suspension of the self is a great equalizer: we are all equal before God and screen. Neither God nor screen is bound by the laws of causality and the discoveries of science. A world of causal explanations is displaced by a world of moral narrative.

There are recurrent millennial movements that explode within communities of faith, just as there are revolutionary moments in politics. But most of the time, and for most people, the point of religion is not to destroy the ordinary but to ground it. Religious narrative offers a way of imagining the self and the community that connects to the sacred. The task is to connect the extraordinary and the ordinary, the sacred and the profane, ultimate meaning to normal affairs. What appears as the sacred and the profane to faith appears as sovereignty and law in politics. In our personal lives this distinction appears as identity and role. In each domain we face a similar problem of legitimacy: to ground the ordinary in the extraordinary. We must see through the multiple representations of the self to the truth of identity; we must see through law to sovereignty, and we must see through the profane to the sacred. This is the work of narrative, from the great myths of origins, to the national myth of the founding, to personal narratives of finding the self in and through love.

The trust that one puts in the church is the trust that the message will respect the narrative conventions. Faith is betrayed if the conventions are breached. The same is true of film.[3] In the last two chapters I argued that the conventions are aided by normalizing forms of anxiety. Even the church had a doctrine of sin; it had also to offer a theodicy. We might think of horror and porn, for example, as normalized expressions of anxiety. They rely on problematizing the relationship of representation to identity, which structures the dominant narrative form.

Of course, any particular film can set itself deliberately in opposition to the expected archetypal forms. It can do so to make the point that these are conventions that could be otherwise. Doing so, the film does not escape the paradigms; rather, it forces them on our attention. *The Hurt Locker*, which I discussed in chapter 2, is a good example of a film that deliberately violates our expectations about the social function of the soldier's heroism in order to make us confront those conventions. The same is true of *Greenberg*, a film about a forty-year-old man, recently released from a mental institution, who is house-sitting in Los Angeles for his wealthy brother.[4] The film is a romantic comedy that is neither very romantic nor very comic—just the point. Greenberg and Florence, the omnicompetent personal assistant to the brother's family, come close to falling in love. We expect them to, but they do not. He remains narcissistic, alienating, and unpleasant. There is no recovery of a true self in and through love. Instead of an authentic self, we see glimpses of a prior self—a failed rock musician. Nothing about him seems any more true than anything else. He is a problem to himself, but then so is she. She remains a rather confused twenty-something who has no idea of where she will end up or what she should do. Neither changes as a result of their encounter. They do not live "happily ever after." We are forced to wonder what the movie is about. Its narrative is, most importantly, an absence, which is the failure of the romantic comedy that we expect.

Ordinarily, a film, like a sermon, contains a moral lesson by virtue of its resolution of the problem around which its narrative is organized. We trust that the resolution will not be arbitrary, capricious, or wrong. This does not mean that endings must always be happy. Love, I have argued throughout, can lead to pain, as well as happiness. The trust we put in the film is not a naive expectation of happiness. Rather, we trust that we will come to see a morally ordered world. *Greenberg* and *The Hurt Locker* are deliberately frustrating because they don't show us the meaningful resolution we expect. Along the same lines, some horror films make a convention out of deliberately frustrating the end; they leave open the possibility of return of the seemingly defeated monster.[5]

In film it is not enough to see evil defeated by a random accident. History may be determined by accidental causes: a change in the weather, a navigational disaster, a chance meeting. Any particular person can be struck down by disease or by a speeding car. A film, however, is about reasons, not causes.[6] We trust the reasons to carry the plot and to move the characters. There are to be no "acts of God," except by a knowing god. What this god knows is what we know. A film depends, we might say, on "good fortune" but not on mere chance.[7] The world that operates in the film is one in which causes and reasons have already been aligned. Nature always cooperates; the trains always run on time. Or, when they don't, that, too, must be a matter of good fortune. There must be a reason.

No one should confuse the representations in popular films with history or reporting. Nor should these representations be confused with "honest" psychological evaluations. This would be like believing we can learn history from Bible stories. Films may be based on historical events or actual people, but they are not offering history or biography. They are doing what drama has always done: offering a moral narrative. They establish order by offering a discrete story with beginning, middle, and end. That structure is the necessary condition of a moral narrative: there must be a problem, and it is to be resolved. We learn from film how to imagine our world, for we are all constantly constructing narratives of our lives and of the communities in which we find ourselves. If we cannot, we are quite literally lost. We will not know what to do or how to think about ourselves. An explanation of causes will not tell us what to do or what to make of our past and future. As moral agents, we need reasons; to have reasons, we must have a narrative.

Films offer training in the constructive function of the social imaginary. We exercise our imaginations by trusting to the narrative construction that is the film. We are drawn in, but we are never left to our own devices. We put ourselves in the world that the film creates. We attend to the characters. There are certain questions we can ask, others we cannot. As long as we are attending to the film, we don't think of it as a financial venture. We don't think of it as a technological achievement. All of this can be said of the practice of religious faith as well. It, too, is a form of training in imaginative construction. We put ourselves in the world that faith creates and religious narrative sustains. Finally, the same can be said of political beliefs: political rhetoric is the construction of the moral narrative of the community. This is just the point: the social imaginary is working across all these fields of experience; it is working in similar ways and forms.

The trust extended upon entering the church is answered by the promise of a redemptive grace. We trust the church, and it responds with a narrative of rebirth. The same is true of film. The trust we extend to film is met by a similar narrative: no longer faith in God's grace but in the power of love. Through love we will be born again.

Faith is the internal experience of narrative completeness. Traditionally, God was the simplest expression of this need for narrative. Faith in God was faith in the power of an author to script a narrative that is whole and complete. People believe in God because they must believe that our lives have a meaning, that something more is at stake in our lives than causes in a material world. Faith moves from causes to reasons, from laws of behavior to free actions. Reasons are sources of persuasion to a free subject. Thus, the Old Testament shows us the patriarchs arguing with God. Why not? God is a free subject who must, therefore, be open to persuasion. Sometimes they do persuade Him.

If we believe that the world operates according to reasons, we easily imagine that they must be reasons for an agent, that is, for someone capable of acting in response to these reasons. That would be God. Faith, however, is not in need of a personal god. It is in need of narrative: a narrative is always the story of a free subject or subjects acting according to reasons. Thus, our own lives are informed by faith when we believe that we are free subjects acting for reasons that constitute the narrative arc of our lives. The same is true of the nation as a historical subject capable of acting for reasons: that nation only exists as the object of the imagination, and it will continue to exist only as long as we sustain a faith in it—no longer faith in God but faith in the popular sovereign. Here, too, we find a free subject capable of acting for reasons.

One of the deepest lessons that our contemporary evangelical atheists refuse to learn is that the choice for God is never the conclusion of an argument. It is not a subject of proof. Most important, it is not defeated by a counterproof. There is no logic to the sacred. There is only faith and the failure of faith. Without faith we will not lack for explanations of experience: science investigates the causes of our actions and beliefs. Causes, however, are not reasons. The law of gravity is not a reason for, but a cause of, movement. It is true or false; it is not to be given weight as an element of a persuasive argument. It is, rather, to be discovered in its actual operation. An explanation that refers to causes operates without any moment of decision and thus without any regard for freedom. When we act for a reason, we have been persuaded.

A reason is, in this sense, always the product of an argument—although not necessarily of a demonstration. Accordingly, reasons always have reasons: they are embedded in arguments.

We can no more understand the relationship between causes and reasons, body and soul, than could Kant. We cross the divide between the two of them through an act of faith. In the absence of faith we stand before a thought that is simply unacceptable: that there is nothing but causes, which simply recede into an infinite past and continue into an indefinite future. We appear and we disappear in the endless chain of causes. Human history, including each of us, is nothing more than a set of points in this chain of events. No one can actually think this thought without experiencing a kind of existential revulsion. People cannot be indifferent to those they love or to their own life as a project that has value, nor can they think that they lack free agency. Everyone believes that there are choices to be made and that his or her life constitutes the narrative in which those choices make sense—or fail to make sense. As long as causes alone govern the world, there is only darkness over the deep. The world begins with a free act of narrative: a performative utterance. Our beginning is in the word. There we find the origin of faith. As I have argued throughout, faith moves us from representation to identity. Identity, whether of self or nation, is always a matter of ultimate value.

Faith is not, as some Enlightenment figures thought, a failure of freedom.[8] It is, rather, the condition of freedom. Without faith we would be bound by causes. To think that science will eliminate faith is like thinking that nonfiction will defeat fiction. The products of the social imaginary are all fictions; they do not show up in a scientific account. But these fictions are matters for which we live and die. We have no other world than that which we imagine. We cannot choose to live in the world of causes revealed in the laboratory. At the end of the day we go home to family, friends, and community. We leave the lab and find ourselves living within multiple narratives. We go to the movies. There even the scientist suspends disbelief.

For the Christian imagination, faith is met by grace. Identity is constituted not by the free choice alone but by the union of that free act with the sacred. One does not save oneself but comes to grace through the free act of confession. This is one way of affirming an experience of ultimate meaning that is not merely subjective. Grace comes from without. We affirm the world at the same time that we affirm ourselves. When I speak of love, sovereignty, or identity, I am always pointing to an experience of ultimate meaning *of the world*. These are the contemporary forms of grace. From these sources we build contemporary narratives of a free subject acting in a world of transcendent value. Here we find the grounds of a sacrifice that creates and sustains a world.

While the idea of grace may no longer be useful for many people, I have tried to show throughout this book that love has stepped into its place. If we think of film as the modern counterpart to the sermon, then, across various genres films offer endless sermons on love. Love, too, requires faith; and love, too, affirms the freedom of the subject. The pattern of confession met by grace remains. Strip away all roles, propositions, and judgments—the moment of confession—and we find the comfort of an inexplicable, because uncaused, love. We must free ourselves of the ordinary; we must turn to the exceptional space of identity, for there alone will we be met by love. Love always has an element of "at first sight" because it has no cause. Just as with grace, it comes as if from nowhere. What else would we expect from a Judeo-Christian culture that has entrusted the social imaginary to the cinema?

Each of the last two chapters took up one of the two dominant themes of our social imaginary. Chapter 4 looked at films through the Old Testament idea of sacrifice; chapter 5 looked at film through the New Testament idea of rebirth. Isaac and Jesus are the deep figures at work here. The story of Isaac is that of sacrifice founding nationhood; that of Jesus is the familial drama of innocence and rebirth. Of course, these stories merge at multiple points, which is exactly what we saw in film as well. We cannot easily separate the imagination of politics from that of family—although the reverse proposition is not true. We can imagine the innocence of family apart from the political. This is just another way of saying that we can imagine ourselves without politics but not without family.

There are deeply conservative religious groups in this country that fear film as a force that would contaminate their children with the germ of secular humanism. Whether films are capable of undermining their fundamentalism, I don't know. It is, however, certainly a mistake to think that films are out of line with the deeply Judeo-Christian nature of our social imaginary. The narratives we find in film are the contemporary forms of the same narratives that have sustained the West for millennia. We find family and state, love and sacrifice, innocence and renewal. We find the call to faith as a call to identity over representation. Of course, we also find films expressing anxiety with respect to these narratives, but doubt is hardly a modern invention. The roots of the social imaginary are as deep as the West itself.

The point of popular films is certainly not to encourage rebellion against these traditional values. Neither, however, is the point to encourage a kind of conservative quietism. Films are not efforts to repress revolution through the construction of false consciousness. Rather, they are efforts to remind and to recall. The reminder is of the promise of faith; the recall is the memory of love. Of course, one might think that this entire imaginary construction is a matter of false consciousness. That is an argument to be made, but come the revolution there will be bigger game to hunt than what is playing at the local cinema.

I want to conclude by speaking of *Avatar*, the most financially successful movie ever. It tells us a good deal about the operation of faith in film. The scene is a planet light years away. The planet possesses a mineral with unique properties that make it enormously valuable back on Earth. The planet is home, however, to a hominoid-like species. They form communities rich in traditions, including religion. Their world is full of natural—and spiritual—wonders with which they live in deep respect and harmony. This is the setting for a contemporary retelling of what is essentially the story of European exploitation of the New World. It is not about gold or Native Americans, but it is the same story of a crossing of political power and economic exploitation, of a turn to brute force in support of crass economic ends, of a willingness to commit genocide, and of the careless destruction of a marvelous nature and ancient tradition. When the natives won't cooperate, they are to be destroyed. Resistance, they are to be made to believe, is useless.

One interesting difference with the earlier story of colonial exploitation is that science has now taken the place of the church. The Spanish colonial apparatus of exploitation had the ideological cover of a religious mission to convert the savages. The church legitimated the colonizers. One of the ways in which it did this was by expressing concern for the indigenous peoples. Different priests and missionaries took different positions along a continuum that extended from justifying slavery to seeing the natives as innocent and thus closer to God than the Europeans. At the extreme some missionaries reversed the colonial order, believing that the Europeans were evil and should learn the ways of true faith from the indigenous peoples.[9] The New World, in this view, could save the Europeans from the sins of the Old. Needless to say, this was not the prevailing view.

In *Avatar* there is no formal religious presence among the humans: only force, economics, technology, and science. Money and technology have created a kind of political order, although it seems to be a privatized order run by corporate interests. The armed forces appear to be largely ex-military personnel, who are now operating as private contractors. There is a hierarchy of leadership that wields the instrumentalities of coercive force. Like every government, it is striving for a monopoly on legitimate coercion. In place of priests, however, there are now scientists. Just as the pope once legitimized the colonial efforts of the Spanish and Portuguese in the name of spreading Christianity to those who would otherwise be lost to sin, the relationship of exploitation and care is replicated by the scientists of the future. The whole of the mining and colonial enterprise requires an unimaginably sophisticated science. Technical knowledge has replaced religious knowledge as the ground of power. Yet the scientists we see are trying to extend to the indigenous the benefits of their knowledge. They are writing books and building schools, while the mining company is killing and destroying. We again have the threat of genocide coupled with an ethics of concern.

The scientists are not just technological enablers but also instruments of legitimation precisely because they care for the natives. The corporate interests understand that peaceful exploitation is easier and cheaper than genocidal destruction. But if the scientists cannot accomplish the former, the soldiers will accomplish the latter. The clock is ticking as the movie begins, for some sort of low-scale war is already being waged between the corporation and the natives. Unable to pacify the natives, the scientists are, for the most part, peripheral to the conflict. They are ignored by the company interests: they are suspected by the indigenous people.

The scientists turn out to be no better at protecting the native population than the priests were in the Americas. Like the church, the scientists unleash forces that they do not control. Indeed, they cannot even save themselves when they stand in opposition to the ends of exploitation. They cannot save themselves because they are caught in between: they reject the corporate ethos of exploitation, but they do not really identify with the natives. The indigenous communities are their objects of study; the scientists want to help them, not become them. Like the church in the Americas, the scientists recognize a hierarchy of knowledge and civilization. They are on a "mission." This idea is perfectly expressed in the avatar that the scientist occupies: it has the body of the indigenous but the mind (soul) of the scientist. It allows the scientist to be an observer but does not allow him to "go native"—the great fear on any frontier.[10]

In the Americas the indigenous peoples had nothing with which to defend against steel and powder, let alone against disease and alcohol. In *Avatar* they are shooting arrows at massive machines of destruction. They can dream of freedom, of a return to a preinvasion time, but they are primitives fighting an advanced technology. *Avatar* replicates this sorry history in what we might call a form of neo-neocolonialism. The patterns are all the same, along with the assumption that the indigenous cannot save themselves. They do not have the power to defeat the invader absent the leadership of the foreigner turned native. They must be saved not just by an outsider but by one who betrays his own people. Of course, it is only love that can cross this divide—not the love of God that the missionaries had but the love by which two people become one. The heroic transformation is a giving up of one world for another: that giving up and taking on is the action of sacrifice for love.

The structure of *Avatar*'s narrative is entirely ordinary: not politics, economics, science, or violence, but love is the foundation on which the world must rest. The striking feature of the movie is not the story but the visual effects of the distant planet and the creative device used to transit from one world to another: the avatar. It is made from the crossing of the DNA of a human and of a native from the planet. This makes the avatar capable of living on the planet without the technical assistance ordinarily needed by humans. It is, however, body without mind. The avatar is only complete—body and soul—when it is "occupied" by the mind of the person from whose DNA it arose. That "mind link" is accomplished through entering what looks like a high-tech casket. To enter the avatar is to enter a sort of dreamworld of wonders, of incredible beauty, and ultimately of a kind of intelligence. The scientist ordinarily awakes, however, back inside the protected space of the colony.

Despite the avatars the scientists have not been successful, for what they offer is not needed in this world. They are needed only by the exploiters. Things change only when an ordinary person—a paraplegic veteran—finds himself, by virtue of the accidental death of his scientist twin brother, cast into the role of avatar. Without the burdens of science, and without the interests of corporate gain, he is innocent. Immediately, he falls in love with the daughter of the native leader. He "goes native." The story is as old as our own endless reworking of the story of Pocahontas. Together, they create their own army, which defeats the corporation. The film ends with its own story of death and rebirth as he becomes permanently the avatar he previously could only occupy with the help of the machine. He is freed of his broken body and born again, made whole through love.[11]

This beautiful planet of strange and wondrous creatures offers more than a replication of colonial affairs. It is an image of the world created by film. The process of entering the high tech casket parallels the process of entering the theater: we are reborn into the spectacular world of the film. We, too, must enter a closed box; we, too, must work the "mind link" that puts us in the world of the film; we, too, rely on a technology that we don't understand; and we, too, trust that it will only be temporary. We, like the occupants of the avatars, must give up our limited, broken bodies of this world and come into the truth and beauty of the film world. We must trust those who create the film, just as they must trust the technicians of the avatar. The question for us, as it is in the film, is whether we enter as scientist-observers or as potential converts open to rebirth.

In the film Sully, the veteran turned avatar, must decide where his identity lies: is he the paraplegic in the box or the avatar in this new world? Science and technology will not answer this question for him. They make it possible for him to move back and forth between worlds, but which world has the better claim? The film answers that love is the foundation of the world. Where we are claimed by love, we find the truth of the self. He must die to live. This resurrection requires faith that through love he will be saved. The two-become-one of the avatar—a technological achievement—must be transcended by the two-become-one of love. The avatar had always been a kind of projected image—a representation—of the self. Love moves from representation to identity. Love makes us whole.

Dying to one world and being reborn in another is the archetype of Christian faith. Christ says, "He who believes in me shall never die." For us the power of these words has shifted to love. Love, no less than grace, requires faith. Sully takes the step to rebirth only through a leap of faith: he cannot be sure if the result will be death or renewal. This is the fundamental message of countless films: we must have faith that love will save us. Through faith there will be rebirth in a marvelous world—the world that love creates. This is a world that is infused with an ultimate meaning that is not captured by technology and that lies beyond economics, politics, or interests.

In working this theme the director James Cameron is returning directly to the themes of *Titanic*—his film of a decade earlier that had previously been the all-time leader in gross revenue.[12] There, the themes of technology, corporate imperialism, love, and identity were played out across a difference of class rather than species. There, the gender roles were reversed: the woman had to cross classes, while the man taught the lesson of the simpler virtues of love. He sacrifices himself for her as the ship goes down, but she is reborn into this world founded on love. She leads the life he opened for her, giving up forever her previous class position. There, too, Cameron uses a framing device that draws our attention to the experience of film as film. The story of love on the *Titanic* is told by the woman at its center. She is now an old woman narrating the story to a group of scientists exploring the wreckage of the ship. They must trust her, just as we must trust the film.

A faith founded in love, not grace, shifts our attention from theodicy to contingency. The Christian faithful unavoidably confronted the question of why God allowed suffering into his creation. Could we sustain faith in the face of that suffering?[13] Today it is not suffering but contingency that threatens to undermine the possibility of meaningful narrative. In a world set free of God, contingency threatens to invade every dimension of our lives, beginning with the question of how we got here and ending with that of where we are going. The answer to the first question seems to be "by chance" and to the second, "nowhere." Can we have faith under these postmodern conditions of disbelief?

A world created by God may be a mystery, but it is not contingent. It may stand under the threat of destruction, but whether it survives or not is posed as a moral issue: does humanity deserve to survive? Today, when we speak of contingency, we mean just the opposite: what happens is a matter of moral indifference. There is no plan, no progress, no judgment. The only explanation for where we are is chance; the only thing we know with certainty about the future is that it is wholly indifferent to human reasons, cares, and hopes. Like the dinosaurs, we are at the mercy of chance events.

The normative crisis of contingency is a product of a scientific attitude that equates causal explanation with understanding. A contingent event is not uncaused; rather, it happens without regard to reasons. When we describe something as contingent, we are acknowledging that it is the product of causes too numerous to ground an account, too diffuse for prediction, and too obscure to control for the sake of our own narratives. We simply don't know what will happen because too much is happening at once. The more we learn of causes, the smaller the domain of contingency. Contingency marks the boundaries of our grasp of causes. An example is predicting the weather. There was a time when it seemed a matter of contingency whether it rained or not. As we get better at predicting the weather, it seems more a matter of cause than chance. Yet weather predictions still come with probabilities attached.

That contingency and necessity are bound together was precisely the threat to the religious imagination represented by Darwin. The evolution of species is simultaneously wholly determined by natural causes and wholly contingent. That humans exist is a purely contingent matter, having nothing to do with creation in the image of God. How we came to be is a problem for science. It will be answered by tracing a series of causal links at multiple levels, from the cellular to the environmental. This relationship of contingency to necessity is true of any accident: the car crash is entirely contingent and entirely caused.

An entirely determined world and an entirely contingent world come to the same thing from the perspective of human action. A human world is one that rests on narrative, and narrative cannot operate in a world determined by causes. Contingency and causality, accordingly, represent the same threat to the imagination. In neither can the free subject take responsibility for his or her actions; in neither can he or she imagine being claimed by an ultimate meaning. In neither can we distinguish between representation and identity.

In philosophy the problem of morality has long been linked to the problem of causality: how can we be free actors making morally significant choices if we are fully determined in our behavior? Posing the problem, instead, as one of contingency shifts the felt threat from the moral to the erotic imagination: How can I think of myself as finding an ultimate meaning in and through love, when the object of my love appears to be entirely contingent? We fall in love with those whom we happen to meet, and those meetings are the product of random events or of actions taken for completely different purposes. Can we recognize contingency and find ultimate meaning in the same events?

Just as causal determinism is met by the moral imagination, contingency is met by the aesthetic imagination, which today includes film. In films questions of free will and moral choice tend to be linked to the dominant theme of responding to the problem of contingency through love.[14] The most recent of the *Terminator* series, *Terminator Salvation*, shows us this movement from the moral problem to the erotic problem, from free will to sacrifice.

Like its predecessors in the series, this film continues the war between machines and persons. The new character introduced here is not the machine that protects humans—as in *Terminator 2*—but a character who thinks he is human but is actually a combination of the human and the machine. He, too, is a kind of avatar. How he got that way matters less than the fact that his course of action, which is seemingly taken to protect the beleaguered human community, has actually been programmed—that is, it is a function of causes, not reasons. The program's real purpose is to trap those whom he thinks he is aiding. What appear to be free choices have actually been aspects of an elaborate deception, not by him but by those who "made" him. If he does not know what he is "really" doing, do any of us? That would be the moral message—free will is an illusion—but the film cannot stop there. Instead, it has to move from the moral to the erotic. He proves himself free—and thus human—by sacrificing himself for the thoroughly human leader. He gives up his human heart in a transplant operation to save the suffering leader. Here love defeats necessity and contingency. His resurrection is complete only at the moment of sacrifice. Through that death he gains the truth of himself. Thus, love founds identity. Faith is an entirely human quality that cannot be programmed, for it rests on reasons, not causes.

In film we see the natural giving way to the erotic imagination—or, more precisely, to the romantic imagination. Usually, this is not linked to a failure of the moral imagination. Rather, it is tied directly to the problem of contingency. When the contingent appears necessary in the human world of reasons, we speak of "fate." *Oedipus* presents this transformation as tragedy: the chance encounter with his unknown father on the road was Oedipus's fate; it was constitutive of his identity. For us this transformation of chance into fate is more likely to produce comedy. This, too, has an ancient root: Aristophanes's speech in Plato's *Symposium*.

Aristophanes tells us that long ago people were circular, possessing a double complement of all the body parts they have now. All were complete in themselves. In that state of autonomous self-fulfillment they challenged the gods. In response to their hubris the gods split them in two, leaving each person desperately searching for his or her other half. Thus, we are each of us only half of a whole. We long to find our other half. If and when we do, we say we are in love. Love is that state in which we want only to be joined with the beloved forever and so return to that state of completeness that is the two-become-one. In this state of identity we have no needs and speak no words. We can forgo entirely the world constructed in and through representation. Lovers need no one else. They have no regard for roles because they have found their true identity. Their lives look to others like a kind of death, for they have died to their former, incomplete selves and been reborn in and through each other.

Aristophanes's myth captures the existential loneliness of the individual, on the one hand, and the world-creating power of love, on the other. Looking back across the millennia, we can see in it the movement from contingency to necessity. Memory—we remember our prior state of wholeness—is a metaphor for an existential necessity. Thus, the myth tells us that our other half exists. She or he is out there to be found in just the same way that I am here. We are two halves of what was a whole, and our loneliness is a longing for the other. Thus, love converts the apparently contingent—a chance meeting—into the deepest necessity. The story we tell of "falling in love" always carries this burden of converting contingency into necessity. We must have the faith that our other half exists, if we are even to imagine the possibility of love. Absent that faith, we may form relationships, but we will not found the new world of the two-become-one.

Aristophanes's myth may be the earliest expression of the archetype of the necessity of love that we discover in countless films. Love is not a matter of beauty, wealth, or power. It is not the conclusion of an argument or a lesson learned. In film love seizes the characters as a result of utterly contingent events. In *Titanic* Jack wins a ticket for the Atlantic passage in a game of cards; in *Avatar* Jake Sully takes on the role of avatar after his brother's accidental death. In neither case was there any planning. In neither case was the object of their love waiting for them. Rather, they were living their own lives, with their own plans. The meeting is always by chance. We cannot choose love. We must have faith that love will find us and that once found, we will be reborn. We are possessed as if by grace.

Contingency become existential necessity is the lesson of the movies. The world that films show us is one in which the two halves of Aristophanes's circle-people find each other. This is the reward of our trust in film, but it is also the formation of the social imaginary that we take with us as we leave the theater. In a contingent world we must have faith in love. Kant asks, after his inquiries into what we can know and what we must do, "For what can we hope?" Our answer is that we can hope for love.

Theaters are not centers of didactic indoctrination. They are rather dreamworlds of narrative. We put our trust in the movies, and we trust our children to the movies. Doing so, we see and hear repeated once again that which we must believe. *Avatar* and *Titanic* were both directed at a young audience, although both were deeply attractive to that audience's parents as well. As long as we trust ourselves to film, our faith will be met by love. Contingency is banished; reasons replace causes; and narrative organizes our world.

NOTES

1. PHILOSOPHY, DEMOCRACY, AND THE TURN TO FILM

1. These complaints have a very long history. Socrates was ridiculed by Aristophanes; see "Aristophanes' *Clouds*," in Plato and Aristophanes, *Four Texts on Socrates*, trans. Thomas G. West and Grace Starry West, rev. ed. (Ithaca, NY: Cornell University Press, 1998), 115–76. Burke charged the extremism of the French Revolution to philosophy. See Edmund Burke, *Reflections on the Revolution in France*, ed. L. G. Mitchell (Oxford: Oxford University Press, 2009).

2. Rousseau speaks of a need for the legislator "to persuade without convincing" (Jean-Jacques Rousseau, *On the Social Contract, with Geneva Manuscript and Political Economy*, ed. Roger D. Masters, trans. Judith R. Masters [New York: St. Martin's, 1978], 69). Philosophy, he thinks, convinces through logic and proof, while what moves citizens is rhetoric and examples. I am suggesting that philosophy, too, must take up a task of persuasion without proof.

3. *The Artist*, directed by Michel Hazanavicius (2011; Culver City, CA: Sony Pictures Home Entertainment, 2012), DVD.

4. It recalls the genre in using black-and-white cinematography as well.

5. The suggestion that isolation, whether literal or figurative, is equivalent to nonbeing shows up in many films, including the classics *Casablanca*, directed

by Michael Curtiz (1942; Burbank, CA: Warner Home Video, 2010), DVD; and *Citizen Kane*, directed by Orson Welles (1941; Burbank, CA: Warner Home Video, 2011), DVD.

6. Many dystopian films highlight the oppressive emptiness of a social world unmoored from the possibility of love. See, e.g., *The Matrix*, directed by Andy Wachowski and Larry Wachowski (1999; Burbank, CA: Warner Home Video, 2007), DVD; *Blade Runner*, directed by Ridley Scott (1982; Burbank, CA: Warner Home Video, 1997), DVD; and *THX 1138*, directed by George Lucas (1971; Burbank, CA: Warner Home Video, 2004), DVD. In each, social hope is restored when the possibility of love is recovered.

7. Many people today think the same of the relationship of religion to politics. For an expression of this sort of judgment see Mark Lilla, *The Stillborn God: Religion, Politics, and the Modern West* (New York: Vintage, 2007).

8. See Robert Post, "Meiklejohn's Mistake: Individual Autonomy and the Reform of Public Discourse," 64 *University of Colorado Law Review* 1109 (1993).

9. This was the idea behind the Supreme Court's decision in *Rosenberger v. Rector and Visitors of the Univ. of Va.*, 515 U.S. 819, 839 (1995), which held that the school could not distinguish between religious and secular student publications for purposes of financial support.

10. One sees a literal embodiment of the homogenization effected by our practice of free speech when philosophy, religion, and the occult appear on the same shelf in the bookstore. You read Plato, I read L. Ron Hubbard: what is the difference in a democratic society?

11. This is the view behind the protection of corporate political speech in *Citizens United v. FEC*, 558 U.S. 50 (2010).

12. Justice Holmes, dissenting in *Abrams v. United States*, 250 U.S. 616, 630 (1919), provided the classic expression of this view: "the best test of truth is the power of the thought to get itself accepted in the competition of the market."

13. Cass Sunstein began a lively debate on this point in *Republic.com 2.0* (Princeton, NJ: Princeton University Press, 2009).

14. See, e.g., Jack Balkin, "Digital Speech and Democratic Culture: A Theory of Freedom of Expression for the Information Society," 79 *New York University Law Review* 1 (2004); and Thomas Emerson, *The System of Freedom of Expression* (New York: Random House, 1970).

15. Isaiah Berlin famously described two competing ideas of liberty: freedom from external constraints versus freedom as the realization of the truth of the self. See Isaiah Berlin, "Two Concepts of Liberty," in *Liberty: Incorporating Four Essays on Liberty*, ed. Henry Hardy (Oxford: Oxford University Press, 1969), 166–217. Philosophy as a practice of critical deliberation offers a third

idea in which both the external and internal concepts of freedom are subject to the same process of analysis and critique.

16. I am not alone in exploring a contemporary, democratic role for philosophy. Perhaps the most prominent recent effort has been the series "The Stone," in the *New York Times*, in which philosophers speak to contemporary issues: http://opinionator.blogs.nytimes.com/category/the-stone (accessed Sept. 20, 2012).

17. See Alexander Bickel, *The Least Dangerous Branch: The Supreme Court at the Bar of Politics* (New Haven, CT: Yale University Press, 1986); Charles Black, *Structure and Relationship in Constitutional Law* (1969; repr., Woodbridge, CT: Ox Bow Press, 2000).

18. See Thomas Kuhn, *The Structure of Scientific Revolutions* (1962; repr., Chicago: University of Chicago Press, 1996).

19. See John Rawls, *A Theory of Justice* (1971; repr., Cambridge, MA: Belknap, 2005). For Rawls, schemes of unequal distribution are to be measured by the "maximin" principle, under which the basic rules of society should generally be arranged so that inequalities they produce are "of the greatest benefit to the least-advantaged" members of society (302).

20. See Jürgen Habermas, *Moral Consciousness and Communicative Action*, trans. Christian Lenhardt and Shierry Weber Nicholsen (1990; repr., Cambridge, MA: MIT Press, 1999).

21. As of 2007 the top 1 percent of households owned 34.6 percent of all privately held wealth in the United States. As I write this, the Murdoch press scandal is unfolding in the United Kingdom. See Edward N. Wolff, "Recent Trends in Household Wealth in the United States: Rising Debt and the Middle-Class Squeeze—an Update to 2007" (working paper, Levy Economics Institute of Bard College, 2010), 44.

22. For a classic, conservative expression of this view see Michael Oakeshott, "Political Education," in *Rationalism in Politics and Other Essays* (1962; repr., Indianapolis, IN: Liberty Fund, 1991), 43–69. For a similar view from the left see Michael Walzer, *Spheres of Justice* (New York: Basic Books, 1983).

23. Michael Walzer describes a liberalism of individual rights being "chosen" as an expression of a community's values. See Michael Walzer, "Comment," in Charles Taylor, *Multiculturalism: Examining the Politics of Recognition*, ed. Amy Gutman (Princeton, NJ: Princeton University Press, 1994), 99–104.

24. See Paul Kahn, *Law and Love: The Trials of King Lear* (New Haven, CT: Yale University Press, 2000).

25. Plato and Aristotle took different positions on the role of reason and character in producing virtue.

26. On the idea of the social imaginary see Charles Taylor, *Modern Social Imaginaries* (Durham, NC: Duke University Press, 2003).

27. Clifford Geertz, *The Interpretation of Cultures* (New York: Basic Books, 1977), 5.

28. I don't mean to suggest that science has a uniquely privileged way of knowing. There is no need for me to take up the problem of the nature of scientific knowledge here. See, generally, Kuhn, *Structure of Scientific Revolutions*; Wilfrid Sellars, "Philosophy and the Scientific Image of Man," in *Frontiers of Science and Philosophy*, ed. Robert Colodny (Pittsburgh, PA: University of Pittsburgh Press, 1962), 35–78; and Richard Rorty, *Philosophy and the Mirror of Nature* (Princeton, NJ: Princeton University Press, 1979).

29. The same point can be made with respect to the corporation. Oliver Williamson explains the incompleteness of neoclassical economics in *The Economic Institutions of Capitalism* (New York: Free Press, 1985). He looks at the internal mechanisms of the private institutions that make up the market (New Institutional Economics, or NIE).

30. One of the best-known efforts to rationalize language is the invention of Esperanto. Utopian schemes for reorganizing family, particularly child rearing, go back to Plato's *Republic*—none have succeeded.

31. On interpretation see chapter 3 infra.

32. The existentialists expressed this idea in the phrase "existence precedes essence." See Jean-Paul Sartre, "Existentialism Is a Humanism," in *Existentialism from Dostoevsky to Sartre*, ed. Walter Kaufmann (1956; repr., New York: Penguin, 1975), 345–68.

33. The scholar's insistence that history meet the standard of a science will push inquiry in this direction. The French Annales school attacked the role of narrative in historical accounts on just this ground.

34. On reasons versus causes see chapter 2 infra.

35. This connection of postmodern inquiry to fiction has been emphasized by Foucault and Geertz, among others. See Paul W. Kahn, *The Cultural Study of Law: Reconstructing Legal Scholarship* (Chicago: University of Chicago Press, 1999), 39.

36. This description of philosophy—its contributions and its limits—resonates with Max Weber's inquiry in "Science as a Vocation," in *From Max Weber: Essays in Sociology*, ed. and trans. H. H. Gerth and C. Wright Mills (Oxford: Oxford University Press, 1946), 129–58. Weber, too, is skeptical about the effort to link philosophy to practice, in part because of the pluralism of ultimate values that compete with reason. He, too, offers a defense of philosophy that rests on its critical function in relation to something very like the social imaginary: "[Philosophy] can force the individual . . . to give an account of the ultimate

meaning of his own conduct. [The teacher] fulfills the duty of bringing about self-clarification and a sense of responsibility" (152).

37. See Leo Braudy, *The World in a Frame: What We See in Films* (New York: Doubleday, 1976), 180: "Allowing us to know the way we see and have seen ourselves has been one of the great contributions of films to culture."

38. For additional information on the sources in this chapter see "Bibliography: Essays on Sources."

2. FREEDOM AND PERSUASION

1. For just such an inquiry into the relationship of a free politics to free thought see Paul W. Kahn, *Political Theology: Four New Chapters on the Concept of Sovereignty* (New York: Columbia University Press, 2011).

2. This proposition begins to break down at the extremes: quantum mechanics and cosmology. Some have sought to use this indeterminacy to understand the possibility of divine, creative intervention in a causally determined world. See John Polkinghorne, *Belief in God in an Age of Science* (New Haven, CT: Yale University Press, 1998).

3. There is a corresponding theological puzzle: is God's omniscience compatible with his omnipotence?

4. This distinction of reasons from causes goes back at least to G. E. M. Anscombe, *Intention* (1957; repr., Cambridge, MA: Harvard University Press, 2000), 23–24: "Roughly speaking . . . the more the action is described as a mere response, the more inclined one would be to use the word 'cause'; while the more it is described as a response to something as *having a significance* that is dwelt on by the agent in his account, or as a response surrounded with thoughts and questions, the more inclined one would be to use the word 'reason'" (emphasis in original). Reasons for Anscombe are generally answers to the question "why," and acts based on such reasons are "intentional."

5. Immanuel Kant, *Groundwork of the Metaphysics of Morals*, trans. H. J. Paton (New York: Harper and Row, 1964).

6. See Karsten Harries, *Infinity and Perspective* (Cambridge, MA: MIT Press, 2001).

7. Gillespie explores the scholastic origins of this idea of God, as well as the challenges posed to it by the rise of nominalism. See Michael Gillespie, *The Theological Origins of Modernity* (Chicago: University of Chicago Press, 2008).

8. See John Rawls, *A Theory of Justice* (Cambridge, MA: Harvard University Press, 1971).

9. Wittgenstein puzzles over something similar when he imagines the child who fails to understand what it is to follow a formal sequence of numbers

generated by a rule. See Ludwig Wittgenstein, *Philosophical Investigations*, ed. P. M. S. Hacker and Joachim Schulte, trans. G. E. M. Anscombe (Oxford: Wiley-Blackwell, 2009), 80–81.

10. Here one should also consider Islam, which literally means "submission."

11. Dissatisfaction with the idea of a God so bound to reason as to lack all particularity was one aspect of the nominalist reaction to the scholastics. We can think of this as a turn from a God of reason to one of will. On the Augustinian roots of this conception see Diarmaid MacCulloch, *The Reformation: A History* (New York: Viking, 2003), 106.

12. All three of these points can be illustrated in terms of H. L. A. Hart's classic example of a legal rule: "No vehicles in the park." See H. L. A. Hart, "Positivism and the Separation of Law and Morals," 71 *Harvard Law Review* 593, 606–15 (1958). The rule coexists with other rules: for example, mow the grass weekly. It requires decision before it can be applied to particular cases: roller skates, a bicycle, a statue. Finally, we might acknowledge its application to an ambulance but still believe the ambulance should enter the park under some circumstances. For a recent discussion of the example see Frederick Schauer, "A Critical Guide to Vehicles in the Park," 83 *New York Law Review* 1109 (2008).

13. Important works exploring the persuasive character of factors beyond rational argument include Martha Nussbaum, *Upheavals of Thought: The Intelligence of Emotions* (Cambridge: Cambridge University Press, 2001); Eugene Garver, *For the Sake of Argument: Practical Reasoning, Character, and the Ethics of Belief* (Chicago: University of Chicago Press, 2004).

14. *The Sweet Hereafter*, directed by Atom Egoyan (1997; Los Angeles, CA: New Line Home Video, 1998), DVD.

15. "Loss without reason" is the theme of one of our oldest narratives that takes up the contrast between reasons and causes: the book of Job.

16. Another such condition is psychopathological—most vividly in amnesia but perhaps more painfully in depression.

17. Until quite recently, the continental, judicial tradition prohibited the publication of dissents in order to create the appearance that the outcome is a product of legal necessity. The moment of decision was suppressed from view, creating an image of the court as a subjectless expert in the law. See Kevin M. Stack, "The Practice of Dissent in the Supreme Court," 105 *Yale Law Journal* 2235 (1996).

18. A cell can present the geography of freedom—for example, in the practice of the religious monk who retreats from the world. The origins of the modern penitentiary are as much in penitence as in the denial of freedom. See Michel Foucault, *Discipline and Punish: The Birth of the Prison*, trans. Alan Sheridan (New York: Vintage, 1995).

19. Of course, it is entirely possible, indeed likely, that a human world of agency—of reasons and persuasion—emerges within the boundaries of the penitentiary. See Wilbert Rideau, *In the Place of Justice: A Story of Punishment and Deliverance* (New York: Random House, 2010).

20. See Judith Butler, *Giving an Account of Oneself* (New York: Fordham University Press, 2005).

21. Ricoeur captures this aspect of narrative when he writes, "The logical connection of probability cannot . . . be detached from the cultural constraints of acceptability" (Paul Ricoeur, *Time and Narrative: Volume 1*, trans. Kathleen McLaughlin and David Pellauer [Chicago: University of Chicago Press, 1984], 47).

22. The vote is another form of coercion, which is to say there are better and worse ways of bringing an argument to an end.

23. This movement back and forth between the general rule and the intuition of the normative character of the particular is what Rawls described as the process of reaching "reflective equilibrium." See Rawls, *Theory of Justice*, 180–82.

24. See Richard Rorty, *Philosophy and the Mirror of Nature* (Princeton, NJ: Princeton University Press, 1979), 362: "The utility of the 'existentialist' view is that by proclaiming we have no essence, it permits us to see the descriptions of ourselves we find in one of . . . the *Naturwissenschaften* as on par with the various alternative descriptions offered by poets, novelists, depth psychologists, sculpturists, anthropologists, and mystics."

25. Perhaps we can create a computer language or a cyber world.

26. On philosophy as continuing a conversation see Rorty, *Philosophy and the Mirror of Nature*, 319.

27. These loosely correspond to three levels identified in film theory as recording, composing, and screening. See Dudley Andrew, *What Cinema Is!* (Oxford: Wiley-Blackwell, 2010), xxv–xxvi.

28. The "auteur theory" of cinema—originally associated with the French New Wave—takes this idea to its extreme, arguing that despite the variety of forces and influences involved in film production, the director's act of free expression defines a film.

29. Because we have a spectator's, rather than a character's, perspective, we may know more than the characters as to the likely consequences of a decision. But that is no less true of those with whom we interact in ordinary life: we may see better than they, but still they must decide.

30. More recently this theme was pursued in *Incendies*, directed by Denis Villeneuve (2010; Culver City, CA: Sony Pictures Home Entertainment, 2011), Blue-ray DVD, now from the perspective of a Jocasta-like character. Here the

mother orchestrates her children's discovery that their father is the torturer/ rapist of their mother. He is also her own son and thus their half-brother.

31. *The Secret in Their Eyes*, directed by Juan José Campanella (2009; Culver City, CA: Sony Pictures Classics, 2010), DVD.

32. This idea of freedom in interpretation is just what is at stake in liberal education: students are held accountable for their interpretive essays. They are asked to consider a range of interpretive possibilities and to defend a position. The object is not to leave them with some set of knowledge claims but to make them morally responsible for their character by having them defend their interpretations of works of normative complexity. The object is to produce liberal citizens: individuals who subject their own beliefs to criticism, are open to persuasion, and are willing to engage others in a common project of self-government. See Anthony Kronman, *Education's End: Why Our Colleges and Universities Have Given Up on the Meaning of Life* (New Haven, CT: Yale University Press, 2007).

33. See Benedict Anderson, *Imagined Communities: Reflections on the Origin and Spread of Nationalism* (New York: Verso, 1983).

34. *Saving Private Ryan*, directed by Steven Spielberg (1998; Universal City, CA: DreamWorks, 1999), DVD.

35. *The Manchurian Candidate*, directed by Jonathan Demme (2004; Hollywood, CA: Paramount, 2004), DVD, is a possible exception, but the film actually has less to do with the Korean conflict than with the subsequent Cold War. The popular television show *Mash*, although located in Korea, was actually about the situation in Vietnam. See David Halberstam, *The Coldest Winter: America and the Korean War* (New York: Hyperion, 2007).

36. For a compelling exploration of the role of the western film in framing American political experience, see Robert Pippin, *Hollywood Westerns and American Myth: The Importance of Howard Hawks and John Ford for Political Philosophy* (New Haven, CT: Yale University Press, 2010).

37. Ernest Renan, "What Is a Nation?" in *Nation and Narration*, ed. Homi K. Bhabha (New York: Routledge, 1990), 11.

38. *The Hurt Locker*, directed by Kathryn Bigelow (2008; Universal City, CA: Summit Entertainment, 2010), DVD.

39. There is no single view about how a film can or should achieve narrative unity. Classic Hollywood—1910–1960—attempted to keep the visual narrative smooth, continuous, and linear. Contemporary cinema has become increasingly elliptical, less concerned with linearity and relying more on cues.

40. See Roger Leenhardt, "Cinematic Rhythm," in Richard Abel, *French Film Theory and Criticism: A History/Anthology*, 2 vols. (Princeton, NJ: Princeton University Press, 1988), 2:203: "The essence of cinema [is] *ellipsis*." An early

cinematic exploration of this theme is Jean-Luc Godard's *Breathless* (1960; New York: Criterion, 2007), DVD.

41. "The viewer's interpretation of edited sequences is largely a matter of cross-referencing possible interpretations against a broader context (i.e., the larger story in the movie itself, together with corresponding situations from real life and other movies). . . . Interpretation is driven by the narrative context, not the *code*" (Paul Messaris, *Visual Literacy: Image, Mind, and Reality* [Boulder, CO: Westview Press, 1994]; quoted in Stephen Prince, "The Discourse of Pictures: Iconicity and Film Studies," in *Film Theory and Criticism: Introductory Readings*, ed. Leo Braudy and Marshall Cohen, 6th ed. [New York: Oxford University Press, 2004], 95).

42. Pippin at one point suggests a similar concern for archetypes, although usually he prefers to speak of myth: "The film shows this in a way that continues the archetypical, representative framework suggested by many of its elements and I am interested in following the nature of that framework" (Pippin, *Hollywood Westerns and American Myth*, 9). He, too, poses this inquiry into archetype as a kind of supplement to political theory in its contemporary form, which tends to ignore issues of "political psychology."

43. Gilles Deleuze makes a similar point, referring to the function of clichés in creating and maintaining unity: "What consolidates all this . . . are the current clichés of an epoch or moment. . . . They are these floating images, these anonymous clichés, which circulate in the external world, but which also penetrate each of us and constitute the internal world. . . . " (Deleuze, "The Origin of the Crisis: Italian Neo-realism and the French New Wave," in Braudy and Cohen, *Film Theory and Criticism*, 244).

44. *Crazy Heart*, directed by Scott Cooper (2009; Los Angeles: 20th Century Fox, 2010), DVD.

45. *Elegy*, directed by Isabel Coixet (2008; Culver City, CA: Sony Pictures Home Entertainment, 2009), DVD.

46. Carl Schmitt writes of this: "the exception is more interesting than the rule. The rule proves nothing; the exception proves everything: It confirms not only the rule but also its existence which derives only from the exception" (Carl Schmitt, *Political Theology: Four Chapters on the Concept of Sovereignty*, trans. George Schwab [Cambridge, MA: MIT Press, 1985], 15).

47. In emphasizing the possibilities within an expected narrative form, my approach resembles work on "genre" in film theory and criticism. See Leo Braudy, *The World in a Frame: What We See in Films* (New York: Doubleday, 1976), 104–81. The archetypes I investigate, however, cut across traditional genres. Moreover, I have no concern with long-fought disputes over the aesthetic value of genre films as opposed to something thought to be "high art."

48. MacIntyre makes a similar point: "There is no way to give us an understanding of any society, including our own, except through the stock of stories which constitute its initial dramatic resources" (Alistair MacIntyre, *After Virtue: A Study in Moral Theory* [Notre Dame, IN: University of Notre Dame Press, 1984], 216). See also Ricoeur, *Time and Narrative*, 76 ("The received paradigms structure readers' expectations and aid them in recognizing the formal rule, the genre, or the type exemplified by the narrated story. They furnish guidelines for the encounter between a text and its readers").

49. See Moshe Halbertal, *People of the Book: Canon, Meaning, and Authority* (Cambridge, MA: Harvard University Press, 1997).

50. Speaking of Truffaut, Braudy captures this point: "Truffaut defined the genre conventions as a frame within which he was free to do as he pleased, at the same time that he could ironically reflect on the reasons the conventions existed" (Braudy, *The World in a Frame*, 165).

51. For additional information on the sources in this chapter see "Bibliography: Essays on Sources."

3. ON INTERPRETATION

1. See Richard Rorty, *Contingency, Irony, and Solidarity* (Cambridge: Cambridge University Press, 1989), 5: "The world is out there, but descriptions of the world are not. Only descriptions of the world can be true or false. The world on its own—unaided by the describing activities of humans—cannot." The language Wilfrid Sellars uses to make this distinction ties the epistemic point back to the practical point of the last chapter. He distinguishes the field of sensation from that of perception. The former is the "space of causes," the latter of "reasons" (Wilfrid Sellars, "Empiricism and the Philosophy of Mind," in *Science, Perception and Reality* [London: Routledge, 1963], 127).

2. See Ernst Cassirer, *An Essay on Man* (New Haven, CT: Yale University Press, 1944); Suzanne Langer, *Philosophy in a New Key: A Study in the Symbolism of Reason, Rite, and Art* (Cambridge, MA: Harvard University Press, 1942).

3. See chapter 2 supra on the difference between causes and reasons.

4. On the idea of the ready-to-hand and its distinction from that which is present-to-hand, see Martin Heidegger, *Being and Time*, trans. J. Macquarrie and E. Robinson (1927; repr., Oxford: Basil Blackwell, 1962), 15–16.

5. This manner of exploration of the everyday is illustrated in Bill Bryson, *At Home: A Short History of Private Life* (New York: Doubleday, 2010).

6. Alfred Hitchcock's work often explores this theme. Consider *Rear Window*, directed by Hitchcock (1954; Universal City, CA: Universal Studios Home

Entertainment, 2001), DVD, which follows a man who, convalescing from an injury, can do nothing all day but observe the city through his window. When he witnesses what he believes to be a murder, he becomes obsessed with piecing together the narrative, just as someone watching a film might be.

7. *Caché (Hidden)*, directed by Michael Haneke (2005; Culver City, CA: Sony Pictures Home Entertainment, 2006), DVD.

8. The closest we can get to a singular act of representation is naming, but even that is far from singular. When we name the child, we welcome her into the world as a member of a family, community, and nation. A proposition can be just one word long.

9. This is true socially as well. The symbolic order of language, for example, is beyond our ability deliberately to invent.

10. A variation on this idea appears in jurisprudence in Ronald Dworkin's metaphor of the "chain novel": each judge decides a case by writing "the next chapter" in this collective enterprise. See Ronald Dworkin, *Law's Empire* (London: Fontana, 1986), 239.

11. God has a similar problem. Because man has language, God's command can be reinterpreted by the Serpent.

12. See chapter 2 supra on freedom in film.

13. We saw this in the scenes of self-destruction in *The Artist*, discussed in chapter 1.

14. See Paul Ricoeur, *Interpretation Theory: Discourse and the Surplus of Meaning* (Fort Worth: Texas Christian University Press, 1976).

15. See Stanley Fish, "Fish v. Fiss," 36 *Stanford Law Review* 1325 (1984).

16. See Leo Tolstoy, "Appendix: 'A Few Words Apropos of the Book *War and Peace*,'" in *War and Peace*, trans. Richard Pevear and Larissa Volokhonsky (New York: Vintage, 2008), 1217–24.

17. See conclusion infra.

18. Technically, it is a transcendental condition of representation.

19. See Michael Gillespie, *The Theological Origins of Modernity* (Chicago: University of Chicago Press, 2008).

20. See Carl Schmitt, *Political Theology: Four Chapters on the Concept of Sovereignty* trans. George Schwab (Cambridge, MA: MIT Press, 1985), 36. The relationship of identity (identification) to representation was also central to Freud's theory of psychoanalytic development. Prelinguistic identification with an erotic object is the earliest form of relating to the world, while representation is a later development of the ego function. See Sigmund Freud, *Group Psychology and the Analysis of the Ego*, trans. James Strachey (1960; repr., New York: Norton, 1990), 46–53.

21. Winslow Homer, *The Veteran in a New Field*, oil on canvas, 61.3 cm × 96.8 cm (New York: Metropolitan Museum of Art, 1865), www.metmuseum .org/toah/works-of-art/67.187.131.

22. Abraham Lincoln, "The Gettysburg Address," in *The Collected Works of Abraham Lincoln*, ed. Roy P. Basler (New Brunswick, NJ: Rutgers University Press, 1955), 234–38.

23. The point is famously made by Jorge Luis Borges in 1939 in his short story "Pierre Menard, Author of Don Quixote," in *Ficciones*, ed. Anthony Kerrigan, trans. Anthony Bonner (New York: Grove, 1994), 45–56.

24. See Emmanuel Levinas, *Totality and Infinity: An Essay on Exteriority*, trans. Alphonse Lingis (Pittsburgh, PA: Duquesne University Press, 1969).

25. *Memento*, directed by Christopher Nolan (2000; Culver City, CA: Sony Pictures Home Entertainment, 2004), DVD.

26. In law these arguments constantly reproduce the distinction of interpretation from invention. Judges will accuse those with whom they disagree of inventing new law in the guise of interpreting existing law. Of course, the rhetorical label hardly matters: an "invention" that succeeds in gathering a majority is an "interpretation" by virtue of its authority.

27. *The Box*, directed by Richard Kelly (2009; Burbank, CA: Warner Home Video, 2010), DVD.

28. "Lacking absolute laws, filmic intelligibility nevertheless depends on a certain number of dominant habits: A film put together haphazardly would not be understood. . . . 'Cinematographic language' is first of all the literalness of a plot. Artistic effects, even when they are substantially inseparable from the semic act by which the film tells us its story, nevertheless constitute another level of signification, which from the methodological point of view must come 'later'" (Christian Metz, "Some Points in the Semiotics of the Cinema," in *Film Theory and Criticism: Introductory Readings*, ed. Leo Braudy and Marshall Cohen, 6th ed. [New York: Oxford University Press, 2004], 69).

29. *The Other Man*, directed by Richard Eyre (2008; Chatsworth, CA: Image Entertainment, 2009), DVD.

30. For additional information on the sources in this chapter see "Bibliography: Essays on Sources."

4. VIOLENCE AND THE STATE

1. Of course, in both cases injustice can become so extreme that we abandon the relationship, but to disown a child is as exceptional as to abandon one's state because of its injustice.

2. These ideas also work in their privative form: the failure of love, for example, gives us our idea of evil. I explore this concept of evil in Paul W. Kahn, *Out of Eden: Adam and Eve and the Problem of Evil* (Princeton, NJ: Princeton University Press, 2007).

3. I explore this concept of the relationship of law to sovereignty in my *Putting Liberalism in Its Place* (Princeton, NJ: Princeton University Press, 2005), 228–90; and in Paul W. Kahn, *Political Theology: Four New Chapters on the Concept of Sovereignty* (New York: Columbia University Press, 2011), 141.

4. See Carolyn Marvin and David W. Ingle, *Blood Sacrifice and the Nation: Totem Rituals and the American Flag* (Cambridge: Cambridge University Press, 1999).

5. Hannah Arendt makes a similar point about the failure of representation. See Hannah Arendt, *On Revolution* (New York: Viking, 1963), 176–78.

6. In films a frequent point of differentiation between a mob and the people is the willingness to sacrifice. For example, in *The Patriot*, directed by Roland Emmerich (2000; Culver City, CA: Sony Pictures Home Entertainment, 2000), DVD, the militia must prove itself against the skeptical British by standing firm in battle and taking losses. Mel Gibson, who plays the titular character, had played the same role of leader of a mob become the people—also against British authority—in *Braveheart*, directed by Mel Gibson (1995; Hollywood: Paramount Pictures, 2000), DVD.

7. Roberto Mangabeira Unger presents a similar view of the double nature of law as product of politics and of reason. See Roberto Mangabeira Unger, *What Should Legal Analysis Become?* (New York: Verso, 1996), 52–59.

8. See Hans Kelsen, *Pure Theory of Law*, trans. Max Knight (Clark, NJ: Lawbook Exchange, 2009); and Paul W. Kahn, *The Reign of Law: Marbury v. Madison and the Construction of America* (New Haven, CT: Yale University Press, 1997).

9. The Hague Convention governing occupied territory formalizes this relationship: an enemy occupying force is to leave the domestic law in place "as far as possible." Hague Convention (IV) Respecting the Laws and Customs of War on Land and Its Annex: Regulations Concerning the Laws and Customs of War on Land, art. 43, Oct. 18, 1907.

10. See Paul W. Kahn, *Sacred Violence: Torture, Terror, and Sovereignty* (Ann Arbor: University of Michigan Press, 2008), 21–41.

11. *Gran Torino*, directed by Clint Eastwood (2009; Burbank, CA: Warner Home Video, 2010), DVD.

12. A classic example of this point occurs in Fellini's *Amarcord*: the village children are forced to attend a yearly confession, but the church, which collaborates with the fascists, can comment on only one sin: masturbation. See *Amarcord*, directed by Federico Fellini (1973; New York: Criterion, 2006), DVD.

13. A classic example of this trope is *True Grit*, directed by Henry Hathaway (1969; Hollywood: Paramount, 2007), DVD.

14. See Marshall Sahlins, "The Stranger-King or, Elementary Forms of the Politics of Life," *Indonesia and the Malay World* 36, no. 105 (2008): 177–99.

15. Classic films of this genre include *The Man Who Shot Liberty Valance*, directed by John Ford (1962; Hollywood: Paramount, 2001), DVD; and *Shane*, directed by George Stevens (1953; Hollywood: Paramount, 2000), DVD.

16. *Taken*, directed by Pierre Morel (2008; Century City, CA: 20th Century Fox, 2009), DVD.

17. *Harry Brown*, directed by Daniel Barber (2009; Culver City, CA: Sony Pictures Home Entertainment, 2010), DVD, takes up this theme as well. Harry Brown, a long-retired British marine must kill the criminal who has become the enemy, while fending off the police who would treat him as a criminal. The theme is central to Christopher Nolan's second contribution to the Warner Bros. *Batman* franchise, *The Dark Knight* (discussed below).

18. For a somewhat quieter consideration of this theme see *In the Bedroom*, directed by Todd Field (2001; New York: Miramax, 2002), DVD. A young adult is murdered by his older lover's ex-husband. While the drama is about the parents' evolving relationship after the murder, the film ends with the father killing the son's murderer before the latter can have a trial. The enemy must be killed, not tried.

19. Success and failure in killing for the state seem equally problematic for the familial order when we compare *Taken* and *Gran Torino*. This is an old theme: killing is both sacred and polluted.

20. Among the most iconic treatments of this theme is the opening scene of *The Godfather*, directed by Francis Ford Coppola (1972; Hollywood: Paramount, 2004), DVD, when Don Corleone excoriates the man asking him for a favor because the proposition is framed as business ("murder for money") rather than "friendship."

21. Had the threat been located in the United States, there is no doubt that the family triumph would also have been a triumph for the direct recovery of the state. Instead of Liam Neeson recovering his daughter and returning home from a corrupt France, we would have Harrison Ford, playing a president, using the same skills of sacrificial violence to recover his daughter from terrorists. Less subtle, but the point is the same: the unity of the familial and the political at the foundation of the state. Here, identity and representation make contact. See *Air Force One*, directed by Wolfgang Petersen (1997; Culver City, CA: Sony Pictures Home Entertainment, 1998), DVD.

22. In *A Few Good Men*, directed by Rob Reiner (1992; Culver City, CA: Sony Pictures Home Entertainment, 2001), DVD, the dramatic confrontation

between the commanding officer and the military lawyer centers on just this point, as the former accuses the latter of a kind of willful blindness: "Son, we live in a world that has walls, and those walls have to be guarded by men with guns. . . . My existence, while grotesque and incomprehensible to you, saves lives."

23. On veterans' guilt see Kahn, *Sacred Violence*, 159–61.

24. *The Dark Knight*, directed by Christopher Nolan (2008; Burbank, CA: Warner Home Video, 2008), DVD; *Batman*, directed by Tim Burton (1989; Burbank, CA: Warner Home Video, 2009), DVD.

25. Interestingly, *The Dark Knight Rises*, released on July 20, 2012, by Warner Bros. Pictures, directed by Christopher Nolan, the sequel to *The Dark Knight* (and the third film of the trilogy), ends with a faux sacrifice. Batman appears to sacrifice himself for the sake of his new lover, and for all of Gotham, but in fact, his "sacrifice" is really an elaborate gambit. He saves the city *and* he survives to live out the rest of his days in calm luxury in Italy.

26. To force the sacrificial warrior to choose between family and state is a necessary theme, producing the figure of the tragic warrior when the choice is for the state. The extreme pathological version of this tragedy of choice is represented in *Sophie's Choice*, directed by Alan J. Pakula (1982; Santa Monica, CA: Lionsgate, 1998), DVD. In its comic form choice is for the family, but it is the quality of comedy to extend the saving act to the state as well.

27. René Girard, *The Scapegoat*, trans. Yvonne Freccero (Baltimore, MD: Johns Hopkins University Press, 1986).

28. Walter Benjamin, "Theses on the Philosophy of History," in *Illuminations: Essays and Reflections*, ed. Hannah Arendt, trans. Harry Zohn (1968; repr., New York: Schocken, 1969), 256.

29. That the first reaction to loss will always be private is a theme developed recently in *The Messenger*, directed by Oren Moverman (2009; New York: Oscilloscope Laboratories, 2010), DVD, a film following two men who have the task of informing families that a loved one has been killed in combat.

30. *Apocalypse Now*, directed by Francis Ford Coppola (1979; Hollywood: Paramount, 1999), DVD; and *Born on the Fourth of July*, directed by Oliver Stone (1989; Universal City, CA: Universal Studios, 2004), DVD.

31. *Inglourious Basterds*, directed by Quentin Tarantino (2009; Universal City, CA: Universal Studios, 2009), DVD.

32. See chapter 2 supra on the distinction of causes from reasons. Violence in *Inglourious Basterds* is about causes, not reasons.

33. For a list, by no means definitive, of film references in *Inglourious Basterds* see Clovis8, "*Inglourious Basterds*: List of Film References," *Filmspotting Forum* (blog), www.filmspotting.net/forum/index.php?topic=6410.0.

34. *Forest Gump*, directed by Robert Zemeckis (1994; Hollywood: Paramount, 2001), DVD.

35. *Zelig*, directed by Woody Allen (1983; Santa Monica, CA: MGM, 2001), DVD, also follows a protagonist who plays the role of "universal spectator" of twentieth-century history. In *Zelig*, however, the locus of meaningless violence is not Vietnam but the Holocaust.

36. In *Forrest Gump* Jane Fonda goes to North Vietnam, while the erotic community of the counterculture sets itself against domestic law. Criminal and enemy no longer structure the political imaginary.

37. *A History of Violence*, directed by David Cronenberg (2005; Los Angeles: New Line Home Video, 2006), DVD.

38. This view is associated with Hannah Arendt's distinction of power from violence. See Arendt, *On Violence* (Orlando, FL: Harcourt Brace, 1970). Today, her view is powerfully continued in Jonathan Schell, *The Unconquerable World: Power, Nonviolence, and the Will of the People* (New York: Henry Holt, 2003).

39. See Kahn, *Sacred Violence*.

40. This was all too apparent in the decision in *Kiyemba v. Obama*, in which the D.C. Circuit Court ruled that a group of Uighur men being detained at Guantanamo are entitled to habeas rights under *Boumediene v. Bush*, 553 U.S. 373 (2008), but nevertheless cannot be released. *Kiyemba* 555 F.3d 1022 (D.C. Cir. 2009).

41. Abraham Lincoln, "The Perpetuation of Our Political Institutions: Address Before the Young Men's Lyceum of Springfield, Illinois, January 27, 1838," in *Abraham Lincoln: His Speeches and Writings*, ed. Roy P. Basler (1946; repr., Cleveland, OH: Da Capo, 2001), 76–85.

42. This is the attitude toward law of aliens who happen to find themselves within a jurisdiction that is not their own. The legal code is like a puzzle: they must determine the rules, but they have no sense that their identity is at stake in the rules. They will not defend this code.

43. See chapter 2 supra.

44. See Alec Stone Sweet, "Proportionality Balancing and Global Constitutionalism," 47 *Columbia Journal of Transnational Law* 73 (2008).

45. See Felix S. Cohen, "Transcendental Nonsense and the Functional Approach," 35 *Columbia Law Review* 809 (1935).

46. *2001: A Space Odyssey*, directed by Stanley Kubrick (1968; Burbank, CA: Warner Home Video, 2011), DVD.

47. A comic version of the same theme of rebellion against representation is found in *The Truman Show*, directed by Peter Weir (1998; Hollywood: Paramount, 2005), DVD.

48. Rene Descartes, *Meditations on First Philosophy*, trans. John Cottingham (Cambridge: Cambridge University Press, 1986), 15.

49. *The Terminator*, directed by James Cameron (1984; Santa Monica, CA: MGM, 2001), DVD. The comic version of this theme is *Wall-E*, directed by Andrew Stanton (2008; Emeryville, CA: Disney/Pixar, 2008), DVD.

50. The same malleability of shape appears in the second of the *Terminator* movies. See *Terminator 2: Judgment Day*, directed by James Cameron (1991; Santa Monica, CA: Lionsgate, 2009), DVD.

51. The future of code and machine is subject to a progressive reevaluation in the series of *Terminator* movies. In the first film human must triumph over machine, the free act over the code. Indeed, man must create himself. In the second film we have a battle between machines. Freedom may have triumphed in the first, but humankind can only defeat the machine by harnessing the power of the machine to humanity's own freely assumed ends. The machine that saves the human being learns the lesson of sacrifice, destroying itself after its mission in order to save the present from the future. In the latest in the series we are left with the question of whether a machine that can operate by itself will come to have a free will. See *Terminator Salvation*, directed by McG (2009; Burbank, CA: Warner Home Video, 2009), DVD. At that point the story offers a modern myth of new beginnings: from a causal world will emerge the free person. What we cannot know is whether the free agent who transcends the code will be good or evil.

52. Representative of this view is Anne-Marie Slaughter, *A New World Order* (Princeton, NJ: Princeton University Press, 2004).

53. On the controversy over the domestic effects of human rights treaties compare Oona Hathaway, "Do Human Rights Treaties Make a Difference?" 111 *Yale Law Journal* 1935 (2002); and Beth Simmons, *Mobilizing for Human Rights: International Law in Domestic Politics* (Cambridge: Cambridge University Press, 2009).

54. Kahn, *Sacred Violence*, 56–60.

55. See Kofi Annan, "Balance State Sovereignty with Individual Sovereignty!" Opening Address of Annual Report to the United Nations General Assembly, New York City, Sept. 20, 1999.

56. For additional information on the sources in this chapter see "Bibliography: Essays on Sources."

5. LOVE, ROMANCE, AND PORNOGRAPHY

1. Thomas Hobbes, *Leviathan* (Mineola, NY: Dover, 2006), 70.

2. The better classical analogy is to Solon, who is reported to have left Athens after rewriting their laws. He did not himself exercise rule.

3. See Hobbes, *Leviathan*, 93–95.

4. On the central role of war to American history and political identity see Stanley Hauerwas, *War and the American Difference: Theological Reflections on Violence and National Identity* (Grand Rapids, MI: Baker Academic, 2011). For a longer view of war and state development see Philip Bobbitt, *The Shield of Achilles: War, Peace, and the Course of History* (New York: Vintage, 2002).

5. See David Luban, "Liberalism, Torture, and the Ticking Bomb," 91 *Virginia Law Review* 1425 (2005).

6. *Unthinkable*, directed by Gregor Jordan (2010; Culver City, CA: Sony Pictures Home Entertainment, 2010), DVD.

7. The same scene is represented in an episode of the second season of the television series *24*. See episode no. 36, first broadcast Feb. 11, 2003, on Fox, directed by Frederick King Keller and written by Evan Katz. This time, though, the terrorist chooses family over politics.

8. *The Road*, directed by John Hillcoat (2009; Culver City, CA: Sony Pictures Home Entertainment, 2010), DVD.

9. *Children of Men*, directed by Alfonso Cuarón (2006; Universal City, CA: Universal Studios, 2007), DVD, develops this theme quite explicitly. In a world where there are no more children, politics has become brutal violence. Without hope for the future, politics turns to violence against immigrants, as if friend and enemy can still matter in a world with no future. Only the reappearance of a child—the first to be born in eighteen years—can promise suspension of the violence.

10. This is the suggestion, as well, of *Eastern Promises*, directed by David Cronenberg (2007; Universal City, CA: Universal Studios, 2007), DVD. In an underworld of rampant human cruelty only an infant, not God, offers salvation.

11. Interestingly, Hobbes saw no particular significance to the conditions under which the founding act of consent is given. Consent produced by defeat is still consent. See Hobbes, *Leviathan*, 111–16.

12. That "religious aura" is personified in the figure of Bishop Desmond Tutu, who headed the South African Truth and Reconciliation Commission.

13. This can be the perspective of the documentary—for example, Michael Moore's films on health care, capitalism, and guns. See *Sicko*, directed by Michael Moore (2007; New York: Weinstein Company, 2007), DVD; *Capitalism: A Love Story*, directed by Michael Moore (2009; Beverly Hills: Starz/Anchor Bay, 2010), DVD; *Bowling for Columbine*, directed by Michael Moore (2002; Santa Monica, CA: MGM, 2003), DVD.

14. *The American President*, directed by Rob Reiner (1995; Beverly Hills: Castle Rock Entertainment, 2008), DVD.

15. This point is curiously brought to our attention in the film by an act of denial. Just after the president orders a military attack on a Libyan installation, he responds to his aides' sense of power redeemed by saying that this was "the least presidential act" he has performed. Hardly. Were he not president, this would be an act of murder.

16. The space of the connection, in the film, takes him through the Rose Garden. The figure of the rose plays a comic mediating function in the film. Can the president engage in a private act of gift giving? Not easily, for he has been removed from a market economy. If he is to give a gift, it must be figuratively "of himself." The rose he gives is not purchased but cut from his own garden.

17. Kennedy himself contributed to this narrative. See Edward M. Kennedy, *True Compass: A Memoir* (New York: Hachette, 2009).

18. Aristotle thought the polis has a priority over the family and the individual, for it is the natural end of the family. The polity is the whole, while the family is only the part. See Aristotle, *The Politics*, ed. Stephen Everson, trans. Jonathan Barnes (1996; repr., Cambridge: Cambridge University Press, 2002), 16–29.

19. See Paul W. Kahn, *Putting Liberalism in Its Place* (Princeton, NJ: Princeton University Press, 2005), 183–227.

20. Robert Pippin's analysis of the mythology of westerns takes him to a similar point: "The *psychological* reality of political life turns out to be bonds not themselves political but private and romantic, only indirectly and secondarily political. They are crucial to political life, but our stake in a political fate is not only mediated and motivated by such affective bonds, it is wholly dependent on and fueled by them" (Robert Pippin, *Hollywood Westerns and American Myth: The Importance of Howard Hawks and John Ford for Political Philosophy* [New Haven, CT: Yale University Press, 2012], 91).

21. The classic treatment of this theme is *It's a Wonderful Life*, directed by Frank Capra (1946; Hollywood: Paramount, 2006), DVD.

22. Liberal theorists often see this equation as an expression of ethnic nationalism. The point, however, is broader and deeper than the genetics of race or ethnicity.

23. See Philippe Aries, *Centuries of Childhood: A Social History of Family Life* (New York: Knopf, 1962); Hugh Cunningham, *Children and Childhood in Western Society Since 1500* (Harlow, UK: Longman, 1995); and Robin Bernstein, *Racial Innocence: Performing American Childhood from Slavery to Civil Rights* (New York: New York University Press, 2011).

24. See Stephen Greenblatt, "The Cultivation of Anxiety: King Lear and His Heirs," *Learning to Curse: Essays in Early Modern Culture* (London: Routledge, 1990), 80–98.

25. This theme often receives a lighthearted treatment in Christmas comedies in which the adults have lost touch with "the Christmas spirit." The classic film is *Miracle on 34th Street*, directed by George Seaton (1947; Century City, CA: 20th Century Fox, 2006), DVD. Contemporary versions include *The Santa Clause*, directed by John Pasquin (1994; Burbank, CA: Walt Disney Home Video, 2002), DVD; and *Elf*, directed by Jon Favreau (2003; Universal City, CA: New Line Home Entertainment, 2004), DVD.

26. See, e.g., *No Reservations*, directed by Scott Hicks (2007; Burbank, CA: Warner Home Video, 2008), DVD; *Fly Away Home*, directed by Carroll Ballard (1996; Culver City, CA: Sony Pictures Home Entertainment, 2001), DVD; *Life as We Know It*, directed by Greg Berlanti (2010; Burbank, CA: Warner Home Video, 2011), DVD; and *The Boys Are Back*, directed by Scott Hicks (2009; Burbank, CA: Miramax Films, 2010), DVD.

27. See, e.g., *Australia*, directed by Baz Luhrmann (2008; Century City, CA: 20th Century Fox, 2009), DVD; and *Up*, directed by Pete Docter and Bob Peterson (2009; Emeryville, CA: Disney/Pixar, 2009), DVD.

28. See, e.g., *Knocked Up*, directed by Judd Apatow (2007; Universal City, CA: Universal Studios, 2007), DVD; and *Juno*, directed by Jason Reitman (2007; Century City, CA: 20th Century Fox, 2008), DVD.

29. *Don't Look Now*, directed by Nicholas Roeg (1973; Hollywood: Paramount, 2002), DVD. Another film on this theme is *Ordinary People*, directed by Robert Redford (1980; Hollywood: Paramount, 2001), DVD.

30. *I've Loved You So Long*, directed by Philippe Claudel (2008; Culver City, CA: Sony Pictures Home Entertainment, 2009), DVD.

31. There is a parallel here to *Sophie's Choice*, in which a mother becomes the agent of the death of her child. Speaking of a violation of moral norms fails to capture the destruction of identity.

32. *In the Line of Fire*, directed by Wolfgang Petersen (1993; Culver City, CA: Sony Pictures Home Entertainment, 2001), DVD; *The Sentinel*, directed by Clark Johnson (2006; Century City, CA: 20th Century Fox, 2006), DVD.

33. See Immanuel Kant, "To Perpetual Peace: A Philosophical Sketch," in *Perpetual Peace and Other Essays on Politics, History and Morals*, trans. Ted Humphrey (Indianapolis, IN: Hackett, 1983).

34. *Brothers*, directed by Jim Sheridan (2009; Santa Monica, CA: Lionsgate, 2010), DVD.

35. *Defiance*, directed by Edward Zwick (2008; Hollywood: Paramount, 2009), DVD.

36. *Doctor Zhivago*, directed by David Lean (1965; Burbank, CA: Warner Home Video, 2011), DVD, is a classic film on this theme.

37. *An Officer and a Gentleman*, directed by Taylor Hackford (1982; Hollywood: Paramount, 2000), DVD.

38. The absence of separation of the private and the public also has a pathological form, often associated with failure of recognition of the innocent love of the child. See, e.g., *The Great Santini*, directed by Lewis John Carlino (1979; Burbank, CA: Warner Home Video, 1999), DVD, in which a pilot/father runs his family as if it were a military unit.

39. See Paul W. Kahn, *Out of Eden: Adam and Eve and the Problem of Evil* (Princeton, NJ: Princeton University Press, 2007), 13–14.

40. See Terry Eagleton, *Reason, Faith, and Revolution: Reflections on the God Debate* (New Haven, CT: Yale University Press, 2009).

41. A famous scene in *The Godfather* expresses this idea. It is a montage that brings together images of Michael Corleone at his son's baptism with images of Michael Corleone murdering members of a rival family.

42. The idea of natality is central to the political philosophy of Arendt and her concept of free action. See Hannah Arendt, *The Human Condition* (Chicago: University of Chicago Press, 1958), 176–78.

43. See chapter 2 supra on the distinction of reasons from causes.

44. For a science fiction meditation on the meaning of this distinction see Ridley Scott's *Blade Runner*.

45. *Sleepless in Seattle*, directed by Nora Ephron (1993; Culver City, CA: Sony Pictures Home Entertainment, 2003), DVD.

46. *The Parent Trap*, directed by David Swift (1961; Burbank, CA: Walt Disney Home Entertainment, 2005), DVD; and *The Parent Trap*, directed by Nancy Meyers (1998; Burbank, CA: Walt Disney Home Entertainment, 2005), DVD.

47. *The Kids Are All Right*, directed by Lisa Cholodenko (2010; Universal City, CA: Focus Features, 2010), DVD.

48. *Everybody's Fine*, directed by Kirk Jones (2009; Burbank, CA: Miramax Films, 2010), DVD.

49. Other recent films on this theme include *About Schmidt*, directed by Alexander Payne (2002; Universal City, CA: New Line Home Entertainment, 2003), DVD; and *The Descendants*, directed by Alexander Payne (2011; Century City, CA: Fox Searchlight, 2012), DVD.

50. *Casablanca* works with this double-character of the ex. A recent film, *It's Complicated*, directed by Nancy Meyers (2009; Universal City, CA: Universal Studios, 2010), DVD, is complicated along precisely these lines of ambiguity in the relationship of a divorced couple.

51. Hannah Arendt, *The Origins of Totalitarianism* (1951; repr., New York: Harcourt Brace, 1968), 177.

52. In this way the extra approximates Agamben's idea of homo sacer. See Giorgio Agamben, *Homo Sacer: Sovereign Power and Bare Life*, trans. Daniel Heller-Roazen (Palo Alto, CA: Stanford University Press, 1998).

53. *The Burning Plain*, directed by Guillermo Arriaga (2008; New York: Magnolia Home Entertainment, 2010), DVD.

54. *Avatar*, directed by James Cameron (2009; Century City, CA: 20th Century Fox, 2010), DVD.

55. See chapter 4 supra.

56. *Somewhere*, directed by Sofia Coppola (2010; Universal City, CA: Focus Features, 2011), DVD, develops along similar lines, except now it is the father leading an empty life before the entry of his eleven-year-old daughter.

57. See Milton Regan Jr., *Alone Together: Law and the Meanings of Marriage* (New York: Oxford University Press, 1999).

58. *Rosemary's Baby*, directed by Roman Polanski (1968; Hollywood: Paramount, 2000), DVD; *The Omen*, directed by Richard Donner (1976; Century City, CA: 20th Century Fox, 2001), DVD; *Children of the Corn*, directed by Fritz Kiersch (1984; Beverly Hills: Starz/Anchor Bay, 2001), DVD; *The Exorcist*, directed by William Friedkin (1973; Burbank, CA: Warner Home Video, 1998), DVD. The films are also labeled "family horror," and they are characterized as expressing an "apocalyptic horror." The negation of the infant as a source of all meaning is indeed a vision of the end of the world. See Peter Hutchings, *The Horror Film* (London: Longman, 2004), 182–83.

59. See Kahn, *Out of Eden*, 207–10.

60. *Rebel Without a Cause*, directed by Nicholas Ray (1955; Burbank, CA: Warner Bros. Pictures, 1999), DVD; *Halloween*, directed by John Carpenter (1978; Beverly Hills: Anchor Bay, 2007), DVD; *Hell Night*, directed by Tom DeSimone (1981; Beverly Hills: Anchor Bay, 2008), DVD. For a discussion of this theme in film see Jon Pahl, *Empire of Sacrifice: The Religious Origins of American Violence* (New York: New York University Press, 2010).

61. *Scream*, directed by Wes Craven (1996; Burbank, CA: Walt Disney Video, 1997), DVD. See also Robin Wood, *Hollywood from Vietnam to Reagan* (New York: Columbia University Press, 1986), 195.

62. Freud sketched out the psychological mechanics of such a split in *Totem and Taboo*, trans. James Strachey (1913; repr., New York: Norton, 1950).

63. *American Beauty*, directed by Sam Mendes (1999; Universal City, CA: DreamWorks Video, 2000), DVD, develops this theme. A father, in a midlife crisis, gives up his job and his ordinary familial roles. He becomes wholly narcissistic, using his daughter to try to seduce her best friend. The conclusion is as expected: he must come back to love, not self-regard, if he is to be whole.

64. See note 61 above; *Zombieland*, directed by Ruben Fleischer (2009; Culver City, CA: Sony Pictures Home Entertainment, 2010), DVD, similarly includes a list of "rules" for surviving amid zombies. The rules are derived from previous zombie films, and they are presented as such.

65. Fittingly, the finale of *Scream 3*, directed by Wes Craven (2000; New York: Dimension, 2000), DVD, occurs on a film set—and the film-within-the-film is called "Stab 3."

66. See the zombie parody *Shaun of the Dead*, directed by Edgar Wright (2004; Universal City, CA: Universal Studios, 2004), DVD, which does this explicitly.

67. *Reefer Madness*, directed by Louis J. Gasnier (1936; Century City, CA: 20th Century Fox, 2004), DVD; *The Texas Chainsaw Massacre*, directed by Tobe Hooper (1974; Orland Park, IL: Dark Sky Films, 2006), DVD.

68. Hutchings describes two models of horror audience, one of which imagines itself as victim. The other "is altogether more raucous . . . and less submissive. . . . We might scream here but we also laugh, shout, throw popcorn . . . with the auditorium transformed into a kind of performance space" (Hutchings, *The Horror Film*, 82).

69. *The Rocky Horror Picture Show*, directed by Jim Sharman (1975; Century City, CA: 20th Century Fox, 2000), DVD; and *The Sound of Music*, directed by Robert Wise (1965; Century City, CA: 20th Century Fox, 2005), DVD.

70. Sequels have become popular across many genres of films, but the horror film may have been the earliest genre to pursue the sequel. See Hutchings, *The Horror Film*, 16–27.

71. This anxiety forms the literal plot of *Videodrome*, directed by David Cronenberg (1983; Universal City, CA: Universal Studios, 1998), DVD, in which people are exposed to a video signal that makes them incapable of distinguishing hallucination from reality. A similar theme forms the plot of *The Ring*, directed by Gore Verbinski (2002; Universal City, CA: DreamWorks Video, 2003), DVD.

72. *Hostel*, directed by Eli Roth (2005; Culver City, CA: Sony Pictures Home Entertainment, 2006), DVD.

73. In *Hostel: Part II*, directed by Eli Roth (2007; Culver City, CA: Sony Pictures Home Entertainment, 2007), DVD, we see that it can happen that the "highest bidder" is a would-be victim. One of the kidnaped women offers to pay more for her survival than her torturer paid, with the result that her torturer is put to death instead of her.

74. Interestingly, *Hostel: Part II* begins with the beheading of the only survivor of *Hostel*. There can be no end in a closed system of representation—only repetition.

75. "These films tend to dispense with or drastically minimize the plot and character development that is thought to be essential to the construction of the

novelistic" (Tania Modleski, "The Terror of Pleasure: The Contemporary Horror Film and Postmodern Theory," in *Film Theory and Criticism: Introductory Readings*, ed. Leo Braudy and Marshall Cohen, 6th ed. [Oxford: Oxford University Press, 2004], 769).

76. Paul Wells comments that these films show us "valueless worlds informed by boredom, inadequacy and the sense that nothing is surprising anymore. . . . There are no values, standards, ideals or traditions with which to challenge [the monster]" (Paul Wells, *The Horror Genre: From Beelzebub to Blair Witch* [London: Wallflower, 2000], 96–97).

77. Is not the current craze for vampire films offering the same mocking, ironic tone toward the conventional ethos of multiculturalism?

78. Modleski, "The Terror of Pleasure," 771; *Dawn of the Dead*, directed by George A. Romero (1978; Beverly Hills: Starz/Anchor Bay, 2004), DVD.

79. See Steven Shaviro, *The Cinematic Body* (Minneapolis: University of Minnesota Press, 1992), 92–94.

80. *House of 1000 Corpses*, directed by Rob Zombie (2003; Santa Monica, CA: Lionsgate, 2003), DVD; *Deliverance*, directed by John Boorman (1972; Burbank, CA: Warner Home Video, 2007), DVD.

81. For a discussion of pornography as a form of antipolitics see Kahn, *Putting Liberalism in Its Place*, 202–18.

82. The link between murder and sex was already at issue in my discussion of *Brothers* supra.

83. Linda Williams links a third genre to these two: melodrama. She argues that each is a "system of excess," featuring a spectacle of bodily ecstasy to which the viewer responds "in an almost involuntary mimicry of the emotion or sensation of the body on the screen" (Linda Williams, "Film Bodies: Gender, Genre, and Excess," in Braudy and Cohen, *Film Theory*, 730).

84. That pornography portrays a sort of antihistory does not mean that pornography itself does not have a history. See Linda Williams, *Hard Core: Power, Pleasure, and the "Frenzy of the Visible"* (Berkeley: University of California Press, 1989). This history would indeed speak to particular films.

85. Sexting is the contemporary technological displacement of the word by the image.

86. There is, of course, a business of pornography, members of which have a good deal to talk about.

87. This is the explicit theme of two HBO series: *Cathouse*, directed by Patti Kaplan, first broadcast Dec. 8, 2002, by HBO; and *Real Sex*, directed by Patti Kaplan, first broadcast May 5, 2000, by HBO.

88. The snuff film is the ultimate example in this direction. The endless, self-reproducing quality of porn, and the idea that porn finds its monstrous limit in

snuff, is explored in *8MM*, directed by Joel Schumacher (1999; Culver City, CA: Sony Pictures Home Entertainment, 2005), DVD.

89. See Kahn, *Putting Liberalism in Its Place*, 208.

90. The accusation is posed most famously by Catharine MacKinnon and Andrea Dworkin. See Catharine MacKinnon, *Only Words* (Cambridge, MA: Harvard University Press, 1996); and Andrea Dworkin, *Pornography: Men Possessing Women* (New York: Plume, 1991).

91. For additional information on the sources in this chapter see "Bibliography: Essays on Sources."

CONCLUSION

1. *The Blind Side*, directed by John Lee Hancock (2009; Burbank, CA: Warner Home Video, 2010), DVD.

2. The same themes are reflected from the perspective of pathology in *The Fighter*, directed by David O. Russell (2010; Hollywood: Paramount Pictures, 2011), DVD. The deep failure of the family makes it impossible for the youngest son to succeed as a boxer, despite his natural talent. Only when he falls in love outside of his family can he succeed. With that success, of course, comes recovery of his family.

3. Robert Kolker uses the metaphor of contract to make a similar point: "Genres . . . are complex contractual events drawn between the film maker and the film viewer" (Robert Kolker, *Film, Form, and Culture* [New York: McGraw-Hill, 1999], xiv). Thomas Schatz uses the same metaphor: "genre exists as a sort of tacit 'contract' between filmmakers and audience" (Thomas Schatz, *Hollywood Genres: Formulas, Filmmaking, and the Studio System* [New York: Random House, 1981], 16).

4. *Greenberg*, directed by Noah Baumbach (2010; Universal City, CA: Focus Features, 2010), DVD.

5. For example, *Carrie*, directed by Brian De Palma (1976; Santa Monica, CA: MGM, 2001), DVD, ends with a hand reaching out from the grave, just as *Hostel: Part II* begins with a beheading, reminding us that *Hostel* failed to close.

6. See chapter 2 supra.

7. This, too, can be inverted such that a film depends on "misfortunes" aligned with its narrative. For example, in *The Square*, directed by Nash Edgerton (2008; Los Angeles: Apparition, 2010), DVD, two adulterous lovers plan to run off together after stealing some already-stolen money from one of their spouses. At every step a fatal accident occurs, which powers the film's downward slide toward the failure of their plan and the inevitable fatal accident of one of them.

8. See Immanuel Kant, "An Answer to the Question: What Is Enlightenment?" in *Kant: Political Writings*, ed. H. S. Reiss, trans. H. B. Nisbet (Cambridge: Cambridge University Press, 1970), 54–60.

9. See, e.g., Bartolome de Las Casas, *A Short Account of the Destruction of the Indies*, trans. Nigel Griffin (London: Penguin, 1992), 71. For a representation in film see *The Mission*, directed by Roland Joffé (1986; Burbank, CA: Warner Home Video, 2003), DVD.

10. Consider, e.g., *Little Big Man*, directed by Arthur Penn (1970; Hollywood: Paramount, 2003), DVD; or *The Last of the Mohicans*, directed by Michael Mann (1992; Century City, CA: Fox Home Entertainment, 2007), DVD.

11. Love conquering death is reminiscent of *The Matrix*, which also created a mind-avatar structure.

12. *Titanic*, directed by James Cameron (1997; Hollywood: Paramount, 2012), DVD.

13. See Susan Nieman, *Evil in Modern Thought: An Alternative History of Philosophy* (Princeton, NJ: Princeton University Press, 2002).

14. See my discussion of *The Sweet Hereafter* in chapter 2 above.

BIBLIOGRAPHY: ESSAYS ON SOURCES

1. PHILOSOPHY, DEMOCRACY, AND THE TURN TO FILM

This chapter brings our earliest model of philosophy into contact with our latest: it brings Socrates to the postmoderns. Because the history of philosophy might be thought of as a long conversation, the difference between the end points is not as great as one might think, particularly if one emphasizes the dramatic and dialogical. Some scholars draw a distinction between Socrates and Plato: the former practices discursive engagement; the latter advances an abstract metaphysics and merely uses the dialogues as a vehicle to convey his ideas. From this point of view my reading is Socratic.

My opening pages refer to Plato's *Euthyphro* and *Republic*. For a dialogue that takes up directly the nature of philosophy—and how it differs from other practices of speech—look to the *Gorgias*. For a sense of the drama that philosophy can be, there is no better place to begin than with the *Apology* and *Crito*.

At the postmodern end I have been particularly interested in works in legal theory. Important works of this genre include Robert Cover, "The Supreme Court Term 1982, Foreword: Nomos and Narrative," 97 *Harvard Law Review* 4 (1983); and Stanley Fish, *Is There a Text in This Class? The Authority of Interpretive Communities* (Cambridge, MA: Harvard University Press, 1980). On the critical idea that thought itself has a history that philosophy should bring to light, see Michel Foucault, *The Archaeology of Knowledge and the Discourse on Language*, trans. A. M. Sheridan Smith (1971; repr., New York: Vintage, 1982); as well as his classic studies *The Birth of the Clinic: An Archaeology of Medical Perception*, trans. A. M. Sheridan Smith (New York: Vintage, 1994); and *Discipline and Punish: The Birth of the Prison*, trans. Alan Sheridan (New York: Vintage, 1995). I have tried to bring these insights to bear on the general practice of legal studies in Paul W. Kahn, *The Cultural Study of Law: Reconstructing Legal Scholarship* (Chicago: University of Chicago Press, 1999). See also Arthur Austin, "The Postmodern Infiltration of Legal Scholarship," 98 *Michigan Law Review* 1504 (2000).

The idea of philosophy as an interpretive practice, the object of which is the imaginative world of meaning, draws equally from the modern disciplines of psychoanalysis and anthropology. On the former, Freud's works on culture are particularly useful; see, e.g., *Civilization and Its Discontents*, trans. David McLintock (1930; repr., Mansfield Centre, CT: Martino Publishing, 2010); and *Group Psychology and the Analysis of the Ego*, trans. James Strachey (1959; repr., New York: Norton, 1990). On the latter I have been particularly influenced by the work of Clifford Geertz, including his *Interpretation of Cultures* (New York: Basic Books, 1973) and *Local Knowledge: Further Essays in Interpretive Anthropology* (New York: Basic Books, 1983).

For more on the specific concept of the social imaginary, Charles Taylor's work is essential—not just the short text *Modern Social Imaginaries* (Durham, NC: Duke University Press, 2003) but, more importantly, his magisterial *Sources of the Self: The Making of the Modern Identity* (Cambridge: Cambridge University Press, 1989). A similar, although somewhat narrower, idea was suggested by Hannah Arendt in her description of what she thought of as that form of human activity—"action"—that is uniquely characteristic of a political life. She referred to the "in-between" world of meaning that binds people together through words and deeds as a "'web' of human relationships" (Hannah Arendt, *The Human Condition* [Chicago: University of Chicago Press, 1958], 182–83).

For the idea that philosophy should turn from foundational principles to a more modest enterprise of self-examination, there are sources in both the analytic and the pragmatic traditions. On the former, Ludwig Wittgenstein's *Philosophical Investigations*, ed. P. M. S. Hacker and Joachim Schulte, trans. G. E. M. Anscombe (Oxford: Wiley-Blackwell, 2009), is the place to begin. On the latter, one can look to Richard Rorty, *Contingency, Irony, and Solidarity* (Cambridge: Cambridge University Press, 1989).

The controversy over the role of narrative in historical work is well summarized in Hayden White, "The Question of Narrative in Contemporary Historical Theory," *History and Theory* 23, no. 1 (1984): 1–33. A more detailed discussion of the critique and defense of narrative in historical work is presented in Paul Ricoeur, *Time and Narrative: Volume 1*, trans. Kathleen McLaughlin and David Pellauer (Chicago: University of Chicago Press, 1984), 95–174. For classic examples of the Annales' approach (supra note 33), which disavows narrative, see Ferdinand Braudel's three-volume work, *The Mediterranean and the Mediterranean World in the Age of Philip II*, trans. Siân Reynolds (New York: Harper, 1972); and Marc Bloch, *The Royal Touch: Monarchy and Miracles in France and England*, trans. J. E. Anderson (New York: Dorset Press, 1990).

My own past work has touched on many of the themes proposed here. In particular, *Putting Liberalism in Its Place* (Princeton, NJ: Princeton University Press, 2005) challenges the usefulness of a political theory that seeks a foundation of the state in abstract, first principles.

2. FREEDOM AND PERSUASION

There is a long debate in contemporary philosophy over the relationship of causes to reasons. This has been of particular interest to those writing in the analytic tradition. This discussion may have begun with G. E. M. Anscombe's *Intention* (1957; repr., Cambridge, MA: Harvard University Press, 2000), in which she accepts the distinction for what she calls "full-blown" cases (24). Donald Davidson argued that reasons, properly understood, are causes. See Donald Davidson, "Actions, Reasons, and Causes," *Journal of Philosophy* 60, no. 23 (1963): 685. For an inter-esting response to Davidson that emphasizes, as I do, the possible in an account of reasons, see Mark Risjord, "Reasons, Causes, and Action Explanation," *Philosophy of the Social Sciences* 35, no. 3 (2005): 1–13.

The discussion of Kant's effort to ground morality in reason contin-ues in some excellent books, including Christine Korsgaard, *The Sources of Normativity* (Cambridge: Cambridge University Press, 1996); and Susan Nieman, *The Unity of Reason: Rereading Kant* (Oxford: Oxford University Press, 1994). Challenges to Kant's moral theory, which rely on the idea that a person is always situated in a particular historical community, begin as early as Hegel. The modern challenge that pur-sued this sort of an argument was formulated by the communitarians. Particularly important were Michael Sandel, *Liberalism and the Limits of Justice* (Cambridge: Cambridge University Press, 1982); and Charles Taylor, *Hegel* (Cambridge: Cambridge University Press, 1975). Alistair MacIntyre's *After Virtue: A Study in Moral Theory* (Notre Dame, IN: University of Notre Dame Press, 1984) pursued a similar sort of cri-tique but appealed to an Aristotelian conception of moral character or what is sometimes called "virtue ethics." See, generally, *The Liberalism-Communitarianism Debate: Liberty and Community Values*, ed. C. F. Del-aney (Lanham, MD: Rowman and Littlefield, 1994).

Much of what I have to say about the role of narrative in the con-struction of individual and social identity follows paths opened by Paul Ricoeur in multiple works, including *Time and Narrative*, trans. Kathleen McLaughlin and David Pellauer, 3 vols. (Chicago: University of Chicago Press, 1984); *Interpretation Theory: Discourse and the Sur-plus of Meaning* (Fort Worth: Texas Christian University Press, 1976); and *Oneself as Another*, trans. Kathleen Blamey (Chicago: University of Chicago Press, 1992). MacIntyre also has a very useful discussion of narrative in *After Virtue*. Like Ricoeur he argues, "Narrative his-tory of a certain kind turns out to be the basic and essential genre for the characterization of human actions" (MacIntyre, *After Virtue*, 208). This claim is central to my approach. Although I turn from this insight to an exploration of the social imaginary, both MacIntyre and Ricoeur want to put the claim to ethical use, investigating the rela-tionship of narrative to the human good and particularly to relation-ships of recognition.

Narrative has also had an important role in contemporary jurisprudence. Despite Dworkin's substantive liberalism, his idea of the judicial opinion as a chapter in a "chain novel" points to the importance of narrative in judicial decision making. See Ronald Dworkin, *Law's Empire* (London: Fontana, 1986), 239. Narrative was also central to Robert Cover's idea of the jurisgenerative character of every legal text. See Robert Cover, "The Supreme Court, 1982 Foreword: *Nomos* and Narrative," 97 *Harvard Law Review* 4 (1983). Consideration of the multiple and changing possibilities of interpretation in law—the element of surprise alongside that of continuity—has led me to understand narrative as far less stable than MacIntyre suggests. This deep instability makes it difficult to posit normative claims based on the narrative structure of the imagination.

The ideas in this chapter of the relationship of narrative to persuasion and persuasion to action also draw on the work of Hannah Arendt, who put the idea of man as a "storyteller" at the center of her account of action. The capacity to tell a story is for her inseparable from the capacity to bring something new into the world: without the story there would be no memory of the act. To show oneself, accordingly, requires the possibility of memory, and that requires the story. See Arendt, *The Human Condition* (Chicago: University of Chicago Press, 1958), 184.

An excellent work on the way persuasion draws on narrative and character is Eugene Garver's *For the Sake of Argument: Practical Reasoning, Character, and the Ethics of Belief* (Chicago: University of Chicago Press, 2004). An excellent work trying to recover the role of persuasion in the history of Western political theory is Bryan Garsten's *Saving Persuasion: A Defense of Rhetoric and Judgment* (Cambridge, MA: Harvard University Press, 2006).

3. ON INTERPRETATION

The main sources for this chapter are largely the same as those for the prior chapter. Both chapters examine the concepts of imagination, narrative, and interpretation. What unites persuasion and interpretation is narrative. Particularly relevant to my emphasis on the conversation as a model of the role of narrative in understanding is Hans-Georg Gadamer,

Truth and Method, trans. Joel Weinsheimer and Donald G. Marshall (London: Sheed and Ward, 1975).

On the idea of and diversity among symbolic forms see Ernst Cassirer, *The Philosophy of Symbolic Forms*, trans. Ralph Manheim, 4 vols. (New Haven, CT: Yale University Press, 1965); and Suzanne Langer, *Philosophy in a New Key: A Study in the Symbolism of Reason, Rite, and Art* (Cambridge, MA: Harvard University Press, 1942). Several recent books on Cassirer are particularly interesting: Deniz Coskun, *Law as Symbolic Form: Ernst Cassirer and the Anthropocentric View of Law* (Dordrecht: Springer, 2010); Peter Gordon, *Continental Divide: Heidegger, Cassirer, Davos* (Cambridge, MA: Harvard University Press, 2010). On the necessity of interpretation in dealing with the range of meaningful behavior and experience that constitute the human world, one should look to Charles Taylor's essay "Interpretation and the Sciences of Man," in *Philosophy and the Human Sciences: Philosophical Papers II* (Cambridge: Cambridge University Press, 1985), 15–57.

The distinction I draw between creativity and planning is loosely based on Hannah Arendt's distinction between making and acting. See Hannah Arendt, *The Human Condition* (Chicago: University of Chicago Press, 1958). My emphasis on the work as drawing forth its creator takes her distinction in quite a different direction.

The issue of the "bearer" of political history has become a central problem in work on national self-determination. How exactly do we determine who or what is the nation, which has a right to self-determination? A claim of national identity easily becomes a polemical, political claim, for there is no natural unity that is the nation. Works exploring this problem include Ivor Jennings, *The Approach to Self-Government* (Cambridge: Cambridge University Press, 1956); Benedict Anderson, *Imagined Communities: Reflections on the Origin and Spread of Nationalism* (New York: Verso, 1983); Eric Hobsbawm, *Nations and Nationalism since 1780: Programme, Myth, Reality* (Cambridge: Cambridge University Press, 1992); and Martti Koskenniemi, "National Self-Determination Today: Problems of Legal Theory and Practice," 43 *International and Comparative Law Quarterly* 241 (1994).

To explore further the nature and significance of the dispute between the nominalists and the scholastics on the nature of God, the best place to begin is Michael Gillespie, *Theological Origins of Modernity* (Chicago:

University of Chicago Press, 2008). The nominalist idea of a radically indeterminate God that can act in ways that appear wholly arbitrary to human beings becomes central to Luther's theology and, of course, continues in much of Protestantism. See Diarmaid MacCulloch, *The Reformation: A History* (New York: Viking, 2003).

4. VIOLENCE AND THE STATE

The subjects of this chapter are at the center of much of my recent work in political theory. My views on the relationship of sovereignty to law have been elaborated in two books: *Putting Liberalism in Its Place* (Princeton, NJ: Princeton University Press, 2005); and *Political Theology: Four New Chapters on the Concept of Sovereignty* (New York: Columbia University Press, 2011). My views on the nature of political violence and its relationship to sacrifice, on the one hand, and torture, on the other, are developed in Paul W. Kahn, *Sacred Violence: Torture, Terror, and Sovereignty* (Ann Arbor: University of Michigan Press, 2008).

Other important recent works on the general theme of the relationship of violence to law include Giorgio Agamben, *Homo Sacer: Sovereign Power and Bare Life*, trans. Daniel Heller-Roazen (Palo Alto, CA: Stanford University Press, 1998); Jacques Derrida, "Force of Law: The 'Mystical Foundation of Authority,'" in *Deconstruction and the Possibility of Justice*, ed. Drucilla Cornell, Michael Rosenfeld, and David Gray Carlson (New York: Routledge, 1992); and René Girard, *Violence and the Sacred*, trans. Patrick Gregory (London: Continuum, 2005). Important earlier texts include Walter Benjamin, "Critique of Violence," trans. Edmund Jephcott, in *Walter Benjamin: Selected Writings*, ed. Marcus Bullock and Michael Jennings, 4 vols. (Cambridge, MA: Harvard University Press, 1999), 1:237; and Carl Schmitt, *The Concept of the Political*, trans. George Schwab (Chicago: University of Chicago Press, 1996). For a critique of the politics of sacrificial violence see Hannah Arendt, *On Violence* (Orlando, FL: Harcourt Brace, 1970); and Jonathan Schell, *The Unconquerable World: Power, Nonviolence, and the Will of the People* (New York: Henry Holt, 2003).

On the continuing place of sacrifice in the modern nation-state see Moshe Halbertal, *On Sacrifice* (Princeton, NJ: Princeton University

Press, 2012); and Carolyn Marvin and David W. Ingle, *Blood Sacrifice and the Nation: Totem Rituals and the American Flag* (Cambridge: Cambridge University Press, 1999).

The dispute over the continuing place of a politics of sovereignty has also produced a substantial body of work. The attack on the modern relevance of sovereignty is well expressed in Stephen Krasner, *Sovereignty: Organized Hypocrisy* (Princeton, NJ: Princeton University Press, 1999). Earlier, David Luban criticized the moral integrity of the concept of sovereignty in a debate with Michael Walzer, who argued in favor of international humanitarian law's presumptions about sovereignty. See Michael Walzer, *Just and Unjust Wars* (New York: Basic Books, 1977); and David Luban, "The Romance of the Nation-State," *Philosophy and Public Affairs* 9, no. 4 (1980): 392–97. This debate over the relevance of sovereignty to law entered international legal scholarship in the 1990s through work on the emergence of a new, transnational legal order. See Harold Koh, "Why Do Nations Obey International Law?" 106 *Yale Law Journal* 2599 (1997); and Ann-Marie Slaughter, *A New World Order* (Princeton, NJ: Princeton University Press, 2004).

The disappearance of sovereignty from jurisprudence was exactly the complaint that Schmitt brought against Hans Kelsen. See Carl Schmitt, *Political Theology: Four Chapters on the Concept of Sovereignty*, trans. George Schwab (Chicago: University of Chicago Press, 2005), 16–35. Contemporary analytic jurisprudence continues in the vein of Kelsen (and H. L. A. Hart), seeing no great need for a concept of sovereignty in order to understand law. See H. L. A. Hart, *The Concept of Law* (Oxford: Oxford University Press, 1961); and Scott Shapiro, *Legality* (Cambridge, MA: Belknap, 2011).

Also relevant to the concerns of this chapter is some of the work of modern, cultural anthropology. The beginning point is Clifford Geertz, *The Interpretation of Cultures* (New York: Basic Books, 1973); and Victor Turner, *The Ritual Process: Structure and Anti-structure* (Ithaca, NY: Cornell University Press, 1969) (on the liminal). More contemporary work on issues of political meaning and sacrifice includes Mateo Taussig, "Outsourcing Sacrifice: The Labor of Private Military Contractors," 21 *Yale Journal of Law and the Humanities* 103 (2009); and "Sacred Property: Searching for Value in the Rubble of 9/11," in *After Secular Law*, ed.

Winnifred Sullivan, Robert Yelle, and Mateo Taussig-Rubbo (Palo Alto, CA: Stanford University Press, 2011), 322–45.

CHAPTER 5. LOVE, ROMANCE, AND PORNOGRAPHY

In the *Symposium* and the *Phaedrus* Plato placed love at the center of philosophical inquiry. Philosophy not only took up the subject of the character of love, but doing philosophy was itself to be accounted for as a practice of eros. There has been a dramatic turn away from love, and to reason, in Western philosophy—as if these two were in tension. Presumably, this has had to do first with the Christian inflection on the nature and role of love but second with Freud's intervention on the nature of eros. Love has become a topic for theologians and psychoanalysts. Recent exceptions include Harry Frankfurt, *The Reasons of Love* (Princeton, NJ: Princeton University Press, 2004); Jonathan Lear, *Love and Its Place in Nature: A Philosophical Interpretation of Freudian Psychoanalysis* (1990; repr., New Haven, CT: Yale University Press, 1998); and my own works *Law and Love: The Trials of King Lear* (New Haven, CT: Yale University Press, 2000), and *Out of Eden: Adam and Eve and the Problem of Evil* (Princeton, NJ: Princeton University Press, 2007).

Hobbes's problem with sacrifice and conscription was identified by Michael Walzer some time ago. See Michael Walzer, *Obligations: Essays on Disobedience, War, and Citizenship* (Cambridge, MA: Harvard University Press, 1970), 80–88. In *Putting Liberalism in Its Place* (Princeton, NJ: Princeton University Press, 2005) I argue that liberalism can have no adequate concept of sacrifice, and this produces a fundamental mischaracterization of the nature of the political experience. I develop these themes further in *Political Theology: Four New Chapters on the Concept of Sovereignty* (New York: Columbia University Press, 2011).

There is a substantial body of work on the nature of the exception. The place to begin is Carl Schmitt, *Political Theology: Four Chapters on the Concept of Sovereignty*, trans. George Schwab (Chicago: University of Chicago Press, 1986). Contemporary work includes Giorgio Agamben, *State of Exception*, trans. Kevin Attell (Chicago: University of Chicago Press, 2005); Bonnie Honig, *Emergency Politics: Paradox, Law, and Democracy*

(Princeton, NJ: Princeton University Press, 2009); and Richard Posner, *Not a Suicide Pact: The Constitution in a Time of National Emergency* (Oxford: Oxford University Press, 2006).

Philosophical reflection on the tension between the family and the polity goes back at least to Plato's *Republic*. On the role of family in modern democratic theory see Brian Duff, *The Parent as Citizen: A Democratic Dilemma* (Minneapolis: University of Minnesota Press, 2011). Recent work on childhood in American political and cultural life includes Steven Mintz, *Huck's Raft: A History of American Childhood* (Cambridge, MA: Belknap, 2004); and Steven Mintz and Susan Kellogg, *Domestic Revolutions: A Social History of American Family Life* (New York: Free Press, 1988).

Speaking of the role of fortune in the world of love, I am indirectly invoking Machiavelli, who saw fortune—mostly misfortune—as a threat to political order and success. See Niccoló Machiavelli, *The Prince*, trans. N. H. Thompson (New York: Dover, 1992), 66–67.

INDEX

Note: Page references followed by the letter *n* indicate notes.